Style, Identity and Literacy

CRITICAL LANGUAGE AND LITERACY STUDIES

Series Editors: Professor Alastair Pennycook (*University of Technology, Sydney, Australia*), Professor Brian Morgan (*Glendon College/York University, Toronto, Canada*) and Professor Ryuko Kubota (*University of British Columbia, Vancouver, Canada*)

Critical Language and Literacy Studies is an international series that encourages monographs directly addressing issues of power (its flows, inequities, distributions, trajectories) in a variety of language- and literacy-related realms. The aim with this series is twofold: (1) to cultivate scholarship that openly engages with social, political, and historical dimensions in language and literacy studies, and (2) to widen disciplinary horizons by encouraging new work on topics that have received little focus (see below for partial list of subject areas) and that use innovative theoretical frameworks.

Details of all the books in the series can be found below and of our other publications on http://www.multilingual-matters.com, or by writing to Multilingual Matters, St Nicholas House, 31–34 High Street, Bristol BS1 2AW, UK.

Other books in the series

Collaborative Research in Multilingual Classrooms
Corey Denos, Kelleen Toohey, Kathy Neilson and Bonnie Waterstone
English as a Local Language: Post-colonial Identities and Multilingual Practices
Christina Higgins
The Idea of English in Japan: Ideology and the Evolution of a Global Language
Philip Seargeant
Gendered Identities and Immigrant Language Learning
Julia Menard-Warwick
China and English: Globalisation and the Dilemmas of Identity
Joseph Lo Bianco, Jane Orton and Gao Yihong (eds)
Language and HIV/AIDS
Christina Higgins and Bonny Norton (eds)
Hybrid Identities and Adolescent Girls: Being 'Half' in Japan
Laurel D. Kamada
Decolonizing Literacy: Mexican Lives in the Era of Global Capitalism
Gregorio Hernandez-Zamora
Contending with Globalization in World Englishes
Mukul Saxena and Tope Omoniyi (eds)
ELT, Gender and International Development: Myths of Progress in a Neocolonial World
Roslyn Appleby
Examining Education, Media, and Dialogue under Occupation: The Case of Palestine and Israel
Ilham Nasser, Lawrence N. Berlin and Shelley Wong (eds)
The Struggle for Legitimacy: Indigenized Englishes in Settler Schools
Andrea Sterzuk

CRITICAL LANGUAGE AND LITERACY STUDIES

Series Editors: Alastair Pennycook, *University of Technology, Sydney, Australia,* Brian Morgan, *Glendon College/York University, Toronto, Canada* and Ryuko Kubota, *University of British Columbia, Vancouver, Canada*

Style, Identity and Literacy
English in Singapore

Christopher Stroud and Lionel Wee

MULTILINGUAL MATTERS
Bristol • Buffalo • Toronto

Library of Congress Cataloging in Publication Data
A catalog record for this book is available from the Library of Congress.
Stroud, Christopher.
Style, Identity, and Literacy: English in Singapore/Christopher Stroud and Lionel Wee.
Critical Language and Literacy Studies:; 13
Includes bibliographical references and index.
1. English language–Study and teaching–Singapore–Foreign speakers. 2. Native language and education–Singapore. 3. Multilingualism–Singapore. I. Wee, Lionel, 1963- II. Title.
PE1128.A2S867 2012
427'.95957–dc23 2011035425

British Library Cataloguing in Publication Data
A catalogue entry for this book is available from the British Library.

ISBN-13: 978-1-84769-596-3 (hbk)
ISBN-13: 978-1-84769-595-6 (pbk)

Multilingual Matters
UK: St Nicholas House, 31–34 High Street, Bristol BS1 2AW, UK.
USA: UTP, 2250 Military Road, Tonawanda, NY 14150, USA.
Canada: UTP, 5201 Dufferin Street, North York, Ontario M3H 5T8, Canada.

The policy of Multilingual Matters/Channel View Publications is to use papers that are natural, renewable and recyclable products, made from wood grown in sustainable forests. In the manufacturing process of our books, and to further support our policy, preference is given to printers that have FSC and PEFC Chain of Custody certification. The FSC and/or PEFC logos will appear on those books where full certification has been granted to the printer concerned.

Typeset by Techset Composition Ltd., Salisbury, UK.

Contents

Preface   ix

1   Social Practices and Linguistic Markets   1
    Language, Gatekeeping and Monolingual Ideologies   6
    Language Education as Social Reproduction   11
    Literacy as a Site of Contestation   19
    The Organization of this Book   22

2   Multilingualism in Late-Modern Singapore: A Portrait   26
    Modern Discourses of Multilingualism   27
    An Ethnicity-based Politics of Language   28
    Monolingual Ideology in Multilingual Singapore   30
    The Inevitability of Orders of Indexicality   33
    English and Social Class   35
    Late Modernity and Singaporeans' Multilingual Practices   37
    The Language Practitioner in Late-Modern Singapore   41
    New Figurations of Language, Class and Ethnicity   45
    Singaporean Official Policy in Late Modernity: From Two
        Languages to One   47
    Monolingualism in Singapore   48
    Conclusion   50

3   Multilingualism in Late Modernity: Literacy as a Reflexive
    Performance of Identity   52
    A Poststructuralist Approach to Identity   53
    Reflexivity Debates   54
    Bohman and the Transformative Potential of Critical Reflexivity   58
    Multiple Markets, Ambivalence and Reflexivity   61
    Performance and Identity   63

Style, Literacy and Identity 65
Linguistic Markets 68

4 Some Data About Our Data 72
Framing Parameters 72
Narratives in the Research Interview 74
Style, Stylization and the Interview 75
Data Sets and Procedures: The Primary Data Sets 78
Choosing the School 79
Transcribing and Interpreting the Data 83
Secondary Data Sets (Engaging with the Narrative
Voice of Voices): Hing (2004) and Ong (2003) 85
Closing Remarks 87

5 Fandi and Ping: Literacy Practices and the Performance
of Identities on Ambivalent Markets 88
Aligning the Home with the Dominant Market 88
Orders of Indexicality 90
Parental Help with English Language Proficiency 92
Multilingualism in Fandi's and Ping's Households 97
Entertainment at Home 101
Interaction with Peers 104
Reading for Leisure: Choice of Language and Material 114
Concluding Remarks 120

6 Edwin, Wen and Yan: Styling Literacy Practices Inside and
Outside the Classroom 123
Introducing Edwin, Wen and Yan 124
Informal Literacy Practices 125
Literacy Practices in the Classroom 130
Reading Aloud 132
(Not) Asking the Teacher for Help 134
Off-Floor Interaction in a Singapore Classroom 138
On-Floor Interaction 142
Conclusion 144

7 Sha: A Comparison 147
English at Home and among Friends 147
The Relative Values of English and Punjabi 150
Pride in 'Standard' English 154

Reading for Pleasure   156
Language Performances as Peer Activity   157
Reading Aloud   160
Asking the Teacher for Help   162
Against Code-Switching in Off-Site Arenas   163
Public Speaking   163
Conclusion   165

8   Pedagogy, Literacy and Identity   168
    Two Approaches to Language Education   169
    Assumptions about Literacy   172
    Anxiety and Identity in the Language Classroom   180
    Some Examples of Identity-based Anxiety   181
    Implications for Language Teaching   183
    Stylization   185
    Some Pedagogical Possibilities   186
    Concluding Remarks   188

9   The Dynamics of Language Distribution in Late-Modern
    Multilingual Singapore   190
    Consuming Singapore   191
    Rescaling Singapore   197
    Revisiting Language Policy in Late-Modern Consumerist
        Singapore   202
    Sociolinguistic Consumption   205
    Reflexive Citizenship and Deliberation   207
    Language Groups as Bivalent Collectivities   210
    National Identities and the Deconstruction
        of Mother Tongues   213
    Language Policy in Late-Modern Singapore   216
    Conclusion   218

References   220
Subject Index   236

Preface

The last few years have seen a growing number of attempts to reconsider what multilingualism means in an era of globalization. Changing social, cultural and economic conditions under late modernity have led to changing conditions of language. The ways in which capital has come to operate in these new times has shifted, leading not only to financial insecurity and crises as a result of bad debt, but also to increasing disparities between over-paid elites and disenfranchised workers; neoliberal policies have not only eroded social support for medicine, unemployment, pensions and disability, but have changed the discourses of what were formally thought of as public institutions [hence the use, for example, of KPI (Key Performance Indicators)-speak in universities]; large-scale immigration and changing political discourses about difference have led to new regimes of nationalist identity across Europe and elsewhere. Amid all this, languages and the roles ascribed to them have shifted: they have become commodified, tools of inclusion and exclusion and carriers of neoliberal discourse. Indeed, multilingualism itself has become a commodity in the new economy (Duchêne & Heller, in press; Duchêne & Piller, in press).

One reaction to these changing conditions, particularly the hegemony of English and the concomitant decline in other languages, has been to take to the ramparts with the old tools of modernity. Hence, the way forward for some has been to focus a critique on English as a neoliberal and imperialistic language while arguing for support for other languages through a framework of linguistic human rights (Phillipson, 2009). From this neo-Habermasian position, the quandary of late modernity is not in modernity itself but rather where it went off the rails in recent times. The problem, therefore, is the manipulation of modernity, not its epistemologies. An alternative tack, however, has been to ask whether the ways we think about languages, either as a result of changing social conditions or as a long-term epistemological concern, have been adequate. From this point of view, the way forward is not to use the same tools of modernity to struggle against it, but to rethink language and multilingualism as part of that struggle. As Hoy (2004) reminds us, any endeavour of critical resistance has to engage in a project to rethink the terms of the debate.

It is in this space of addressing concerns about language and inequality in late modernity, and trying to find alternative ways of thinking our way out of these dilemmas, that this book by Chris Stroud and Lionel Wee needs to be understood. Key ideas that they bring to this debate are *voice* and *linguistic citizenship*. Drawing on Bakhtin, they suggest that voice may be a more useful point of departure than language. This position sits very well with similar arguments by Blommaert (2010) for understanding how speakers use resources rather than languages, or with Blackledge and Creese's (2010) focus on the Bakhtinian carnivalesque as part of their critical approach to multilingualism. Blommaert is highly critical of work that continues to deal with large reifications of languages as entities in competition with each other, and that assume the 'spatial "fixedness" of people, language and places' (Blommaert, 2010: 44). The 'linguistic-ideological dimension' to these views of fixed languages and worldviews are anathema to the analyses of mobile linguistic resources needed for a sociolinguistics of globalization.

A common strand across this new generation of work on the sociolinguistics of multilingualism is that it is not so much languages (as reified entities) as it is linguistic (and non-linguistic) resources such as genres, discourses and styles where the interesting work of identity formation and semiotic construction occurs. Stroud and Wee's focus on voice makes a related point and ties to the idea of linguistic citizenship. Here the central concern is not state citizenship so much as the kind of reflexive citizenship that underlies all those smaller decisions we make around language resources as we shift between linguistic communities. The idea of linguistic citizenship points at once to questions of consumption, choice and reflexivity as well as to the fact that linguistic diversity is a central means by which democracy may be achieved. Speakers use and negotiate their linguistic resources across different sites, thereby constituting the terrain for democratic engagement. The idea of linguistic citizenship does not tie language users to static notions of linguistic identity but rather sees this as an open (though also contextually constrained) field of choice, a question of *multilingual portfolios*.

The context for these arguments is Singapore. Language in Singapore, it might be observed, has attracted a great deal of attention over the years, perhaps more than is warranted for a small island state of a few million people stuck at the end of the Malaysian Peninsula. Huge amounts have been written about the particular forms of English that have emerged in Singapore (Singlish), much of this within that exoticizing tradition of World Englishes that dwells so much on those particular features – particles such as *lah* or *lor*, terms from Hokkien or Malay, means other than inflectional morphology for realizing tense and aspect – that distinguish English in Singapore from other varieties. Fortunately, this is not another book in that tradition (they would have had to try another book series if it were). Much too has been written about language policy, multilingualism, education and the various efforts to police English and Chinese (the Speak Mandarin Campaign and the Speak Good English Movement). Why, we might ask has Singapore become such a focus of attention? The answer lies in a mixture of factors: the fact that English is one of the languages in the mix and that a great deal of the writing about Singapore has been in English; the fact that Singapore funds its tertiary institutions well and pays its overseas academics generously, so there are always enough researchers around to delve into language in Singapore; the fact that language policy has always been part of public discourse in Singapore, so that discussions about language, policy and education are frequently aired in newspapers and other public forums; and the fact that the multilingual context of Singapore, the particular contradictions, developments and debates on policy are indeed interesting to many an applied linguist.

What then do these authors bring to this context that adds something new? They point out there is a paradox in Singaporean language policy in that while overtly favouring four official languages (Malay, Mandarin, Tamil and English), Singapore has moved towards a position that hugely favours the hegemony of English. But this we have known for a long time (Pennycook, 1994). More importantly, they seek answers to how this happens in the micro-sociolinguistic interactions of adolescents rather than in the macro-sociolinguistic dictates of government or institutional regulation. Part of this focus is on the ways in which young people seek to reconcile identity conflicts and contradictions. Important in this context is the idea of *sociolinguistic consumption* as a way of understanding the relationships between small-scale sociolinguistic acts, large-scale sociolinguistic orders and the particular values ascribed to languages as part of their commodification. Once languages are subject to commodification and become objects of consumption, questions of language, ethnicity and identity shift towards questions of language and class. Young adolescents are therefore participants (as are we all) in different linguistic markets where different forms of capital (in Bourdieu's sense) are attached to different languages. Given the interest in this book in English language literacy, and particularly as it operates as prime site for exclusionary educational practices, Stroud and Wee's critical project here is able to draw attention to questions of power and social reproduction in relation to language, literacy and identity.

In order to do this, they develop some key further resources, in particular *style* and *language ideologies*. Style has emerged from its earlier delimited domain in sociolinguistics to become a more significant category for the understanding of sociolinguistic variation and identity (Coupland, 2007). The exploration of sociolinguistic identity has thus increasingly been explored through a focus on style, a concept that now embraces not just sociolinguistic variation from vernacular to standard but also a much wider focus on multimodal semiotic practices (Bucholtz, 2009). As Rampton (2011) has recently remarked, however, this focus on style may come at the expense of an analysis of class: style draws attention to questions of agency and a capacity to stylize oneself and thereby may draw attention away from a focus on social structures that limit the capacity for stylization. This is where Stroud and Wee's focus on consumption, class and capital is a useful corrective to a portrayal of style in terms only of personal choice. Important too is an understanding of the different ways in which languages are understood ideologically, or as Seargeant (2009: 26) put it in an earlier book in this series, the 'structured and consequential ways in which we think about language'. Indeed Stroud and Wee's book echoes several of the themes that have emerged in this series: the importance of understanding multivocality and local language practices (Higgins, 2009), the politics and inequalities around literacy in an era of global capitalism (Hernandez-Zamora, 2010) and the struggles around English within globalization (Saxena & Omoniyi, 2010). This is an important book, not only because it brings some new insights into the over-written territory of language in Singapore, but more importantly because it opens up new ways of understanding language and consumption, language and voice, and language and citizenship.

Alastair Pennycook
Brian Morgan
Ryuko Kubota

References

Blackledge, A. and Creese, A. (2010) *Multilingualism: A Critical Perspective*. London: Continuum.

Blommaert, J. (2010) *The Sociolinguistics of Globalization*. Cambridge: Cambridge University Press.

Bucholtz, M. (2009) From stance to style: Gender, interaction, and indexicality in Mexican immigrant youth slang. In A. Jaffe (ed.) *Stance: Sociolinguistic Perspectives*. Oxford: Oxford University Press

Coupland, N. (2007) *Style: Language Variation and Identity*. Cambridge: Cambridge University Press.

Duchêne, A. and Heller, M. (in press) Multilingualism and the new economy. In M. Martin-Jones, A. Blackledge and A. Creese (eds) *Handbook of Multilingualism*. New York: Routledge.

Duchêne, A. and Piller, I. (in press) Mehrsprachigkeit als Wirtschaftsgut: Sprachliche Ideologien und Praktiken in der Tourismusindustrie. In G. Kreis (ed.) *Babylon Europe. Zur europäischen Sprachlandschaft*. Basel: Schwabe Verlag.

Hernandez-Zamora, G. (2010) *Decolonizing Literacy: Mexican Lives in the Era of Global Capitalism*. Bristol: Multilingual Matters.

Higgins, C. (2009) *English as a Local Language: Post-colonial Identities and Multilingual Practices*. Bristol: Multilingual Matters.

Hoy, D. (2004) *Critical Resistance: From Poststructuralism to Post-critique*. Cambridge, MA: MIT Press.

Pennycook, A. (1994) *The Cultural Politics of English as an International Language*. London: Longman.

Phillipson, R. (2009) *Linguistic Imperialism Continued*. New York: Routledge.

Rampton, B. (2011) Style contrasts, migration and social class. *Journal of Pragmatics* 43, 1236–1250.

Saxena, M. and Omoniyi, T. (eds) (2010) *Contending with Globalization in World Englishes*. Bristol: Multilingual Matters.

Seargeant, P. (2009) *The Idea of English in Japan: Ideology and the Evolution of a Global Language*. Bristol: Multilingual Matters.

1 Social Practices and Linguistic Markets

(1)
Yan: You have to know [English] otherwise people will laugh at you.
...
I: What happens if the shop assistant is a Malay؟
Y: Then I will speak in Malay
I: Will you attempt English first؟
Y: No. They will say I am like this spoiled girl. I mean, like, they will know, they can sense that I know they are Malay. Then if, like, I am speaking English, then it is like I am boasting my .. you know.
I: Really؟
Y: I know some people think that way.

The above is an extract taken from an interview with Yan. Yan is a Malay female, about 16 years old, who is growing up and studying in Singapore. In the extract, Yan points out that knowledge of English is crucial in Singapore (*otherwise people will laugh at you*). As the inter-ethnic lingua franca and prestige variety in Singapore (and, of course, in many other societies as well), English serves an important gatekeeping function by allowing selective access to social and economic goods, thus influencing in important ways the social trajectories of those who may (or may not) be considered to speak the language well. This gatekeeping function creates a strong motivation for Yan to improve her English. Yet, one of the problems that she faces comes from the kind of identity she projects if she insists on using English instead of Malay, which is the official mother tongue of her ethnic group[1]. In interactions with her co-ethnics, insistence on using English is associated with snobbery (*They will say I am like this spoiled girl; it is like I am boasting*). Because of this, Yan feels that she has no choice but to use Malay when interacting with a Malay shop assistant. In this way, Yan is responding to what she sees as pressure from a particular social group to privilege ethnic identity even in the context of a commercial transaction (*I know some people think that way*).

Young adolescent Singaporeans, of course, do not deny that there are people and institutions (such as their parents, their teachers, their potential future employers) that deeply value academic qualifications. But it is also the case that for many of these adolescents, the activities involved in acquiring such credentials may sometimes conflict with the activities required to maintain or gain localized peer recognition. In some cases, any formal recognition by school authorities may even mean a loss of popularity or credibility amongst one's peers. And if the two forms of recognition happen to be in conflict, it may sometimes be peer credibility that gets to be prioritized over official recognition by the school.

Yan is therefore most certainly not alone in the kinds of predicaments that she faces and in this book, we focus on a number of other Singaporean adolescents who have to deal with similar dilemmas as well. Our goal here is threefold. First, we are interested in how the micro-interactional identity work performed by our adolescent informants contributes to a macro-sociolinguistic paradox. The paradox is this. Despite the espousal of a multilingual language policy on the part of the state – a policy that recognizes four official languages (English, Malay, Mandarin and Tamil) – Singapore society appears to be moving largely toward a situation that favors the reproduction of English language hegemony. How the collective experiences of adolescents such as Yan can lead unequivocally toward the privileging of English – despite the fact that there exists social pressure to continue using other languages like Malay – can contribute to a broader understanding of the kinds of constraints and pressures that multilingual societies have to cope with, especially in the context of globalization and late-modernity. The main answer to our first question is presented in the following chapter, where the indexical values of different languages in the Singapore landscape are discussed. Here, we see that despite the Singapore government's attempts at arguing for the equal value of English and the official mother tongue, its own policy formulations seem to clearly favor the former over the latter. And these signals of language valuations are picked up by adolescents such as Yan, who then face the challenge of reconciling an official commitment to the equal value of English and the official mother tongue, on the one hand, with a social reality where English seems to be particularly privileged, on the other.

This need to reconcile conflicting linguistic demands leads to our second goal. That is, we also wish to understand how attempts at learning English in Singapore may implicate particular kinds of identities among adolescents, thus possibly creating for them conflicts of various sorts, both inside and outside the classroom. We will see, in Chapters 5 through 7, that there are times when these adolescents resolve conflicting identity demands by favoring their desire to preserve peer-oriented relationships, even though they are aware that this might undermine the very activities that they themselves believe could help them improve their English. But in order to even begin making sense of the data presented in these three chapters, some preliminary remarks about the relevant analytical concepts and the methodology involved in our data collection are pertinent. These preliminary issues are addressed in Chapters 3 and 4.

And third, we are aware that it is not enough to merely note the language-learning problems faced by these adolescents. Because of this, we also wish to explore some of the ways in which identity concerns can be beneficially harnessed by educational institutions so as to develop teaching strategies that can help them acquire a more standard variety of English. In other words, the challenge is to find ways of getting these adolescents to learn standard English while not simultaneously requiring them to compromise on the kinds of identities that they are already heavily invested in (Norton, 1995). We do this in Chapter 8.

As we tackle these three questions, it will become clear that there are broader issues at stake that are being implicated as well. One of these is how assumptions about the nature of language and literacy affect language education policy. For example, it becomes difficult to ignore the fact that much of language education policy is predicated on the unquestioned assumption that language is an ontologically stable and delimitable phenomenon. This kind of assumption tends to encourage a view of language and literacy skills as decontextualized technology that ought to be easily transferred across contexts. And of specific concern to the theme of this book, it also tends to de-emphasize the influence that considerations of identity can have on the successful acquisition of literacy practices. We discuss this issue in Chapter 8 also.

Another issue concerns the broader nature of policy-making in a late-modern society such as Singapore. Language education represents just one aspect of a larger set of policies that the state is aggressively pursuing as it aims to ensure the continued economic growth and wellbeing of the country. The state, for example, is concerned about the low fertility rate and outward migration of Singaporeans, and because of this, has attempted to attract 'foreign talent' to consider taking up Singaporean citizenship. The resulting situation consequently presents a number of challenges for Singapore, as the social and linguistic order that the state has so carefully constructed on the basis of clear historically inherited ethnolinguistic affiliations and boundaries has to come to terms with a society that is opening up economically, socially and culturally. Our assessment of this situation is that the very nature of language education policy itself needs to be reevaluated at a more fundamental level. The challenges posed by the rapid and unpredictable nature of social, political and cultural changes in late-modernity require that greater room be given to notions such as autonomy, individual choice and reflexivity – notions that have not generally been given due consideration when language policy is formulated. We deal with this issue in Chapter 9.

We have chosen in this book to explore these various questions through an in-depth, ethnographic, account of the English language literacy practices and events that the students partake of, both within the classroom and across their activities in peer groups and individually outside of the classroom. In order to do this, we need a theoretical framework that is able to integrate literacy-based practices with nonliteracy-based ones, and further able to relate literacy to the notion of identity. As pointed out by a number of scholars (see especially Moje, 2000: 655), freely broadening the notion of *literacy* to encompass all forms of representation (including activities such as dancing and drawing) runs the risk of making the concept so vacuous that it begins to hold little or no analytical value. Furthermore, while such a broadening may be motivated by the well-intentioned desire to challenge the hegemonic status of print literacy – a status especially prominent in 'folk theories of literacy' (Carrington & Luke, 1997) – in fact, it serves only to reinforce the status quo. This is because by asserting too loosely the variegated nature of literacy practices, print literacy then retains its position as the prototypical point of reference against which other forms of literacy become understood and evaluated (cf. Moje, 2000: 655). Consequently, in our discussion, we limit the term *literacy* to specifically language-related practices such as speaking, reading and writing around texts in the sense of Heath (1983, 1994), namely, literacy events and literacy practices. We, of course, want to be able to recognize that language-based practices do not necessarily occur in isolation from other modalities. Therefore, in talking about how both literacy-based and nonliteracy-based practices come together, we find it useful to draw upon recent sociolinguistic theorizations of the notion of style (see the collection of papers in Eckert & Rickford, 2001; see also Coupland, 2007) and performance (e.g. Bauman & Briggs, 1990). Style has been conceptualized as a form of semiosis, one where disparate elements from different modalities, both literacy- and nonliteracy-based modalities, may be drawn upon in order for the stylist to create and project particular identities, often in response to locally negotiated situations. Style, conceived in this manner, is essentially a form of social practice that partakes of bricolage (Bucholtz, 2002). That is, while individuals may create relatively unique combinations, the particular elements that make up an individual's style are usually drawn from generally shared macro-social categories. It is this that allows each individual to signal his/her uniqueness while still being recognized as affiliated with a particular group or groups.

But while treating style as social practice is valuable because it allows us to link particular behaviors and attitudes to identity work, if we want to go on and further understand how such identity work is differentially valued, we need to be able to place our analyses of style in relation to a theory of power. As Coupland (2007: 82) points out, styling involves 'constrained freedom' since the performance of sociolinguistic resources is not totally up to the idiosyncrasies of individuals, but instead takes place 'within certain tolerances'. The exact nature of these tolerances, however, remains theoretically controversial. For both Bell (1984, 2001) and Labov (1966, 1972), the main constraint on individual style is the speech community. Coupland, however, suggests that such a view of style is both too apolitical – since it does not pay sufficient attention to the ideological implications of variation – and also too restrictive – since it does not sufficiently acknowledge that speakers are 'not limited to recycling pre-existing symbolic meanings [but] can frame the linguistic resources available to them in creative ways, making new meanings from old meanings' (Coupland, 2007: 83–84). To accommodate Coupland's observations about style, constraint and creativity, we find Bourdieu's (1977, 1984, 1990, 1991) social theory (which is also a theory of practice) particularly valuable since it recognizes the existence of multiple fields or markets, multiple forms of capital, and rules of convertibility that allow actors to strategically trade in one form of capital for some other. The existence of institutional structures and the inculcated habitus of individuals speak to the restrictions that operate on possibilities of styling. At the same time, as we explain in Chapter 3, because actors inhabit multiple markets, this inevitably leads to ambivalence and reflexivity. Actors become critically aware of how their own stylistic performances are constrained and may as a consequence, work actively to exploit or subvert these constraints (see also Coupland, 2007: 99).

With the foregoing in mind, adolescents can therefore be seen as participants in multiple markets, among which include families, peer groups and schools. While schools traffic mainly in cultural capital (such as the awarding of academic qualifications and credentials), peer groups traffic mainly in symbolic capital (informal prestige and recognition). And as we shall have occasion to note in the rest of this book, it is the conflict between these forms of capital and the different markets they characterize that often lead to the creation of English language-learning dilemmas for our adolescent subjects.

For now, however, in the rest of this introductory chapter, our aim is to elaborate on some of the issues that serve as a backdrop to our study of Singaporean adolescents.

Language, Gatekeeping and Monolingual Ideologies

Multilingual societies like Singapore are typically characterized by great social and linguistic heterogeneity, and managing both kinds of heterogeneity across constituencies of speakers is an important part of all civil and political activities. In the specific case of Singapore, the management of multilingualism is accomplished by the state's explicit recognition of the country's ethnic and linguistic diversity. The result is that Singapore is an officially multilingual country with a language policy that equates ethnic identity (and political role) with one of four official languages (see Chapter 2).

But despite this official commitment to multilingualism, one over-riding focus of this book is on how language and literacy education in Singapore contributes to the social reproduction of a macro-linguistic order based on a monolingual ideology of multilingualism (see below), thus link-ing an account of the sociolinguistic practices of individuals in their day-to-day lives with the performance and consolidation of a particular modernist order of ethnicity. This relationship between 'macro' and 'micro' levels has constituted one of the central problems of social theory, and as Heller points out, 'the macro/micro dichotomy is not the most helpful way in which to understand how the observable dimensions of social life in the here and now are linked to durable patterns which lie beyond the control or the awareness of individuals ...' (Heller, 2001: 212). Instead, Heller (2001: 212, citing Giddens, 1982) suggests that it is more appropriate to reconceptualize the 'problem of linkage between macro- and micro-levels' as a 'problem of linkage among social interactions over time and (social) space'. Heller elaborates:

> In practical terms, this means identifying the nature and social signifi-cance of the communicative resources people bring to interactions and call into play there, how they draw on them in the course of interactions, and with what consequences, for them and for others, immediately and over time. (Heller, 2001: 213)

In this book, our focus is on the specific kinds of interactions that our ado-lescent informants engage in and in the closing chapter (Chapter 9), we take up this issue of the relationship between the 'macro' and 'micro' levels via the concept of sociolinguistic consumption. The notion of sociolinguistic consumption, we suggest, provides a useful way of understanding the linkage between particular 'micro' social interactions, and how their cumulative force can lead to a particular 'macro' social order. But because we are concerned with exploring the implications of the macro-linguistic order for the multilingual practices of the individuals involved in our study, especially in the ways in which reproducing the social order also means reproducing social and ethnic identities that are associated with differential access to valuable symbolic and cultural capital, one question that interests us, then, is how multilingual practices are able to function as a proxy for socially and ethnically based inequities, or expressed differently, how language can serve as a gatekeeper.

It is widely recognized that language can act as a gatekeeper precisely because it allows selective access to social goods and as a consequence, can significantly affect one's social trajectory. A telling example of this comes from the experience of Helen, a Manchester woman who found her accent to be a problem when it came to looking for employment opportunities in London (Milroy & Milroy, 1999: 152). In Helen's own words:

> ... in the arts where no-one has a regional accent ... my CV was good enough to get me interviews, but ... as soon as they heard me speak ... I wasn't taken seriously ...

But unlike the United Kingdom, where the devaluation of particular linguistic varieties is often implicit, Singapore has, in contrast, a tradition of state-initiated campaigns, where the state explicitly attempts to encourage particular kinds of behavior over others, including linguistic behavior. In fact, Singapore has, for some time, been described as something of a 'nanny state' (Mauzy & Milne, 2002: 35). And Lee Kuan Yew, Singapore's first prime minister has even been quoted as saying (cited in Mauzy & Milne, 2002: 35, italics added):

> We wouldn't be here, would not have made the economic progress, if we had not intervened on very personal matters – who your neighbor is, how you live, the noise you make, how you spit or where you spit, or *what language you use* ... It was fundamental social and cultural changes that brought us here

What this means, then, is that in Singapore, the state is a particularly influential and authoritative institution (Blommaert, 2005) when it comes to adjudicating on ideologies about language. In particular, its views on what kinds of languages are worth learning and why, have been especially formative (Blommaert, 1999) in directing the courses of various language ideological debates (Bokhorst-Heng, 1999; Wee, 2005). This includes the state's embrace of monolingual ideologies, since one significant way in which multilingual realities are being managed by the state is via an appeal to monolingual ideologies or more specifically, by an appeal to language policies that are ultimately grounded in monolingual ideologies (Spolsky, 2004). As a consequence, the nuanced realities of multilingual contexts in much of social life get oversimplified and sit uneasily with the constraints and expectations imposed by monolingual ideologies. This is because monolingual ideologies typically assume that languages can be unproblematically treated as self-contained systems of knowledge, where each such system is clearly and identifiably separable from the other.

Even in cases where language policies are prepared to recognize or encourage multilingualism, the prevailing assumption is still that the different languages can and should be differentially valued (Silverstein, 1977, 1979), and be cognitively separated from each other (in the case of individual multilingualism) or spatio-temporally segregated by being tied to different domains or activities (in the case of societal multilingualism) (cf. Heller, 1999a, b). This leads to the assumption that the relationship between different languages is that of a zero sum game where increased knowledge or use of one language is often seen to be at the expense of some other. Thus, Siegel (1999) points out that in language education, two common justifications given for banning stigmatized or denigrated varieties are 'time on task' and 'interference' arguments. The 'time on task' argument is that the time spent using a stigmatized variety takes away from the time that could have been more productively spent on the improving competence in a more desired variety. This argument therefore 'explains' a learner's lack of proficiency in the desired variety by pointing to the fact that the learner is still using the stigmatized variety. This leads to the conclusion that the most reasonable remedy is to eliminate the stigmatized variety from the learner's repertoire. The 'interference' argument is that the learner experiences confusion between the grammar of the desired variety and that of the stigmatized variety. This inability to distinguish the two leads the learner to mix features of the stigmatized variety with those of the desired variety, thus contaminating the grammar of the desired variety. Again, as with the 'time on task' argument, the 'interference' argument has been used to justify the conclusion that the stigmatized variety ought to be eliminated, because of the confusion and contamination it causes.

We see indications of this monolingual ideology in the two different contemporary language campaigns that the state has been conducting to influence language use in Singapore, the Speak Mandarin Campaign and the Speak Good English Movement. The Speak Mandarin Campaign, which was started in 1979, is aimed at encouraging Chinese Singaporeans to speak their official mother tongue, Mandarin (Bokhorst-Heng, 1998, 1999). In trying to accomplish this, the campaign has at various times in its history, created an opposition between speakers of Mandarin and speakers of other Chinese dialects, and more recently, between speakers of Mandarin and speakers of English (Bokhorst-Heng, 1998). The second and more recent campaign is the Speak Good English Movement,[2] which began in 2000. One of the activities conducted in conjunction with this campaign is a series of internet online lessons (Kwan, 2003: 33) that are ostensibly aimed at improving the general standard of English. But in trying to do so, these lessons typically adopt an approach where a speaker of standard English is compared with a speaker of Singlish, a nativized colloquial variety, so that Singlish is effectively equated with 'bad' English.

Singlish shows a high degree of influence from other local languages, particularly Hokkien, Cantonese, Malay and Tamil. The following are sample Singlish utterances (adapted from Wee, 2005), showing how it is characterized by, among other features, a lack of inflectional morphology (2a), productive use of reduplication (2b) and discourse particles (2c) and lexical items borrowed from Malay and various Chinese dialects (2d). In (2c), the particle *lor* indicates a sense of resignation and in (2d), the word *suay* 'cursed/ unfortunate' comes from Hokkien.

(2)
a. He eat here yesterday.
   [He ate here yesterday.]
b. I like hot-hot curries.
   [I like very hot curries.]
c. I won't get married, lor.
   [I have no choice but to not get married.]
d. Don't make me suay, ok?
   [Don't bring me bad luck, ok?]

The Speak Good English Movement lessons usually involve a variety of contexts (education, professional, interaction with foreigners), and in each case, learners encounter statements such as the following that indicate the workings of 'verbal hygiene' (Cameron, 1995) on the part of the state:

... it is clear that the receptionist's use of Singlish gives the company a bad image

> Singlish speakers often repeat a verb (e.g. 'try-try', 'run-run', 'play-play') to indicate doing something for a short period of time or in a trivial manner. This is not acceptable. (Kwan, 2003: Appendix C)

Thus, while it is a social fact that, in multilingual societies, different linguistic varieties will tend to be differently valued, in Singapore, the presence of language campaigns initiated by the state authoritatively defines particular languages as being of greater value than others. This leads to a system of stratification, with different languages being 'indexically ordered' (Blommaert, 2005; Silverstein, 2003; see below) by their associations with different kinds of social and cultural factors. In the case of both the Speak Mandarin Campaign and the Speak Good English Movement, we see that the promotion of one variety is presented in oppositional terms, such that success in promoting one variety (Mandarin, good English) is seen to depend on the elimination of some other variety or varieties (other Chinese dialects, Singlish).

Monolingual ideologies also generate the expectation that proficiency in a particular language should be marked by a display of linguistic purity, with the consequence that the mixing of elements from different languages, surely the norm in multilingual societies, becomes construed as a form of linguistic contamination. In turn, such contamination can also, via the process of iconization (Gal & Irvine, 1995; Irvine & Gal, 2000), be further construed as pointing to a moral deficiency in the character of the speaker. Cameron's remarks are especially pertinent here:

> Ignorance or defiance of grammatical rules is equated with anti-social or criminal behavior. Grammar needs to be taught ... less to inculcate the norms of polite usage than to encourage respect for persons and property, to keep people clean and law-abiding, to build their 'character' and discourage indiscipline or 'sloppiness' ... (Cameron, 1995: 94)

It is this monolingual ideology that allows the government to consistently contrast Singlish with standard English, so that the former ends up being largely defined by its divergence from the standard. That is, as far as the 'interference' argument is concerned, it does not matter whether Singlish is a colloquial variety that might be rule-governed or whether it is an ad hoc collection of ungrammatical errors. In either case, it is still nonstandard and thus 'incorrect' by virtue of its divergence from the standard variety (Milroy, 2001). Singlish, then, is portrayed broadly as nonstandard English and at this relatively gross level of characterization, the distinction between that which is colloquial and that which is ungrammatical is lost. The distinction between what counts as colloquial and what counts as ungrammatical is admittedly a fluid one that depends on the conventions of particular linguistic markets (Bourdieu, 1990, 1991). But the failure to recognize the distinction allows the labels 'Singlish' and 'standard English' to be construed as identifying different language practices with contrasting moral values. This, then, provides the state with yet another line of argument against those language varieties that have been targeted from elimination from the Singapore linguistic landscape. In this case, the connection with moral values allows the state to target the speakers themselves by raising questions about their cultural integrity or social desirability. In this volume, then, we wish to explore how the state's indexical ordering of languages, with attendant monolingual ideologies, is legitimated in particular linguistic markets, and how access to valued linguistic and symbolic capital is distributed across social and ethnic groups in ways that reproduce the status quo.

Language Education as Social Reproduction

This concern with the social distribution and valuation of linguistic resources is in fact a sociolinguistic issue par excellence (Blommaert, 2005: 9). Perhaps because of this, attempts at addressing the gatekeeping functions of language loom large, especially in the literature on language and education. Explicit valuations by the state of particular linguistic varieties place major constraints on schools in Singapore. Legitimizing some forms of knowledge – including forms of language use – while de-legitimizing others is obviously a significant part of what educational institutions do. These institutions are obligated to provide learners with the 'practical competence' to 'produce expressions which are highly valued on the markets concerned' (Thompson, 1991: 18), while at the same time they cannot be seen to be condoning or endorsing the use of de-valued ones. Schools are consequently expected to endow learners with the necessary linguistic capital that will be of most advantage to them in the society at large even though it is unlikely that the distribution of such capital can ever be achieved with any kind of parity. In Singapore, for example, the prohibition on linguistic mixing is especially clear in educational contexts since ideologies of monolingualism typically lead teachers and, by extension, their students, to accept, often without reflection, the position that the focus on the target language cannot and should not be compromised by any appeal to the students' first language (see above).

In the specific case of English language education, Ferguson points out that 'it has long been regarded (see, for example the Kingman Report 1989) as part of the business of education to impart knowledge of, and skill in using, a standard variety – a variety, that is, that is common and uniform, and has wide currency beyond the local or regional' (Ferguson, 2006: 167). And quoting Davies (1999: 176), Ferguson goes on to note:

> Which model is, of course, a matter for those responsible for the examination, normally those with decision-making powers at national level. The choice may be British English, American English, Singapore English, Zimbabwe English: but a standard English it most certainly will be. (Ferguson, 2006: 167)

But as Bourdieu points out, the standard language is a product created on the assumption that a language can be 'impersonal and anonymous like the official uses it has to serve' (Bourdieu, 1991: 48). Such an assumption ignores the fact that even official uses of language are indexically marked by their associations with the contexts of bureaucracy and administration, and because of this, represent language resources that are not necessarily stylistically suitable for other interactional contexts. This ideology of a standard, aided by the educational system and labor market, helps to 'devalue popular modes of expression, dismissing them as "slang" and "gibberish" and to impose recognition of the legitimate language' (Bourdieu, 1991: 49; see also Milroy, 2001; Milroy & Milroy, 1999). This is despite the fact that many linguists have argued for greater space to be accorded dialects in language education, often on the grounds that the linguistic confidence of students is critical to successful language learning, and this can be best cultivated by demonstrating sensitivity toward the nonstandard varieties that students bring with them into the classroom (Cheshire, 1982; Trudgill, 1975; see also Mesthrie & Bhatt, 2008: 207).

Of course, even leaving aside the relationship between the standard and nonstandard varieties, among the different standard varieties, there are still relations of inequality, so that Singapore English or Zimbabwe English – even the so-called standard versions – are not likely to be considered as valuable as their British or American counterparts. In some cases, their very legitimacy may even be called into question. Thus, Bamgbose, speaking from the Nigerian context, points out the following:

> One noticeable effect of the refusal to accept the existence of a Nigerian English is the perpetuation of the myth that the English taught in Nigeria is the same as, say, British English … In our teaching and examinations we concentrate on drilling out of existence forms of speech that even the teachers will use freely when they do not have the textbooks open before them. (Bamgbose, 1992: 149, cited in Ferguson, 2006: 169)

In the case of Singapore, the state's attitude toward the existence of a standard Singaporean English is ambivalent at best. But what is unequivocal is its view that the colloquial variety of English, often referred to as Singlish, has absolutely no legitimacy because its very existence threatens to undermine the ability of Singaporeans to learn 'good' or 'proper' English (Bokhorst-Heng, 2005; Chng, 2003; Rubdy, 2001; Wee, 2005). The government assumes that Singlish is a fully extensive social language (Gee, 2001: 652), that is it can be used – like standard English – as the medium for conducting entire exchanges (Wee, 2010). For example, the state assumes that there are Singaporeans who are interacting entirely in Singlish because they are unable to speak the standard variety. This assumption legitimizes the claim that there is indeed a Singlish 'problem', since Singlish is then seen as 'poor English [that] reflects badly on us and makes us seem less intelligent or competent' (Goh Chok Tong, 2000 Speak Good English Movement speech). If, on the other hand, Singlish were only a play language – perhaps one that speakers occasionally and deliberately crossed into (Rampton, 1995) so that it was limited to the 'liminal margins of everyday interactional practice' (Rampton, 1998: 229), such as greetings or farewells, then it would be less of an issue because it would be less widespread through not being used for rather more 'substantive' interactions. The state's assumption that Singlish is being used for the conduct of entire exchanges implies that it is a fully extensive social language. This gives credence to the character of the monolingual Singlish speaker, which is then taken to reflect a linguistic reality – one in sore need of redress. Thus, in August 1999, Singapore's Senior Minister Lee Kuan labeled Singlish 'a handicap we must not wish on Singaporeans' (*The Sunday Times* August 15, 1999), and later that same month, the then Prime Minister Goh Chok Tong suggested that 'we should ensure that the next generation does not speak Singlish' (*The Straits Times* August 29, 1999).

The state is aware, of course, that there are also Singaporeans who can easily code-switch between Standard English and Singlish, since it is precisely this particular group of Singaporeans who have been the strongest supporters of Singlish. However, these Singaporeans who deliberately choose to speak Singlish when they can in fact speak Standard English are described as doing the nation a 'disservice' (Goh Chok Tong, 2000 SGEM Speech), since they are not making it easy for their monolingual Singlish-speaking fellow Singaporeans to learn the standard. But the assumption that Singlish is indeed a fully extensive social language is actually problematic. We can see this by comparing Singlish with other varieties that are indeed fully extensive social languages, that is varieties that we know can be used as the medium for entire exchanges. Wee (2010) points out that the Chinese dialects such as Cantonese, Hokkien or Teochew, can all be used to totally constitute the medium for various interactions. These Chinese dialects have also been the target of a language campaign. This is the Speak Mandarin Campaign (referred to earlier), intended to encourage Singaporeans to use Mandarin in place of the other dialects (Bokhorst-Heng, 1999). In attempting to do both discourage the dialects as well as Singlish, the Media Development Authority issued the following advisories (MDA Free-To-Air Television Programme Code (3–4):

(3)
   News, current affairs, and info-educational programmes where dialect interviews are given by older people who are unable to speak Mandarin. Voice-overs should be provided for these interviews.

(4)
   Singlish, which is ungrammatical local English, and includes dialect terms and sentence structures based on dialect, should not be encouraged and can only be permitted in interviews, where the interviewee speaks only Singlish. The interviewer himself, however, should not use Singlish.

However, it has been much easier to implement (3) than (4), for the simple reason that as fully extensive social languages, there are conversations or programs that are entirely in Hokkien or Cantonese. These can then be banned or dubbed. But as a less extensively developed social language,[3] most Singlish usage involves switching between Singlish and standard English; there are few movies or television serials that are *totally* in Singlish. Alsagoff (2007: 40) implicitly recognizes this fact in her discussion of how Singaporeans use Singlish and Standard English, when she refers to the inclusion of Singlish features 'in what would otherwise be recognized as Standard English' rather than the other way round. Returning to (3–4) above, what this means is that while it may be relatively easy to identify movies, serials or news interviews that are presented entirely in the Chinese dialects (and thus either ban them or demand the use of voice-overs), it is in contrast far more difficult to apply the same regulatory practices to Singlish. This is because Singlish is usually interspersed with other lexicogrammatical constructions that are more or less standard, so that the attempt to treat Singlish and Standard English as clearly bounded varieties is in fact problematic (Crowley, 1999; Wee, 2011). This does not invalidate the features described in (2) above (p. 9) as representations of Singlish. However, they are best considered stereotypical features: their presence may be sufficient to index Singlishness, but their absence cannot be taken as an indication of non-Singlishness.

What is lost, as a result, is the pedagogical value of linguistic hybridity, where students can and should learn to manage different linguistic systems even as they appreciate the porous nature of such systems. But in a rapidly globalizing world of highly mobile individuals, the ability to effectively deploy varied linguistic systems in order to achieve particular interactional goals is a valuable skill. And given Singapore's interest in preparing its population to succeed in a globally competitive environment, the cultivation of such 'symbolic competence' (Kramsch & Whiteside, 2008) should be an educational priority.

Unfortunately, the deeply entrenched assumptions that constitute the ideology of monolingualism are hard to discard. As a result, what this means is that students often find that identities associated with lower valued linguistic varieties (such as Singlish) are denigrated wholesale in the language classroom, as opposed being recognized as resources that might yet have value, given the vagaries of cultural encounters in a rapidly changing world. This is a deeply ironic situation, especially if we consider the influential status of what is sometimes described as the 'communicative approach' to language teaching (Clarke, 1989; Wallace, 2002). A major impetus for the rise of the communicative approach came from the recognition that schools cannot merely view their role as one of preparing learners to pass school-based examinations; rather, they must train them to communicate 'authentically' beyond the school (cf. Widdowson, 1979: 162–163). In fact, authentic communication is seen so much as a pedagogical desideratum that Clarke (1989: 73) refers to it as a 'moral imperative'. But while the notion of authenticity has been greatly emphasized and discussed in the field of English Language Teaching (ELT), we find it interesting that there has generally been much less controversy over, or debate about, what actually counts as authentic communication. Thus, Clarke (1989: 76), in summarizing works by various authors (including Canale & Swain, 1980; Littlewood, 1981, among others) notes that it is generally assumed that authentic communication involves 'freedom of choice concerning what to say and how to say it, meaningful context and the purposeful use of language.' Writing almost 10 years later, Skehan (1998: 18) makes similar points when he suggests that in authentic communication, people 'express individual meanings', where meaning is prioritized over form. Also, people are not simply given 'other people's meanings to regurgitate', and there is no concern with 'language display' (Skehan, 1998: 95).

Underlying this emphasis on freedom of choice and individual meaning is what Duranti (1992: 26) refers to as a 'personalist' view of communication. This is a view that assumes that authentic communication takes place only if the illocutionary intent that grounds the communicative act originates from 'within' the speaker himself/herself. As such, the personalist view unduly privileges the speaker's subjective intentions in acts of communication. Duranti (1992: 25–27) suggests that this view is in fact extremely common in the 'Western tradition of linguistic studies' and 'Western epistemologies and theories of social action'. Accordingly, Duranti (1992: 26–27) points out that the personalist view of communication tends to downplay the role of the audience in 'shaping utterances and (re)defining meanings', as well as the fact that there are times when it is 'dramatis personae rather than individuals who are seen as producing meaningful speech acts'. This view of communication, rather unfortunately, treats the individual intention as a fully defined psychological state that exists prior to any act of speaking (Duranti, 1992: 25) and, as a consequence, relegates the addressee to the relatively passive role of simply trying to reconstruct as accurately as possible the intentions of the actor. Also, actor responsibility, in so far as it is even an issue of discussion (rather than being dismissed under the rubric of 'perlocutionary effects') is essentially treated as a function of actor intention. That is, actors are held responsible for the resulting effects of their communicative acts to the extent that they chose to engage in the act despite the fact that they foresaw, or can be reasonably expected to have foreseen, its consequences.

The personalist view of meaning has been criticized, primarily from a linguistic anthropological perspective, for giving insufficient attention to contextual factors. Rosaldo (1982: 203), for example, criticizes speech act theory, particularly the version developed by Searle (1969), for its 'individualistic and relatively asocial biases' (see also the papers in Duranti & Goodwin, 1992; Hill & Irvine, 1992). The main thrust of the criticism is twofold: One, communication is far more interactive than has been recognized so that the addressee often plays an active role in (co-) constructing the meanings of communicative acts. Two, the centrality given to actor intention is unjustified especially if this is presented as a universal statement of how communication works; cultures vary greatly in the degree to which actor intention is even considered a relevant variable in meaning construction. And as many other scholars have observed, the recognition of specific emotions or attributes as being present is dependent on some form of social endorsement. For example, in professional performances discussed by Hochschild (1983) and Leidner (1993) of the airline, insurance and fast food industries, workers are expected to engage in 'emotional labour' (Hochschild, 1983: 7), projecting specific emotions (such as sincerity, enthusiasm or warmth) in ways that are organizationally acceptable. What is deemed a professionally acceptable manifestation of a specific emotion may even be 'styled' or 'scripted' (Cameron, 2000). Similarly, Goodwin and Goodwin's (2004: 225) concept of participation framework focuses on how different parties 'build action together' by reflexively monitoring each other's contributions toward the construction of a situated activity. Such contributions can include the public imputation of intentionality as well as the attribution of qualities such as anger, sadness, integrity and so on. In relation specifically to authenticity, Bucholtz and Hall (2004: 385) point out that the quality of being authentic is in fact a socially negotiated attribute that may be bestowed upon, or denied to, various individuals or groups.

But because the personalist view underlies what is taken to be authentic communication, it is no surprise that when it comes to language teaching, the emphasis becomes one of enthusing learners sufficiently so that they would sincerely want (for themselves) to do things like understand cooking recipes, write science reports, formulate hypotheses, or inquire about the weather, all in the target language (Hall, 1995: 12; Rossner, 1988: 140–141). Unfortunately, this focus on language as a medium for information transfer that privileges the speaker's intentions ignores the socially negotiated nature of communication, including the fact that how language is used in social interaction can critically influence the way in which the speaker's identity is co-constructed by interactional others.

As we saw in our brief discussion of Yan, her choice of language use is not simply constrained by intelligibility, it is also constrained by the desire not to be perceived by others as spoiled or snobbish, with such identities being indexed by the use of English as opposed to Malay. But given the assumption that learners need only worry about using the language for information transfer, it is no wonder that when remedial strategies are proposed, they are mainly concerned with addressing 'competence-based anxieties' rather than 'identity-based anxieties' (see Chapter 8).

Competence-based anxieties have to do with students' worries about how their language competence will be evaluated; these might be alleviated if the teacher appears approachable or if the students are given sufficient time to rehearse their language use. In contrast, identity-based anxieties have to do with the kinds of person one wants to be seen as, including the desire not to appear boastful and the desire for peer approval. Remedial strategies that target competence-based anxieties while ignoring the influence of identity-based ones are therefore unlikely to be of much use in helping language learners since, as we show later, identity issues can have significantly detrimental effects on learner behavior in the language classroom. We suggest here that the personalist, information-focused and individualist conception of 'authentic communication' is, in fact, closely linked to the particular communicative/linguistic ideology of late-modern Singaporean state, and that one important function of the school is to legitimate this view of language. However, the linguistic markets within which our adolescents trade give premium to a very different conception of communication and learning, where the performance of identities in which students have heavily invested and concomitant stylizations of self-sensitive to audience co-craftings across multiple floors is the norm. In this book, we will focus specifically on how these different types of practices are legitimated and de-legitimated, the relationship of these processes to the political economy (of schooling) and the implications these carry for stakeholders social positioning.

Another significant point with this view of authentic communication is that it implicitly assumes that such communication is essentially *monolingual* in nature. That is, while learners are supposed to be given 'freedom of choice in what to say and how to say it', the possibility that this might involve code-switching or crossing (Auer, 1998; Rampton, 1995, 1998) is seldom taken into consideration at all. We would also argue that there are strong reasons for treating code-switching and crossing as being concerned with language display since in such cases, it is not simply the lexicogrammatical structures of the codes that communicate; the transition itself from one code to another also serves to convey implicatures of various kinds (Stroud, 1998). In this study, we show how adolescents persist in carrying their patterns of interaction that take place outside the classroom (such as code-switching) over into the English language classroom as well, though this is done covertly in off-site activities that are conducted away from the teacher's scrutiny. The effects of this carrying over on English language learning cannot be underestimated, and one of our concerns is on how such code-switching (and the kind of identity work that it implicates) can be treated as a pedagogical resource to better engage students.

So while there have been heated arguments in ELT over how best to implement syllabuses and methodologies that prepare learners to communicate 'authentically', the possibility that this might have to take into account manifestations of linguistic hybridity and identity-based anxieties appears to have hardly ever been addressed, and even then only quite recently. Instead, discussions revolving around the notion of authentic communication have covered a range of other issues such as whether the texts being used for instruction should be authentic in the sense of having been already attested in a corpus (Sinclair, 1988: 6) or whether it is more important for the learner to have an 'authentic response' regardless of how contrived the texts themselves may be (Widdowson, 1978: 80); whether the kinds of pedagogical materials and tasks being devised are in fact consistent with the espoused principles of authentic communication (Widdowson, 2003: 124); and whether the issue of authenticity should apply only to syllabuses pertaining to English for specific purposes or those pertaining to English for general purposes as well (Clarke, 1989: 73–74).

In multilingual contexts, however, authentic communication inevitably involves code-switching, the use of mixed codes and crossing, and the management of these codes in the service of identity work. To give learners the impression that these are in some way 'illegitimate' or 'peripheral' uses of language is to do them a vast disservice. In fact, the devaluing or de-legitimizing of linguistic hybridity (implicit or otherwise) is one crucial mechanism by which monolingual ideologies are reproduced. Here, we build on the insights of sociologists such as Goffman and sociolinguists such as Bell, Eckert and so on, who importantly have developed mechanisms for capturing how speakers may be articulating multiple identities in and designing their utterances in relation to multiple interlocutors in multiple languages through practices of switching and bricolage. Furthermore, we attempt on the basis of this model to apply these insights to a classroom practice for English language teaching that builds on the notion of crossing (see Chapter 8).

Literacy as a Site of Contestation

In this book, we are engaging with these themes specifically with respect to English language literacy as it is a prime site for exclusionary educational practices centering around monolingual identities and practices. An important milestone in studies of literacy is, of course, Street's (1984) distinction between autonomous and ideological models of literacy. Under the autonomous model, literacy is treated as a form of 'neutral technology'; written texts are considered highly distinct from speech; it is considered better to be literate than nonliterate, with the distinction between the two understood as a binary attribute so that one can be categorically either literate or not; and research tends to focus on literacy as a cognitive phenomenon, being concerned with disembedded thought and a universalized notion of what it means to be rational. In contrast, an ideological model recognizes the existence of multiple literacies (Collins, 1995; Gee, 1990; Street, 1993), and rather than literacy being 'neutral', it is acknowledged that there are different kinds of literacies and these are necessarily embedded in their socio-cultural contexts. There is no sharp distinction between spoken and written language, and research focuses on the social contexts in which literacies arise, are legitimized and sustained. But while Street's distinction has undoubtedly proven enormously influential and useful in allowing researchers to appreciate the richness of literacy practices, we think it is fair to say that it has been far less successful in overcoming the hegemony of the autonomous model. Paradoxically then, even as literacy scholars continue describing the situatedness of particular literacy practices (Barton & Hamilton, 1998), the world around us, it seems, is fast becoming a place where the autonomous model is ever more prevalent (Hull & Schultz, 2002: 52; Street, 2003: xii), and there are reasons for thinking that this distinction has not been pursued to the point where issues of power are being engaged with in any systematic manner.

One reason, it seems to us, why the autonomous model is not only prevailing but seems to be growing is that, despite more than 20 years of research under the ideological model, the latter historically has focused largely on describing the richness of literacy practices to the point where there has been a reluctance to suggest normative recommendations for either educational strategies or general implications for language policies. For example, Street, in his introduction to a collection of papers, states that 'The ethnographic approach represented here is, then, more concerned with attempting to understand what actually happens than with trying to prove the success of a particular intervention or "sell" a particular methodology for teaching or management' (Street, 2001: 1). Unfortunately, this attitude has seemed to become entrenched to the point where any kind of intervention has been preempted, leaving the study of literacy in a rather unsatisfactory state. Thus, as expressed by Rogers:

> But at times this leaves a sense of unfinished business. Time and again, I was tempted to ask at the end of a chapter, 'So what?' ... But literacy agencies cannot 'suspend judgment'. The question for all literacy learning practitioners is, 'whose side are you on?' If there are dominant and subaltern literacies and different ways in which the dominant literacy is used, which literacies and which uses of literacy are we encouraging? If literacy is tied to the power structures of society, where do we stand? Where do we come from and where are we going? (Rogers, 2001: 217)

Despite these concerns, there is still a general feeling that the study of literacy still needs to be positioned even within the 'next phase' (Street, 2004: 329, see below) of describing and analyzing power relations. Consider, in this regard, Street's more recent remarks:

> The ethnography of literacy, then, has to offer accounts not only of rich cultural forms and 'situated' literacy practices but also broader, more politically charged accounts of the power structures that define and rank such practices. (Street, 2004: 327)

And (Street, italics added):

> The task of ethnographies of literacy in *the next phase*, then, ... is to provide rich and complex accounts of multimodality in the context of

such local/global dimensions. *Once we have sufficient such accounts, we might then, as Baynham argues, return full circle to the ethnography of communication's interest in literacy pedagogy and apply it equally to multimodal pedagogy.* (Street, 2004: 329)

We are generally very much in agreement with the sentiments expressed by Street (2004). Yet, we are concerned that there may be too much of a tendency to defer the engagement with issues of applied literacy pedagogy. Put another way, the focus of much literacy research has been primarily on documenting the specific details of literacy practices rather than taking note of their 'material consequences' (Luke, 2004; see also Brandt & Clinton, 2002) and proposing, where necessary, particular remedial strategies. This is not, we want to emphasize, the same as 'selling' a particular methodology since the methodology does not precede the analysis of literacy practices. Rather, any proposed methodology emerges from a consideration of the particular effects of prevailing practices and it attempts to suggest possible ways in which such effects may be mitigated in order to help individuals transform their own lives in a manner that might serve purposes of their own.

This book is thus intended as an extended investigation into the sociolinguistics of literacy from the perspective of how it mediates the formation of social roles and identities (in various groupings such as the family, the peer group, the school and ultimately, nation-state). Following Luke, we take the conceptualization of literacy as social practice 'as but a starting point for analysis and not as the end point – lest it become a "vanishing point" for a critical political economy of literacy and education' (Luke, 2004: 334). Our interest is in understanding how conceptualizations of literacy at the micro-level of individual interactions are informed by, and contribute to, the structuring of broader macro-level political economies. Our particular focus is on the sociolinguistics of English language literacy in Singapore, and the question of how a multilingual society such as this nevertheless succeeds in reproducing a linguistic market that privileges the English language despite officially subscribing to a policy of 'multiracialism' (Benjamin, 1976; Wee, 2002b; see Chapter 2). We have chosen to research these concerns by focusing on education precisely because it is a key institution found in almost every modern society (Bourdieu & Passeron, 1979; Ferguson, 2006). Education is arguably the most formalized channel by which speakers acquire the symbolic and cultural credentials that are given premium in society at large. By distributing categories of academic achievement differentially across social categories, educational practices comprise 'a key site for the construction of social identities and of unequal relations of power' (Heller & Martin-Jones, 2001: 2). Furthermore, there is a general expectation that whatever else the purpose of education may be, it includes preparing and credentializing learners for the workplace (Bills, 2004: 14).

How students participate in talk around text and their conceptions and use of language, all contribute to what counts as a legitimate display of knowledge, with consequences for their academic roles as learners (Gee, 2000). And classroom practices are very much about authenticating and legitimizing particular ways of talking about, and taking knowledge from, texts (Heath, 1983). Very often, how educational institutions distribute credentials results in a reproduction of the prevailing social structure, since cultural capital tends to be allocated among social classes in such a way as to reflect the status quo. According to Bourdieu, this makes educational institutions especially efficacious as mechanisms of social reproduction:

> ... the sociology of educational institutions ... may make a decisive contribution to the frequently neglected aspect of the sociology of power which consists in the science of the dynamics of class relations. Indeed, among all the solutions provided, throughout the course of history, to the problem of the transmission of power and privileges, probably none have been better dissimulated and, consequently, better adapted to societies which tend to reject the most patent forms of hereditary transmission of power and privileges, than that provided by the educational system in contributing to the reproduction of the structure of class relations and in dissimulating the fact that it fulfils this function under the appearance of neutrality. (Bourdieu, quoted in Jenkins, 1992: 110)

We therefore agree with Bourdieu that any investigation into education needs to pay attention to issues of power and social reproduction, and how these are legitimized as neutral or natural. To this end, we employ a framework that draws on, among others, recent sociolinguistic treatments of identity construction in terms of style (Coupland, 2007; Eckert, 2000) and performance (Bauman & Briggs, 1990; Coupland, 2007) as well as theorizations concerning the semiotic processes by which language ideologies are brought about and sustained (Blommaert, 2005). Throughout, we attempt to be cognizant of how classroom and out-of-school practices of literacy articulate with aspects of late-modern Singaporean society and its *modus operandi* in terms of social class, ethnicity and its multiple trajectories of crossing and transport.

The Organization of this Book

This book is organized as follows. Because our data and analyses are drawn from adolescents living and studying in Singapore, it is only appropriate that in the next chapter, *Multilingualism in Singapore: A Portrait*, we provide a brief description of the multilingual nature of Singapore society. And as indicated above, in doing so, we will also attempt to address the rather paradoxical question of how it is that a policy explicitly committed to multilingualism might in fact be moving toward the privileging of English language hegemony. Our focus in this chapter, then, is on contrasting the official modernist perspective on Singaporean multilingualism expressed in official policy with the realities of a sociolinguistics of multilingualism more typical of a late-modern society. This description will serve as a useful springboard for the subsequent chapters, when we begin looking at the literacy practices of particular individuals. The expositional trajectory of our discussion therefore is very broadly a move from the more general and macro aspects of multilingualism in Singapore to the more specific and micro.

Chapter 3, *Multilingualism in Late Modernity: Literacy as a Reflexive Performance of Identity*, develops an account of our theoretical framework centering on the notion of reflexivity as framed within poststructural notions of identity, and core analytical concepts such as style and performance and an exploration of Bourdieu's notion of market. Together with the discussion in Chapter 2, this chapter lays the groundwork for the analyses to be subsequently presented in Chapters 5 through 7.

Chapter 4, *Some Data About Our Data*, describes the methodology involved in gathering our data, with particular attention being given to the challenges of choosing approaches to data collection that are appropriate to late-modern contexts of multilingualism. In particular, we discuss issues around interpreting our informants' voices through reflexive and multi-sited narratives.

Chapters 5 through 7 introduce the adolescent informants in our study and explore the interactions between their home environments, their peer groups and their classroom behaviors. In Chapter 5, *Fandi and Ping: Literacy Practices and the Performance of Identities in Multiple Linguistic Markets*, we approach our adolescents' literacy practices from the perspective of performance, reflexivity and ambivalence, using the idea of orders of indexicality and its interaction with social class and ethnicity in constructions of self-representation. Here, we focus on the experiences of Fandi and Ping, a Malay male adolescent and a Chinese female adolescent, respectively. By examining the practices of literacy that Fandi and Ping engage in, at home, in school and in their interactions with their peers, we aim to bring out the various demands these adolescent informants face and the ways in which the negotiations of these demands influence the ways they align themselves in different linguistic markets.

Having discussed and analyzed the experiences of Fandi and Ping, Chapter 6, *Edwin, Wen and Yan: Styling Literacy Practices Inside and Outside the Classroom*, goes on to introduce three other adolescents: Edwin, a Chinese male, Wen, a Chinese female and Yan, the Malay female whom we encountered at the very beginning of this chapter. In Chapter 6, we deal in more detail with how literacy practices are performed as style and stylization in identity work, and with the ways in which literacy artifacts (as products for consumption) construct different symbolic spaces for stylization. Whereas Chapter 5 focuses on identity work mediated by performances of literacy in relation to macro-scale categories of class, and ethnicity, Chapter 6 complements this focus by attending to identity work at the local level of the peer group in different interactional spaces, footings and floors.

The notion of performance is also employed in Chapter 7, *Skilled Performances: A Comparison with Sha*, to discuss a particularly facilitating type of orientation to language and language learning among socioeconomically privileged youth in late-modern Singapore. Here, we introduce our final adolescent informant, Sha, an Indian male who, unlike the preceding informants, is distinguished by at least two facts. One, he has a much more confident command of the English language than the rest, and two, he comes from a more socioeconomically privileged background. The connection between these two facts, though obviously not a necessary one, is by no means coincidental. In our discussion of Sha, then, we aim to bring out the connections between language performances, English language competence and social class.

Chapter 8, *Pedagogy, Literacy and Identity*, inserts our work into ongoing discussions about the nature of literacy. In particular, we suggest some possible pedagogical strategies that we think can be usefully brought to bear on the question of how language and literacy teaching can be conducted in ways that do not force students to compromise the peer-oriented identities that they might otherwise heavily value.

Chapter 9, *The Dynamics of Language Distribution in Late-Modern Multilingual Singapore*, serves as a conclusion to the book as a whole. Here, we focus specifically on the broader policy implications of the ideological model of literacy. We return to some of the issues that were raised in Chapter 2, and we attempt to situate our discussions of multilingualism in Singapore in relation to the broader flows of globalization. We pay particular attention to the implications of outward and inward migration for Singapore's language policy. In doing so, we necessarily address the intersection between the official expectations of language competence, including the role to be played by English, and we suggest that the language policy may need to be tweaked in order to give greater space to individual choice autonomy.

Notes

(1) See Chapter 2 for an explanation of the official mother-tongue policy in Singapore.

(2) The term 'movement' is a deliberate attempt to convince Singaporeans, who might be suffering from 'campaign exhaustion', that this is really not another state-initiated campaign. Calling it a 'movement' is thus intended to convey the impression that this is grassroots, bottom-up initiative started by the people rather than one begun by the state.

(3) By treating the dialects as more extensive social languages than Singlish, we do not of course mean to imply that the grammar of the dialects is complete or hermetically sealed. Nor do we mean to suggest that the grammar of Singlish cannot further develop so that it can be used in sustained social interactions. Extensiveness is a relative matter, contingent on the activities of language users, which is precisely what Gee's (2001) notion of social languages is trying to remind us of.

2 Multilingualism in Late-Modern Singapore: A Portrait

In this chapter, we present a scenario of a late modern[1] Singapore, and discuss the wealth of contradictions faced by a traditionally strong (and successful) modernist policy on language in the nation-state, and the everyday late-modern multilingual practices of Singaporeans as they go about their daily lives. What we wish to do is to map how government has attempted (and still attempts) to address diversity in nation-building, particularly how policies are redrawn to meet the changing conditions of trans-nationalism and late-modernism cut to the same cloth as the essential national building blocks of earlier successful policies.

The changing relationship between a modernist state and the late-modern conditions of existence is far from unique to Singapore, and it reflects the shifting ground on which the nation-state attempts to reinvent itself in many contexts of rapid contemporary transformation (Sassen, 2006; Wallerstein, 2000). We do believe, though, that Singapore provides a particularly clear example – in fact, a pristine example – of such a state because of its long tradition of explicit close government and hands-on management of all sectors of public and private life (see Chapter 1), and its desire to be on the cusp of global developments, its ever-readiness to embrace the latest in late-modern entrepreneurialism (Ong, 2006).

This chapter will attempt to address the question of how and why it is that Singapore appears to be moving toward the privileging of English. At the same time, it will also set the scene for the theoretical and methodological framework that we develop in Chapters 3 and 4. Our conceptual understanding of late-modern societies such as Singapore requires that we rethink many social (e.g. social class, reflexivity) and sociolinguistic concepts (style, stylization) and perspectives in order that we may capture the dynamics of nation-building (cf. Heller, 2008a). Furthermore, the nature of late-modernity, specifically the types of relationships and semiotic interactions that people are engaged in, also suggests revisiting questions of research methodologies, a re-weighting of data elicitation types (e.g. the revised significance of the 'interview', the problems of mobility and the difficulties in collecting data in one context only – which therefore point to the value of a multisited approach).

Modern Discourses of Multilingualism

Official Singaporean discourses on multilingualism are pristinely modernist in content and orientation. A modernist take on multilingualism sees language in explicitly structural–functional terms, where each language is presumed to be a bounded and delimitable system that occupies an equally bounded and delimitable space and function (Makoni & Pennycook, 2007). In other words, it views multilingualism in terms of a mosaic model of linguistic distinctiveness, a perspective on language that 'takes the world to be a neat patchwork of separate monolingual, geographical areas almost exclusively populated by monolingual speakers' (De Schutter, 2007: 3). As a consequence, a modernist take ends up treating language as an unproblematic and easily identifiable construct, one that serves as an intrinsic expression of a community or individual identity. There is, in short, an emphasis on a strict compartmentalization of languages, a division that also carries with it different indexical determined according to the distribution of capital in society (see below).

This view of language and multilingualism is an instance of a more general modernist view of society as structured in terms of an integrated conglomerate of ordered and bounded coexisting social entities, such as ethnic groups, social classes, genders and family units. These social entities are the basic building blocs of society, responsible for socializing their members and for monitoring and correcting behavior. In fact, managing diversity comes to be construed as essential to the smooth operation of the nation-state, as diversity is seen as potentially disruptive as well as a disadvantage to those who suffer it. It is therefore seen as something that needs to be controlled, contained and ameliorated, ideally through rational policies of government and the technical knowledge of expert planners.

As we shall see, all this is relevant to understanding the important roles that language plays in the social and ethnic politics of Singapore, allowing us to better appreciate the close links and tensions that exist between social politics and the policies of multilingualism.

An Ethnicity-based Politics of Language

As an ethnically and linguistically diverse society, with a population totaling about 3.2 million, it is no surprise that Singapore has grappled since independence in 1965 with the problem of how to manage its heterogeneity across a range of sociopolitical contexts. One way in which the Singaporean state has seen fit to manage such ethnolinguistic diversity is to divide the population into four ethnicity-based categories, so that the 3.2 million Singaporeans are effectively seen as being made up of 76.8% Chinese, 13.9% Malays, 7.9% Indians and 1.4% Others (2000 Census of Population). Each of the major ethnic categories is then assigned an official mother tongue, with the state treating Mandarin as the official mother tongue of the Chinese, Malay as the mother tongue of the Malays and Tamil as the mother tongue of the Indians. There is no official mother tongue for the 'Others' category since this is really a miscellaneous collection of various ethnicities that cannot be easily fitted into the first three. We note then how this politics of ethnicity and language has all the features of a modernist discourse of society and language. This modernist take on ethnicity also opens up the space for a special treatment of English. In addition to the three official mother tongues, the state also treats English as a fourth official language. Specifically, English is positioned as an inter-ethnic lingua franca and as a language of particular importance in the global economy. Here, then, we see that Singapore's language policy recognizes four official languages (English, Mandarin, Malay and Tamil) with English supposedly an ethnically neutral language since it is the only one of the four that has no official ethnic affiliation (Wee, 2002b).

In the case of education (see Gopinathan et al., 1998 for a critical overview), the implication of this language policy is that students are expected to be bilingual in both the ethnically neutral English and their official ethnic mother tongue. That is, students are expected to know English because it is used as the medium of instruction in the schools and universities, and also because it facilitates communication across the various ethnic communities in Singapore, as well as communication with the world outside, as it were. But in addition to English, students are expected to learn their officially assigned mother tongues as second languages in order that they may have a sense of their own 'true' cultural ancestry. Pakir (1992) refers to this requirement that Singaporeans learn both English and their official mother tongue as a policy of 'English-knowing bilingualism'.

The official notion of mother tongue is obviously problematic since, with the possible exception of the Malays, it does not necessarily reflect the language actually spoken at home (see Tables 2.1 through 2.3). Also, a child

TABLE 2.1 LANGUAGE MOST FREQUENTLY SPOKEN IN CHINESE HOMES (%)

	1980	1990	2000
English	10.2	21.4	23.9
Mandarin	13.1	30.0	30.7
Chinese dialects	76.2	48.2	30.7

TABLE 2.2 LANGUAGE MOST FREQUENTLY SPOKEN IN INDIAN HOMES (%)

	1980	1990	2000
English	24.3	34.3	35.6
Tamil	52.2	43.5	42.9

TABLE 2.3 LANGUAGE MOST FREQUENTLY SPOKEN IN MALAY HOMES (%)

	1980	1990	2000
English	2.3	5.7	7.9
Malay	96.7	94.1	91.6

categorized as belonging to the 'Others' category will still have to learn a second language in order to fulfill the requirement of bilingualism, but this second language may have no connection at all with the child's ethnic identity. These various problems[2] arise because first of all, the policy of multi-racialism overlooks the 'heterogeneous character of each race in favour of a more simplified, multiracial CMIO (Chinese, Malay, Indian and Others) quadratomy' (Siddique, 1990: 36) and second of all, English is increasingly becoming a home language for a significant portion of the population.

As we noted in Chapter 1, the institution of Mandarin as the mother tongue of the Chinese community came at the price of a Speak Mandarin Campaign, where the goal of the campaign was to discourage the use of the other Chinese dialects. The government's motivation for initiating the Speak Mandarin Campaign was that a linguistically heterogeneous Chinese community is also a socially fragmented community. And while a sociolinguistically natural outcome of the increased use of English in any community is the development of a nativized variety (Kachru, 1985, 1986, 2005), the nativized variety of English in Singapore, commonly referred to as Singlish, has been targeted for elimination by the state as part of its Speak Good English Movement (Chng, 2003; Rubdy, 2001). What these all suggest is that the state is keen on maintaining its commitment, for the foreseeable future at least, to a policy where students are required to learn their official mother tongue or a second language (in the case of 'Others'), and where, while proficiency in English is encouraged, this language is simply not officially acceptable at all as a mother tongue.

Monolingual Ideology in Multilingual Singapore[3]

As we have pointed out (Chapter 1), one way in which monolingual ideologies deal with multilingualism is to insist on specific functions for particular languages. To see the monolingual ideology behind Singapore's policy of bilingualism, note that the state insists on the strict compartmentalization of English from the mother tongues. The state's rationale is that knowledge of English is necessary both as an inter-ethnic lingua franca and for global economic competitiveness. Knowledge of the mother tongue, on the other hand, is needed to ensure that Singaporeans remain rooted in their Asian heritage even as they compete globally. In fact, Bokhorst-Heng (1999: 240) observes that there is a belief in Singapore that 'the mother-tongue is seen to somehow inherently embody one's ethnically defined culture.' English, by this same logic, inherently embodies a different (Western) culture, which is why the mother tongues are needed to counter the (undesirable) Western values that supposedly come along with learning English.[4]

The state's insistence that English and the mother tongues serve different functions is ostensibly an attempt to ensure that all four official languages are seen by Singaporeans to be on par with each other. That is, it is an attempt to distinguish the languages from each other while trying to avoid according them differential values. However, we will see below, and in the following chapters as well, that this does not work. This is because our adolescent informants and their family members are quick to note that English is in fact of far greater value than the mother tongues, especially since the former is much more strongly associated with the pursuit of socioeconomic success. But for now, let us see how the state is attempting to project a sense of multilingual equality across the four official languages.

First, by assigning English and the mother tongues to separate domains (technological and economic for English, cultural for the mother tongues), the state hopes that this will also make it meaningless for Singaporeans to try comparing the relative values of the different languages. The state's argument is that *both* English and the mother tongues are equally important since, so the argument goes, the former provides for one's material needs and the latter for one's socio-psychological well-being. Consider, as an example of this argument, the following statement from the then Minister for Education, Tony Tan (1986):

> Our policy of bilingualism that each child should learn English and his mother tongue, I regard as a fundamental feature of our education system ... Children must learn English so that they will have a window to the knowledge, technology and expertise of the modern world. They must know their mother tongues to enable them to know what makes us what we are.

In this statement, we see a division of labor where English functions as the language of modernity while the mother tongues are intended as cultural anchors that ground individuals to traditional values. By assigning English and the mother tongues to different domains, the language policy thus aims to treat the relationship between them as one of complementarity (Rappa & Wee, 2006: 21). That is, there should not be any competition between English and the mother tongues, at least as far as the functions performed are concerned. The belief that the mother tongues are necessary for providing a sense of cultural rootedness continues to be cited as a rationale for Singapore's language policy. This point is put across succinctly by Lee Kuan Yew, the then prime minister, in his 1984 *Speak Mandarin Campaign Speech*:

> One abiding reason why we have to persist in bilingualism is that English will not be emotionally acceptable as our mother tongue. To have no emotionally acceptable language as our mother tongue is to be emotionally crippled .... Mandarin is emotionally acceptable as our mother tongue ... It reminds us that we are part of an ancient civilisation with an unbroken history of over 5,000 years. This is a deep and strong psychic force, one that gives confidence to a people to face up to and overcome great changes and challenges.

The above position problematically assumes that a clear distinction can be made between Asian and Western values, even though the values claimed by the state as Asian (e.g. thrift, honesty, self-discipline and respect for elders) are clearly not unique to Asia at all (Clammer, 1985). Nevertheless, the different functions ascribed to the different languages – English on the one hand, and the mother tongues, on the other – make it necessary that the two never mix. Thus, consider the following remarks by Lee Kuan Yew:

> Please note that when I speak of bilingualism, I do not mean just the facility of speaking two languages. It is more basic than that, first, we

understand ourselves, what we are, where we came from, what life is or should be about, and what we want to do. Then the facility of the English language gives us access to the science and technology of the West. (Lee Kuan Yew, *The Straits Times*, November 11, 1972)

Extrapolating from Lee's remarks about Mandarin to the other mother tongues, we have an appeal to some kind of ethnic primordialism, where the kinds of values and cultural knowledge that Malay and Tamil impart are in some sense also essential to the Malay and Indian identities, respectively (see Han *et al.*, 1998: 163–165). The state is thus resigned to the fact that ethnic and cultural distinctiveness cannot be ignored, which means that, in its strategy for the management of diversity, some form of social cohesion must be attempted that does not require different groups to give up their language or culture. This is why, in addition to its economic value, English is also supposed to serve as Singapore's inter-ethnic lingua franca. It is English, as the ethnically neutral language, which would allow the different ethnic groups to communicate and understand each other even as they strive to maintain their ethnic distinctiveness.

It is in order to accommodate this ethnic primordialism that the state insists on assigning each major ethnic community its own official mother tongue. To its credit, the state has been at pains to avoid any suggestion that one particular ethnic tradition is inherently superior to another. This, in fact, constitutes the very heart of Singapore's policy of multiracialism (Benjamin, 1976), which aims to ensure equality of treatment for the various ethnic communities. Consequently, Singapore's language policy also aims to ensure that the three mother tongues are perceived to be equal value, since each mother tongue is supposedly the repository of its associated cultural tradition.

The state's appeal to a monolingual ideology is thus characterized by a strict assignation of particular languages for particular purposes: English for socioeconomic competitiveness, the mother tongues for particular ethnic identities.[5] This differentiation of purpose is intended to obviate the possibility of competition between English and the mother tongues. And since each ethnic group has its own official mother tongue, there is supposedly no competition amongst the three mother tongues themselves either. In other words, this articulation of a language policy represents a typical instantiation of the structural–functional paradigm of language.

In theory, the structure of Singapore's language policy, as an attempt to manage ethnolinguistic diversity while preparing the population for economic competition, is arguably an ingenious one. In practice, however, things are never quite as neat, and despite the best attempts of the state, the different languages inevitably start to acquire different values.

The Inevitability of Orders of Indexicality

We have seen that Singapore's language policy is clearly predicated on the idea that languages and their associated cultural values, as well as ethnic identities, can and should be strictly compartmentalized. However, the idea that each ethnic community should have a single official mother tongue is obviously a linguistic desideratum, and it is one that is easily inconvenienced by sociolinguistic reality since any community of speakers will in fact be characterized by great variation in communicative resources. And in the 1970s, the Chinese community in Singapore was indeed characterized by the widespread use of many different Chinese dialects. As we pointed out, this led the state to initiate the Speak Mandarin Campaign in 1979, where it insisted that all other dialects be eliminated in favor of Mandarin.

In the course of championing the Speak Mandarin Campaign, the adoption of a monolingual ideology (with its implication that knowledge of one language is always at the expense of some other) was coupled with Lee Kuan Yew's belief that the human brain was genetically wired for exactly two languages. As a result, Lee felt it necessary to present Chinese Singaporean parents with a relatively blunt choice that they needed to make on behalf of their children. They could choose to encourage their children to learn either Mandarin and English, or dialect and English, but it was not possible to encourage them to learn all three (i.e. Mandarin, dialect and English). This would only, according to Lee's logic, stretch the capacity of the human brain beyond what it could reasonably be expected to 'contain'. In the following two extracts (the first from a 1978 speech and the second from a 1984 speech), Lee therefore made the point that Chinese parents needed to consciously limit their children's languages to just two. And given that of the three possible language options, dialects were being actively discouraged by the Speak Mandarin Campaign, it became very clear that the choices most likely to benefit the children's future would have to be Mandarin and English.

But, in fact, for most Chinese students, bilingualism in school means trilingualism in practice. Ninety per cent of parents have chosen the English stream schools. Chinese students spend thirty to forty per cent of instruction time learning or being taught in Mandarin ... At home, mothers speak to their children in one out of over a dozen Chinese dialects ... The average student finds it difficult to master three languages – dialect, Mandarin and English ... Why weigh your child down with three languages? (Lee Kuan Yew, 1978 speech)

If we want our bilingual policy to succeed, we must lighten our children's learning load by using Mandarin as the mother tongue in place of dialect. Studies show that students from Mandarin-speaking families consistently do better in their examinations than those from dialect-speaking homes. It could be that the parents of such students are better educated. It must also be because they have no extra load of dialect words and phrases to carry. (Lee Kuan Yew 1984 speech)

According to Lee, then, three languages constitute an unreasonably demanding learning load while two do not. The reason why two languages are deemed acceptable, but three are not, is because the human brain can (apparently) easily accommodate two languages without any ill-effects:

But let me reassure all parents: your child has a brain bigger than the biggest computer man has ever built. Whilst the world's biggest computer cannot handle two languages, most human beings can, especially if they are taught when young. ... the fact is that your child has a brain which can use two languages, whilst the computer as yet cannot. (Lee Kuan Yew, speech given at the Tanjong Pagar Community Centre Scholarships Presentation March 4, 1978)

There is therefore no way parents can expect their children to learn a Chinese dialect, Mandarin and English. One of these languages has got to go, and the state's exhortation is that the Chinese dialect should be sacrificed, since it has no clear economic or cultural value when compared with the others. What is happening here is that the state, perhaps the most influential institution in Singapore society, is ranking Chinese dialects below Mandarin and English. Blommaert (2005), drawing upon the works of Silverstein (2003) and Foucault (1982), introduces the notion of 'orders of indexicality', to refer to the implications of ranking varieties, defining the notion as:

Systematically reproduced, stratified meanings often called 'norms' or 'rules' of language, and always typically associated with particular shapes of language (e.g. the 'standard', the prestige variety, the 'usual' way of having a conversation with my friends, etc.) ... Stratification is crucial here: we are dealing with systems that organize inequality via the attribution of different indexical meanings to language forms (e.g. by allocating 'inferior' value to the use of dialect varieties and 'superior' values to standard varieties in public speech). (Blommaert, 2005: 73)

However, not only are the languages ranked in terms of ethnic or standard, dialect or standard; they are also ranked along parameters of social class. That is, the different values along which languages are arranged – their indexical values – pertain to typical modernist categories and scales of stratification such as social class.

English and Social Class

Despite the state's intentions that difference in function should not mean a difference in value (at least where English and the official mother tongues are concerned), (standard) English has slowly but surely acquired the status of the most prestigious language in Singapore. Thus far, our discussion has dealt with how the official language policy is intended by the state to be perceived by Singaporeans. But of course, orders of indexicality derive from various sources, with the state as only one among many institutions, though arguably the most influential. Other institutions, such as families, peer groups and workplaces also contribute to the ranking of languages, and in this case, to the higher ranking that English enjoys over the other languages.

English, we recall, is officially positioned as an ethnically neutral language. But ethnic neutrality obviously does not mean social neutrality. Gupta (1998: 120), for example, has noted that '(w)hatever measure of social class is taken, it is still the case that the higher the social class, the more likely it is that English is an important domestic language' (see also Lu, 2005). Citing data from Lau (1993), Gupta observes that as the monthly income of Singaporean households rises, so does the percentage of households using English. In households with more than 10,000 Singapore Dollars per month, 35% of all households use English, to be compared with households earning 1000 Singapore Dollars where only 3% actually use English. As a result of the emphasis on English in Singapore, the number of homes listing English as the home language has slowly been increasing over the past decades (Pakir, 2000: 262), and it threatens to further displace the use of other languages, as shown in the tables below (from 1908, 1990 and 2000 Census of Population; see also Kwan-Terry & Luke, 1997: 294). The rise of English is most pronounced in the case of Chinese and Indian homes (see Tables 2.1 and 2.2). Chinese homes citing English as the home language rose from 10.2% (in 1980) to 23.9% (in 2000). For Indian homes, the corresponding figures are 24.3% (in 1980) and 35.6% (in 2000). Malay homes show a much less pronounced shift to English (Table 2.3), possibly due to the close affiliation between the Malay language and the religion of Islam (Kwan-Terry & Luke, 1997: 296). Nonetheless, Malay homes still show a discernible shift toward the English language. In the case of the Chinese and Indians, the use of English, while significant, does not mean a complete displacement of other languages. For Chinese homes, the presence of Mandarin and other Chinese dialects remains clearly detectable. For Indian homes, Tamil is widely spoken, as are other Indian languages not reflected in Table 2.2, such as Hindi, Punjabi, Bengali (see PuruShotam, 1998).

It is also important to bear in mind that English in the home often does not necessarily mean standard English. Though it is the standard variety that Singaporeans clearly value and aspire toward, for many Singaporeans, the English spoken both at home and amongst peers is a colloquial variety, locally referred to as Singlish. This variety is widely denigrated in official discourses on language use in Singapore, and has been the target of elimination in the Speak Good English Movement (Chng, 2003; Rubdy, 2001; Wee, 2005; see Chapter 1). In other words, local understandings typically treat Singlish as lacking in both prestige and socio-economic value. The other point to note is that even where a particular language has been listed as the home language, this does not mean that there is no code-switching or emerging mixed codes. Thus, in a single household, it is quite common to find different codes being used depending on a variety of situational factors such as the age and education qualifications of the interlocutors or the nature of the topic (Gupta & Siew, 1995; Li et al., 1997; Pillai, 2003). All of these point to the ever adaptable nature of Singapore society in response to global and regional political and economic developments, echoed in a highly dynamic situation with respect to the role played by languages other than English; multilingualism is inserted into the lives of speakers in complex and intricate ways in the jostle for capital-standing. But they also mean that despite the growth of English as a home language, homes where a more standard variety of English is spoken, rather than Singlish, are a minority. Later on, we will see this exemplified in the case of our informants, where only one adolescent, Sha, actually comes from a home where a more standard variety appears to be spoken (Chapter 7). But as far as our other informants are concerned, code-switching between a colloquial variety of English and some other language is more likely to be the norm (Chapters 5 and 6).

Singaporeans therefore are generally aware that homes where 'better' English is spoken tend to also be economically more affluent. This leads quite naturally to the belief that English is extremely important if one wants to move ahead in society, a belief that lends further substance to the state's desire to encourage English language proficiency in the general population. In this regard, we will hear our own informants, in the later chapters, express very similar views: that English is valuable for one's future employment, or even if one does not have a specific career in mind, it is valuable if one wishes to continue moving up the educational system. In all these cases, Singaporeans are in no doubt that by 'English' is meant 'standard English', never 'Singlish'.

Late Modernity and Singaporeans' Multilingual Practices

Late modernity refers to a shift in the material and ideological conditions of social life. Nation-state borders, imagined in modernist discourse as relatively impermeable, solid and intransient have become shifting, permeable and amorphous/ambivalent, as the liberalization of world economies leads to the increased movement of people, goods, technologies across borders. As a result of all these movements across multiple 'scapes' (Appadurai, 2001; see also Pennycook, 2003: 523–524), individuals and groups are able to stay in continuous contact with their points of origin, even as they venture abroad. This leads to the creation of a space for a truly transnational community of citizens. As Marginson points out, 'after transferring location, people are able to maintain instantaneous links with their point of origin through media and communications systems, strengthening the capacity of migrants to manage their own diasporic identities while resisting full assimilation into the new nation' (Marginson, 1992: 2, cited in Rampton, 2006: 7). At the same time, conditions for established minorities have also radically altered, not least due to the flux of transnational regulatory bodies, such as the United Nations, Amnesty International, Doctors without Borders (Brysk, 2002) that protect the rights of national minorities in previously sovereign nation states. Late modernity has traveled hand in hand with the growth of world cities, and this has led Cohen to make the following observation:

[w]hat nineteenth century nationalists wanted was a 'space' for each 'race', a territorializing of each social identity. What they have got instead is a chain of cosmopolitan cities and an increasing proliferation of subnational and transnational identities that cannot easily be contained in the nation-state system. Thus, instead of individuals' life trajectories being determined solely by the dictates of the social groups into which they are officially slotted, life in late modernity is characterized by plurality, variety, contingency and ambivalence as fundamental social conditions, as opposed to order and homogeneity. (Cohen, 1997: 175, cited in Rampton, 2006: 7)

According to Rampton (2006: 17), 'All in all, whether it is age- or ethnicity-based, belonging to a group now seems a great deal less clear, less permanent and less omni-relevant than it did twenty years ago, and this makes it much harder to produce to [sic] an account of "the language of such-and-such a social group", or "language use among the ___", than it used to be'.

In short, while in modernist discourses, the state is the prime societal institution responsible for articulating and sustaining social groupings, in late-modernity, there are many competing groupings motivated and legitimized by many other rationales, and contrary to the situation where politics was once confined to activities of the state organs, politics must now be seen to be the taking place at multiple levels of social organization, both intra-state and transnational.

With this in mind, we can go on to observe that one of the prime drivers more generally in late-modern societies is a culture of consumerism (Bauman, 1998; Baudrillard, 1988), where material culture, its acquisition and appropriation, is an integral part of how social roles and identities in diverse walks of life are constructed and negotiated (Amin & Thrift, 2004: 267; Giddens, 1991). Benwell and Stokoe for instance, state that, 'consumption becomes a means of articulating a sense of identity and, perhaps even more crucially, distinction from others' (Benwell & Stokoe, 2006: 167). The emphasis on consumption is accompanied by the growth of neoliberal discourses more generally in public life (Du Gay, 1996; Keat & Abercrombie, 1991; Ong, 2006; Rose, 1989). Contemporary developments in the new economy, such as privatization and growth of key industries of media, cultural production, tourism and financial and banking services, are changing the functions and values accorded to language(s), as well as ushering in a completely new discourse around identity and linguistic authenticity. The commodification of identities on new markets leads to a similar commodification of languages to the extent that linguistic resources are mobilized to manage a 'multiplicity of social identities' (Da Silva et al., 2007: 185).

Increasingly, and due to processes in the new economy, with its emphasis on language and text as product, tourism and other forms of global activity (arts and crafts, global commercial markets), the links between language, identity and territory-body-personhood is reconfiguring language as a skill and, even more importantly, as a commodity (Da Silva et al., 2007: 184). Heller (1999a, 1999b) has noted how globalization has created a situation where mobility and migration is increasingly leading to the replacement of conventional identity politics associated with language by a position that sees language and culture as commodifiable resources (cf. Wee, 2003: 211). Thus, even though language has always been used to sell products, today it has become a product itself (Da Silva et al., 2007: 187). Da Silva et al. argue that the commodification of language creates the conditions for disentangling language from its traditional associations with social identities such as ethnicity, gender and the like, creating language as 'something that is sepa-rate and external to their personhood' (Da Silva *et al.*, 2007: 185). In fact, to a large extent whether such identities are perceived as legitimate and authen-tic by other actors depends on the how successfully these consumer identities are mediated in new forms of language such as entrepreneurial discourses. The result is a linguistic market that is propelled by the economic value of a language, where such value is further determined by its viability in local and global spheres and salience in the public sphere. This impacts on basic prin-ciples of language use and linguistic prestige. In most contexts, languages are now consumed based on their value, that is, the prospect of success they offer their speakers of material, cultural and symbolic capital.

The fluidity of the notion of identity coupled to the crossing and perme-ability of social boundaries, and the collapse of strict systems of social regula-tion leads to *stylization* and *performance* as core aspects of language use. One way of capturing this ambivalence, reflexivity, stylization and performance is in a sociolinguistics of consumption (Stroud & Wee, 2007; see Chapter 9). According to Eckert (2005), whereas what she distinguished as both 1st wave and 2nd wave studies relate the meanings of variants as identity markers directly to established and reified social groupings, 3rd wave studies shifts attention from discrete linguistic variables to *styles*, or structured con-stellations of (semiotic) resources, exploring how linguistic forms contribute to the stylization of *identities*. The emphasis in 3rd wave studies has thus shifted from an emphasis on speaker categories to the construction of personae or subjectivities. Importantly, the semiotic resources for stylization of identities are no longer confined to linguistic variables, but also include multimodal forms.

Bucholtz (2009) also concurs that '[t]he sociolinguistic study of identity has increasingly become the study of style'. In the Labovian paradigm, style was treated as a continuum of forms ranging from vernacular and less moni-tored and informal speech to more formal, monitored speech that more closely approximates the standard. In contemporary sociolinguistics, style is increasingly seen as the multimodal and multidimensional performance of many different semiotic practices (Bucholtz, 2009; Coupland, 2007). Bucholtz also points out that in the realization or performance of style or stylization, the social meaning of linguistic forms is generated, not from cor-relations with social/demographic categories, but through *indexicality* where speakers 'take stances, create alignments and construct personas' (through interactional practices and *ideological representations*).

Blommaert (2005) suggests that there are two kinds of indexicality that are worth distinguishing. In one sense, connections between linguistic signs and contexts (Blommaert, 2005: 73) are 'ordered' in that these are not random but are also related to other social and cultural features (see the discussion above). For example, the use of Malay in Singapore, as we will see in the following chapters, may point to one's ethnic identity as a Malay, but it may also point to other features like being from an older generation or being less educated. Here, a linguistic sign is indexically ordered in that it points to a cluster of related features rather than just a single property. But in another sense, these already ordered indexicalities are further ordered in being stratified so that some kinds of indexicalities are ranked higher than others, including 'prestige versus stigma; rationality versus emotion; membership of a particular group versus non-membership, and so forth' (Blommaert, 2005: 74). Again, to anticipate our discussion in the coming chapters, we will see that English suggests prestige while the mother tongues either do not or do so to a lesser extent. It is precisely this association of English with prestige that, in specific contexts, as we saw above with Yan's remarks, that the speaker can be accused of being snobbish or elitist. Amongst the various Chinese dialects in Singapore, Mandarin ranks higher than, say, Hokkien, in that the former suggests that the speaker may be educated whereas the latter does not. Blommaert's key point, then, is that:

> 'orders of indexicality' allow us to focus on the level of the concrete, empirically observable, deployment of semiotic means, while at the same time seeing such micro-processes and semiotic features as immediately connected to a wider sociocultural, political and historical space. By orienting to orders of indexicality, language users (systematically) reproduce these norms, and situate them in relation to other norms. Thus, orders of indexicality endow the semiotic process with *indexical order* in the sense of Silverstein (2003): we get conventionalized patterns of indexicality that come to 'mean' certain things. And these, in turn, feed into orders of indexicality, thus creating a dialectics of context and indexicality often captured under 'micro' and 'macro'. (Blommaert, 2005: 74, italics in original)

This notion of orders of indexicality is a late-modern feature of language, identity and consumption par excellence and is therefore particularly useful to our analysis for at least two reasons. One, it allows us to link what takes place in specific contexts of interaction with much larger socio-cultural forces, thereby making it possible to address the issue of social reproduction. And two, it allows us to connect social reproduction with identity work because when actors engage in the management of their identities, they have little or no choice but to draw upon prevailing orders of indexicality as relevant resources.

The Language Practitioner in Late-Modern Singapore

In late-modern Singapore, the influence of this indexical order is very real in the lives of ordinary Singaporeans. One of our informants, Ping (see Chapter 5 for details), is a Hokkien Chinese female. But despite this, her parents made a conscious decision to avoid using Hokkien with Ping and her sister, so as to increase the chances of Ping and her sister doing well academically. As a result of this decision, the Hokkien dialect has been largely eliminated from Ping's household. Ping, of course, is not alone, and expressions of regret about the loss of their dialects has been quite common among young Chinese Singaporeans, even as they seem to accept the state's argument that dialects possess little or no value in modern day Singapore. For example, on June 10, 2001, a local columnist wrote an article lamenting the demise of dialects in Singapore, especially among the younger generation. The following week the newspaper reported that the column had apparently struck a chord, and published a number of responses from readers (*The Straits Times, Life!* June 16, 2001). We present two extracts here. One reader wrote:

Growing up in a generation where English and Mandarin are the main languages spoken at home, I lament that dialects are becoming less frequently used in our everyday lives . . . . Nevertheless, the dialects are a part of my heritage, akin to the name and race I inherited from my parents, and I want to pass them on to my children. Therefore, I try whatever way I can to re-learn and practice my parents' dialects.

And from another reader:

As a 21-year-old Hokkien, I have often felt sad when I was unable to express myself clearly to my grandparents. My grandmother is shrewd and lively, and thank goodness she understands Mandarin or we would barely be able to communicate. This is especially true for the generation before her, my great-grandparents, whom I can only nod painfully to as I struggle to talk about the most basic events in my life when they ask about them . . . I also see a trend of youngsters wanting to learn other dialects. In Xiamen and Taipei, Cantopop is played and sung with gusto. Many of my friends have also wished Hong Kong TVB imports are shown in dual sound, not because we understand Cantonese extremely well but because it is just more entertaining in its original form. Thus, I believe there is a lively interest in dialects among young and old . . . Thank you again for your article. I never knew how strongly I felt about this until I realised I could barely have a conversation with my elders, a frustrating feeling and surely, a pertinent concern if we are to build family harmony across generations.

Like Ping, both readers are aware of their dialect identities, but both have also grown up in households where the Chinese dialects are not spoken. What this shows is that many Chinese Singaporeans are *ambivalent* about the loss of dialects. This ambivalence is a pervasive characteristic of life in late modernity. These Chinese Singaporeans recognize and accept, though not without some reluctance, the state's argument that dialects carry little economic or cultural cachet when compared with English and Mandarin. Yet, for many young Chinese Singaporeans, there is a palpable sense of regret in not being able to speak a language that represents an aspect of their identities as Chinese.

For other Chinese Singaporeans, however, dialects appear to have a somewhat different status compared to their 'official' indexical value. Rather than being seen as signifying some aspect of their identity and evoking a concomitant sense of loss, dialects, for these other Singaporeans, have become resignified as serving a primarily utilitarian or pragmatic purpose. This is because there are still situations where younger Singaporeans may find it necessary to communicate with older Singaporeans who are capable of conversing mainly or only in dialects. Also, in yet other situations, the dialects, Hokkien in particular, appear to be considered more appropriate than either English or Mandarin precisely because they are not associated with being well-educated and are therefore useful codes when speakers wish to avoid drawing attention to differences in social class.

So, even though the dialects have been discouraged by the Speak Mandarin Campaign, and, as seen in the discussion on Ping, some parents have also deliberately chosen to eliminate them from the household, we note that they are in fact still a pervasive feature of many speakers' everyday, modern, orientation to life, such as having a job. This results in a view of the dialects as having a functional–practical value (albeit in highly specific situations) rather than having any relevance toward the Chinese identity. We provide a few illustrations here.

Consider the experience of Leeling, a medical social worker (Hing, 2004). Leeling is a female in her early 20s, and she finds Cantonese extremely useful in her work. It is worth noting here that she does not even come from a Cantonese background; her family is actually Hakka. However, as the data below indicate, Leeling finds Cantonese to be of greater use to her than Hakka because of her work environment. Leeling deals with many elderly patients who speak mainly Cantonese. Without at least a working knowledge of Cantonese, Leeling would find it nearly impossible to help her patients since she would not be able to communicate with them.

(6)

I: You mentioned that you used Cantonese in your work. How important is Cantonese?

L: Very important because I come across a lot of elderly patients as a medical social worker. Some of them only know how to communicate in dialect. Some know only minimal Mandarin. Dialect helps me to bridge the communication, it also makes them feel closer and help them to open up to you.

It is unclear if Leeling would prefer to use Hakka rather than Cantonese, although she does not seem particularly sentimental about not using the former. What seems clear, though, is that her 'zero opportunity' (7) to use Hakka does not in fact result in a situation where dialects are completely absent from her life. Rather, she points out that she anticipates Cantonese will play a greater role in her life, not because it has any bearing on her identity as a Chinese, but because of her professional obligations (*I get to use Cantonese regularly now because the nature of my job requires me to do so*).

(7)

I: So, right now there is less opportunity for you to use Hakka?

L: Yes, so right now there is zero opportunity to speak in Hakka unless there are family gatherings, or when my father communicate with my relatives in Hakka and I want to join in the conversation, then I use Hakka.

I: What about Cantonese? Do you see yourself using more Cantonese in the future?

L: Yes, I get to use Cantonese regularly now because the nature of my job requires me to do so.

Consider, as another example, the remarks of Justin, a Hainanese male, whose attitude toward Hainanese seems to echo that of Leeling's. As shown below, Justin seems to treat Hainanese as a purely incidental or even ancillary aspect of his ethnic identity.

(8)

I: So you consider yourself as a Hainanese Chinese?

J: I just consider myself as Chinese.

I: So … the Hainanese in you is just a extra part [of your identity]?

J: No, I don't see it as a part of my identity, it is just Chinese and it just happens I'm Hainanese.

Unlike Leeling, because he is male, Justin has had to spend about two years in the army as part of his National Service. An important aspect of the National Service experience is that young men of extremely varied socioeconomic backgrounds are forced to work and interact together. National Service therefore provides for many young Singaporean males (mainly Chinese, and to a lesser extent, Malays and Indians) a set of experiences in which officially denigrated varieties, such as Singlish and the Chinese dialects (in particular, Hokkien) have been resignified as important lingua franca for getting along with fellow soldiers as well as for simply getting things done. Thus, like many male Singaporeans, Justin found knowledge of Hokkien to be extremely valuable during National Service. Hokkien is considered important not only because it facilitates the transfer of information, but also because it serves a critical interpersonal function, especially when the speaker wants to avoid being perceived as a snob or elitist (Hing, 2004: 54). As Justin points out, he tends to use Hokkien when speaking to the less education servicemen (*peng*) while switching to English or Mandarin when speaking to those who are more educated.

(10)
J: ... for the Hokkien *peng* [Hokkien for 'soldier'], I will use Hokkien, for higher educated ones, I will use English or Chinese [Mandarin].

Delvin, another Singaporean male who had to undergo National Service, makes a similar point (Hing, 2004: 52, 54). Delvin states in no uncertain terms that it was his experience in National Service that made him appreciate the (practical) value of Hokkien.

(9)
I: At what age did you make a conscious decision to say that dialect is important and you should keep on using it?
D: Around army time. A lot of instructors speak in Hokkien and so do the supervisors. So I realized that if I did not use Chinese dialect, it was difficult to communicate with them.

(11)
I: Relating this to your NS days ... do you think that your ability to speak Hokkien helped you to adapt to NS life easier?

D: I should think so because sometimes in army life, you get people from all walks of life, not everybody is like me ... JC [junior college] educated ... sometimes they think you are from JC, you are very .. erm ... high up there which is not true ... when you use Hokkien, you tell them that you are at the same level as them, so there's no airs between you and your other army friend ... have better friendships.

Notice here that both Justin and Delvin explicitly point to the use of Hokkien as neutralizing class differences (*you tell them that you are at the same level as them, so there's no airs between you and your other army friend*).

New Figurations of Language, Class and Ethnicity

There is a need, then, in certain circumstances, for speakers to be able to switch to a language such as Hokkien or Singlish in order to neutralize class differences, even though such a need appears to have no official recognition in the state's language policy. But this need to address differences arising from class is clearly an echo of Yan's remarks that we presented at the very beginning of the previous chapter. Recall that Yan explained that she felt obligated to use Malay rather than English when interacting with a fellow Malay. Yan was concerned to avoid being perceived as a snob, which she felt would have been indexed by her use of English. The only other option, then, was to speak in Malay, privileging ethnic solidarity over class differences. Ping, too, voices a similar predicament. As she indicates, she also feels obligated to avoid using English with her friends; she is afraid that she might be accused of 'acting ... very educated'. As a result, she makes use of Mandarin (Chinese) instead. Like Yan, the recourse to ethnic identity appears to provide a safe way to avoid accusations of elitism.

(13)
P: Then it's like if I speak English with my Chinese other friends, lah, they will say you are acting, acting like you are very educated. .... Majority they are Chinese, what. Then outside you speak English to them, they will think that ... what are you trying to say ... my English is bad? Trying ... me over English?

However, as our discussion of the dialects and Singlish suggests, decisions about what language to use in order to emphasize or (as is more commonly the case) avoid drawing attention to social class can be rather complex.

Actors are often required to juggle the various linguistic options at their disposal in relation to the specific kinds of situations they find themselves in. Justin and Delvin, for example, make it clear that even Mandarin is perceived as a class marker in the context of National Service. Here, it is Hokkien (rather than Mandarin or English) that one needs to make use of if one wishes to downplay differences in class. Again, however, this use of Hokkien is likely to be more operative when the participants involved in the interaction are all Chinese. The pragmatic force of Hokkien as a class equalizer cannot be presumed to be in operation when the interactions are with Malay or Indian National Servicemen. In the latter kind of interactions, when Singaporeans of different ethnicities are involved, it is Singlish that is more likely to be used as a class equalizer.

These concerns about the choice of language and its concomitant implications for identity work appear to be something that Singaporeans are very much conscious of. This is not surprising given that the state, through its language policies and language campaigns, has consistently reminded Singaporeans of the connections between particular languages, social mobility and ethnic identity. In fact, some observers have expressed concerns that Singapore's policy of multiracialism has actually served to concretize ethnic differences rather than promoting unity or understanding across cultures, and its promotion of 'pragmatism' has in fact created a tendency to 'define everything in terms of economic-technical rationality, rendering antithetical all arguments based on moral or ethical grounds' (Pennycook, 1994: 241; see also Chua, 1983). Speakers therefore may feel obligated to avoid using a language such as English precisely because it is generally acknowledged in Singapore to be a prestige variety. This is because English is far from being an instrumental, purely neutral language – as if such a thing were possible (Blommaert, 2005: 10–11).

What this means is that when adolescents construct identities in the course of various forms of interaction, they are in fact drawing on markers that are already indexically ordered. Some kinds of orderings are widely accepted across society at large while others may be more locally constructed, and may thus be differently ordered from one group/community to another. These different orders are tied to different centering institutions (Silverstein, 1998: 404), which can range from the family to peer groups to the school and, ultimately, even the state (Blommaert, 2005: 75). The characteristic for late-modernity is the ubiquity of many centering institutions. Centering institutions are so-called because they are the main sources of indexicalities, that is, they generate the kinds of social meanings that others have to orient to, depending on their scope. For example, the peer group is not as widely influential as the state, so that indexicalities attributed to a different peer group may be more easily disregarded by some other peer group. In contrast, indexicalities attributed to the state, to 'society at large', or to general global forces are much harder to ignore.

Singaporean Official Policy in Late Modernity: From Two Languages to One

We have thus observed a tension between modernist language planning discourses with their assumption of stable social categories and mappings of language and identities, and a multilingual dynamics of ambivalence, and processes of stylization and performance where speakers readily cross these linguistic boundaries in identity work. The core question here is how is this tension reconciled by the state on an everyday basis in late-modern Singapore? The short answer is that the state continues to attempt to manage diversity through even more monolingualism.

We have seen that the state has, with significant though not complete success, persuaded Chinese Singaporeans to stop using Chinese dialects other than Mandarin, so that they can focus on being proficient in English and their officially assigned mother tongue. But we also saw that despite the attempts by the state to treat both English and Mandarin as being of equal value, a further indexical order develops when Mandarin comes to be seen by many Singaporeans as being of lesser importance than English. In connection with this, we noted that one consequence of emphasizing the value of English is that more and more Singaporeans are beginning to come from homes where English is the spoken language. And this development has forced the state to acknowledge that a significant number of Singaporeans, especially Chinese Singaporeans, actually have great difficulty coping with the bilingual language requirements of the Singapore education system.

This has led Lee Kuan Yew, more than 20 years after the initiation of the Speak Mandarin Campaign, to change his beliefs about bilingualism and the human brain. Lee has recently recanted his earlier view that the human brain is naturally equipped for learning two languages (Wee, 2006). He now believes that the average person can only be expected to master one language and not two:

I used to believe that you can learn two languages at the same time, whatever your IQ. I was wrong. You have to master one language enough to read and to absorb knowledge for all the other subjects. (Lee Kuan Yew, now Minister Mentor, *The Straits Times* November 26, 2004)

But now I believe it's only possible for the exceptionally able and the very determined ... If you spend half-and-half of your capacity on two languages, it's likely you won't master either. (Lee Kuan Yew, now Minister Mentor, *The Straits Times* June 24, 2004)

Lee's reference to 'half-and-half of your capacity' reflects the assumption that languages are self-contained autonomous systems whose purity would be undermined by any form of language mixing. Thus, the shift to the current position (that humans have the propensity to learn one language instead of two) only serves to foreground the state's continuing appeal to an ideology of monolingualism.

This change from treating two languages as the natural capacity of the human brain to just one language is a position that the state has been forced into. This is because the number of Chinese students from English-speaking homes has, in recent years, risen from about 17% in 1985 to almost 50% in 2004 so that English has now overtaken Mandarin as 'the primary language used in homes of Primary 1 Chinese pupils' (Ministry of Education, press release January 9, 2004). This has left the state with little choice but to acknowledge that a significant number of Chinese Singaporeans actually have great difficulty coping with Mandarin, despite the fact that it is supposed to be their mother tongue. Consequently, in early 2004, the Ministry of Education (press release January 9, 2004) announced a number of changes to the mother tongue language requirement. Especially interesting was the introduction of a simplified 'B' syllabus to cater to students with learning difficulties in Mandarin, and the possibility of exempting some Singaporeans from the mother tongue requirement, especially those who were reentering the education system after having lived abroad for some time. It is therefore only a minority, an elite estimated at about 10% of the student population (*The Straits Times* November 26, 2004), who is expected to be fully bilingual in English and the mother tongue.

At present, the state has indicated that similar moves toward a B syllabus are being explored with respect to the other mother tongues (Malay and Tamil) as well. Thus, what originally started out as a language policy with four official languages, all of which are intended to be of equal importance, has slowly but surely acquired an order of indexicality that, in the eyes of many Singaporeans, unambiguously ranks English above the mother tongues.

Monolingualism in Singapore

Because English remains the language used as the medium of instruction and because any simplification in the language syllabus is in the direction of simplifying *mother tongue* learning, there is no doubt that if most Singaporeans are going to be essentially monolingual, this monolingualism should be

English language monolingualism rather than mother-tongue monolingualism.

The spread of English, often at the expense of the mother tongue, is possibly due to the fact that Singaporeans tend to 'put the instrumental value of a language above the sentimental or symbolic value' (Li *et al.*, 1997: 380). This is not unexpected since the mother tongues have been positioned as repositories of traditional knowledge and values in contrast to the modernist orientation associated with English. Perhaps recognizing that instrumental value is an important motivating factor, the state has recently argued that, in addition to heritage reasons, Mandarin should also be learned in order to take advantage of China's growing economy. While there is no danger of Mandarin surpassing English in terms of status, the perceived economic value of Mandarin has created additional problems for the government's desire to maintain parity amongst all three official mother tongues. This is because Mandarin is now becoming so popular that a growing number of non-Chinese parents want schools to allow their children to study the language (*The Straits Times* April 30, 1994), which, of course, creates further difficulties for the state, since this potentially threatens the equal status that all three mother tongues (Mandarin, Malay and Tamil) are supposed to enjoy (Wee, 2003).

A detailed discussion of this issue would take us too far afield. So, here we briefly note the different impacts on the various mother tongues and their communities. For the Malays, the desire to learn Mandarin must be balanced against their obligation to learn Malay. And while Malay is not perceived to be as valuable as Mandarin economically, it is still an important lingua franca both in Singapore and the region. This means that the Malay language is still perceived to be of some social relevance and value, even if this may not compare to that of Mandarin. However, the impact on the Indian community is more severe since even before Mandarin became popular, there had already been concerns about the declining use of Tamil in the Indian community (Mani & Gopinathan, 1983; Saravanan, 1994, 1998). This was in part due to the fact that spoken Tamil tends to have little or no prestige amongst Tamil speakers (Saravanan, 1994: 86) and Tamil itself has little support as an intra-ethnic language of communication within the Indian community, which consists of speakers of other languages such as Malayalee, Hindi, Punjabi and Gujarati. Consequently, many Indians have, with some success, lobbied to offer Malay as the second language in the schools. And in recent years, the state has also responded positively, though with comparatively limited support, to wishes of speakers of other Indian languages (Hindi, Gujarati, Bengali) to have these languages recognized as mother tongues. A child can therefore use these languages in school examinations to fulfill the mother tongue requirement, but it is up to the relevant communities to source for their own language teaching resources, including teachers. These all mean that further complications are potentially in the offing since, even as English is ranked above the mother tongues, all is not necessarily well amongst the mother tongues themselves. There are signs, then, that the mother tongues themselves are in the process of developing an internal order of indexicality.

Here, then, we have our answer to the question of how and why it is that Singapore is moving toward the privileging of English language hegemony. As the society begins to become more aware of global forces, and as it begins to attach greater importance to the ability to compete and succeed on a global level, it is inevitable that English, as the global language par excellence (Crystal, 1997), becomes a 'first among equals' even in a society as committed to multilingualism as Singapore. While other languages are still considered relatively valuable, the reasons for *their* value itself become less than clear in the context of late-modernity. This is because some of these other languages, as we have seen, may be resignified along more pragmatic or instrumental lines. However, such resignifications merely serve to place these languages along the same indexical order as English but on a somewhat lower level. Some other languages may be robustly defended on more traditional grounds as critical bearers and markers of ancestral values. While there are undoubtedly ardent defenders of such a preservationist view of language, the rapidly changing social experiences of many individuals also mean that arguments that emphasize a linguistic and cultural obligation to group belongingness carry far less weight than it used to do, and more important, the kinds of groups that individuals may want to be affiliated with may themselves not have any clear language affiliations (Rampton, 2006: 17, see above).

The cumulative effect of all these factors, then, is to consistently strengthen the move towards English, and to weaken (at least relative to English) any other language's claim towards hegemonic status.

Conclusion

In this chapter, we have provided a background sketch to a new situation on the ground for multilingualism in Singapore, characterized by ambivalence and reflexivity. Given the pervasiveness of late-modernity on all walks of life, how does Singaporean officialdom/government attempt to regulate and control these developments? In order to understand this, we have needed to understand the basics of nation-building at independence in Singapore, and we have seen a marked continuity across historical solutions and current policy, and a coexistence and tension between the competing discourses of modernity and late-modernity. In the next chapter, we will explore in some detail a set of core theoretical concepts that will allow us to describe this type of tension around multilingualism with greater insight.

Notes

(1) The term 'late modernity' is often used to emphasize that some highly developed societies represent continuing developments of modernity rather than a completely distinct stage of 'postmodernity' (Beck, 1992; Giddens, 1991). And as Giddens (1990: 63) observes, 'modernity is inherently globalizing', by which he means that the social transformations associated with modernity lead to the exacerbation of the characteristics associated with globalization.

(2) A detailed discussion of these problems would take us too far afield, and the reader is referred to Gupta (1994), PuruShotam (1998) and Siddique (1990) for studies on how Singaporeans have responded to this oversimplified multiracial classification.

(3) The discussion in this section draws on Wee (2007).

(4) It might appear that there is something of a contradiction between the state's positioning of English as ethnically neutral, on the one hand, and its assertion that English is a vehicle for undesirable Western values. But this contradiction is relatively easy to resolve. English is ethnically neutral vis-à-vis the different ethnic groups in Singapore because it is (supposed to be) equally alien to all of them. But to say this does not necessarily commit the state to the position that English is completely bleached of any cultural traits. This observation, of course, merely highlights the fact that the very idea of language neutrality is a highly ideological one.

(5) An anonymous reviewer raised the question of whether language policy in Singapore is really rigidly subjected to the monolingual ideology of multilingualism. The simple answer is 'Yes'. Even though the state has in recent times admitted to various mistakes in its language policy, these mistakes concern the more specific policy matters such as the level of proficiency that can be expected regarding the official mother tongue (see the discussion below in this same chapter), and the kinds of pedagogical techniques that might be employed to cultivate interest in the mother tongue. The fundamental policy division between English, on the one hand, as a non-Asian language and hence a culturally inappropriate mother tongue, and the ethnic mother tongues, on the other hand, as officially sanctioned heritage identity markers, remains unquestioned.

3 Multilingualism in Late Modernity: Literacy as a Reflexive Performance of Identity

In this chapter, we develop an account of reflexivity that acknowledges its transformative potential.[1] We do this by drawing on Bohman's (1999) reworking of the Bourdieuian habitus, which has been criticized for being overly deterministic. Bohman's reworking of Bourdieu starts with the position that reflexive practices that encourage deliberations and debates can in fact lead to transformative second-order desires, such as the desire to be a certain kind of person, or the desire to have certain kinds of desires and not others. The content of such reflexive deliberations can, of course, include an actor's relationship to particular literacy practices, such as the desire to learn particular languages and the reasons for wanting to learn those languages. And these desires and motivations can be significantly consequential for the ways in which such learning might actually take place. Such reflexive deliberations concerning literacy practices are often implicated in an actor's identity work. Because of this, this reflexively oriented approach to literacy, we suggest, is of particular analytical value since a key idea in this book is that in a late-modern, consumerist context, the practice of literacy can constitute an important channel for the expression of style and identity (Norton, 2000).

We begin our discussion by first situating our understanding of identity within a poststructuralist approach, carefully emphasizing the importance of avoiding an extreme interpretation of poststructuralism. Following that, we move on to review various debates over the notion of reflexivity, paying particular attention to the work of Pierre Bourdieu as well as those works inspired by him. This will set the scene for our discussion of Bohman's rehabilitation of Bourdieu, where we explain how the notion of a habitus benefits from greater attention being given to the mediating roles of reflexivity and ambivalence. We then conclude our discussion by integrating these various concepts in the context of actors' participation and performance in multiple linguistic markets.

A Poststructuralist Approach to Identity

Because we will be concerned with how the agency of individual students in utilizing linguistic and social resources in fashioning/resisting particular identities (cf. Pavlenko & Blackledge, 2004: 27) is constrained either by macro-socio-historical forces or by more locally constructed interpretations of acceptable peer behaviors, we adopt a poststructuralist approach to identity in multilingual learning (Canagarajah, 1999, 2004a; Norton, 1995; Pavlenko, 2001; Pavlenko & Blackledge, 2004). The value of a poststructuralist understanding of identity is that it draws attention to the multiple, fluid, hybrid and linguistically negotiated and constructed nature of identity, sculpted in contexts of power. At the same time, such an understanding informs us that learning is discursively mediated through the same linguistic means that construct identity. Authors such as Lave and Wenger (1991) and Wenger (1998) have all thus underscored the situated nature of cognitive activity, noting how participation in practice is what constitutes learning, and how learning and knowing are ultimately expressions of relations among people.

That being said, it is important that we avoid some of the more extreme interpretations of poststructuralism. This is important because an extreme poststructuralist orientation would lead us to the untenable position that there is no subject or actor beyond its discursive constructions. Arguably, the major motivation behind an extreme orientation is to counter the overly optimistic rationalist position, which tends to attribute an unrealistic degree of freedom or choice to the individual actor to the point where the constraints of socio-historical forces may even be ignored or denied (cf. Tollefson, 1991). However, the consequence of an extreme poststructuralist orientation is that it eliminates the possibility of individual freedom precisely because the individual actor can no longer be located outside of its various interpellations (Althusser, 1971). This is unfortunate because any educationally oriented analysis 'must necessarily ask normative questions about "what should be", about preferred families of discourses and practices, about the material and discourse consequences of such ensembles, and about whose institutional interests these serve' (Luke, 2004: 334). Furthermore, it seems clear to us that the analysis should also attempt to propose possible remedial strategies that can help actors overcome or mitigate the effects of particular forms of linguistic hegemony. But to even coherently begin attempting such a normative enterprise is to already assume that actors have some kind of autonomy. That is, they have some independent control or influence over forms of discourse, which is an assumption that an extreme poststructuralist orientation does not allow for. Assuming the possibility of such independent control leads us to the notion of reflexivity, which is primarily concerned with the kinds of distance actors might attain from their prevailing social conditions.

We shall see later how a sociologically informed understanding of autonomy is deeply bound up with reflexivity. For the moment, however, we want to recognize that different theorists have sought to elaborate on the notion of reflexivity in different ways, since these elaborations carry varying implications for the role of the actor in identity work. It is to these debates therefore that we now turn our attention.

Reflexivity Debates

Adams (2006) provides a useful guide to the debates over reflexivity when he distinguishes between 'two dominant tropes', one claiming that reflexivity 'increasingly constitutes self-identity in late-modern societies' (Adams, 2006: 512), and another suggesting that reflexive awareness is 'necessarily rare' (Adams, 2006: 514). The main contrast between these two positions lies in (1) the extent to which social actors can actually be said to be reflexive, and (2) whether from such reflexivity necessarily follows the possibility for actors to actively fashion their identities. In other words, the points of contention between these positions revolve around the issues of scope (How widespread is reflexive awareness?) and agency (Does reflexivity necessarily mean that individuals now have a greater opportunity to shape their identities?).

The first position is associated prominently with the works of Beck (1992, 1994) and Giddens (1991, 1992). The core idea here is that individuals find it increasingly difficult, if not impossible, to rely on institutional structures and traditions to help make sense of social life. Rapid institutional changes and the detraditionalization of social norms in late-modern societies mean that individuals are increasingly unable to rely on existing social structures for guidance about how to live their lives, leading them to take on greater personal responsibility for the choices they make. This leads to an emphasis on self-reliance and this in turn creates a reflexive awareness of the contingent relationship that individuals bear to their surrounding material conditions. Kennedy usefully summarizes what might be called the 'extended reflexivity thesis' (Adams, 2003) in the following manner:

> ... individuals are *compelled* to take greater control over the kinds of social identities they wish to assume ... because once-powerful solidarities such as class, occupation, church, gender and family are slowly *declining in their ability to define our life experiences*. (Kennedy, 2001: 6, italics added)

Because traditional sources of identity no longer 'define our life experiences', the resulting vacuum creates not just the need for actors to become reflexively aware, it also (at least according to the theorists associated with this position) leaves open a host of possibilities and opportunities for actors to take control of the kinds of identity work they wish to engage in. Hence, for proponents of this extended reflexivity thesis, the increase in the scope of reflexivity is treated as simultaneously marking a concomitant increase in agency, as seen in the claims (cited in Adams, 2006: 513) that 'people have to turn to their own resources to decide what they value, to organize their priorities and to make sense of their lives' (Heelas, 1996: 5) and 'the self today is for everyone a reflexive project' (Giddens, 1992: 30).

In contrast to the extended reflexivity thesis, the second position is much more skeptical about the ubiquity of reflexivity. And even where reflexivity is acknowledged to be present, this position tends to be also more skeptical about the possibility of actors actually shaping their identities. This second position has been most widely explored with respect to the issue of gender, and finds its inspiration from Bourdieu's (1977, 1990) argument that actors in a social field carry with them a habitus that predisposes them to respond in ways that tend to reproduce the existing social structure.[2] The habitus is a set of dispositions inculcated in individuals by virtue of their socialization experiences and so everyone inevitably has a habitus simply because everyone willy-nilly undergoes some form of socialization. What will vary, of course, is the specific nature of the habitus that is acquired since human beings are habituated into different forms of practice by virtue of their exposure to specific experiences. The kind of habitus acquired by particular individuals or classes of individuals therefore varies and this has significant consequences for their social trajectories, as has been empirically demonstrated in a number of studies (Bourdieu & Passeron, 1977; Fowler, 1997; Heath, 1983; Sullivan, 2001).

A good example of a Bourdieu-inspired approach to reflexivity comes from McNay's (1999, 2000; see also Skeggs, 1997) argument that even though ongoing social changes may have led to a mismatch between (gendered) habitus and field, such mismatches and any emergent reflexivity must always be understood in field-specific terms. For McNay, it is not possible to take for granted that reflexivity is an inherently universal capacity of subjects. Instead, reflexivity emerges instead only with the experience of dissonance, as is the case when individuals experience a sufficiently drastic mismatch between the kind of habitus they have acquired and the expectations of the field that they are encountering. Consequently, even as certain aspects of gender relations are destabilized, other aspects may yet be further entrenched (McNay, 1999: 103). In this light, proclamations about the status of reflexivity as a widespread societal condition foisted upon all individuals are deemed premature, since the possibility of reflexivity is supposed to depend on the actual details of the habitus–field interaction.

While these two positions[3] differ importantly in how they approach the issue of reflexivity, the differences internal to each should be noted as well. Amongst theorists associated with the first position, the claim that reflexivity is widespread has led, not surprisingly, to proposals for distinguishing between different types of reflexivity. Lash (1994: 135; see also Lash & Urry, 1994) has, for example, made a distinction between cognitive and aesthetic reflexivity. Cognitive reflexivity refers to agents' monitoring of conceptual symbols ('flows of information') whereas aesthetic reflexivity refers to their monitoring of mimetic symbols ('images, sounds and narratives making up the other side of our sign economics'). In response to Lash, Giddens has disputed this distinction, suggesting that the cognitive–aesthetic separation is not quite as clearcut as Lash makes it out to be:

> Is there such a thing as aesthetic reflexivity? I don't really think so or at least I wouldn't put it this way. I am not at all sure that, as Lash puts it, there is 'an entire other economy of signs in space' that functions separately from 'cognitive symbols'. (Giddens, 1994: 197)

For social theorists coming from the second position, the concern is with addressing the rather pricklier question of how the existence of a habitus can be reconciled with reflexive awareness. If habitus informs practice by being a disposition to act and react in certain ways (Thompson, 1991: 12), a logical question that arises concerns the engine of practice: What drives actors in their varied practices of social life? Bourdieu's answer is that actors are habituated to accept and embrace the normative goals that constitute the field of their habituation. Different forms of capital (symbolic, cultural, linguistic, economic) and the values attached to them are, of course, specific to different fields. Depending on the details of a given field, the actors within are then motivated by the need to retain capital already acquired or the need to pursue capital deemed to be within possible reach. Bourdieu's notion of misrecognition is important here as it captures a fundamental postulate that social interactions, particularly those involving unequal relations of power, must always rest on some set(s) of shared understandings, beliefs or worldviews. Such understandings or worldviews are typically inculcated as part of the habitus, but the concept of misrecognition is worthy of 'recognition' in its own right because it draws our attention to the fact that such inculcation concerns not only content but also modality, where actors come to have a *shared commitment* to certain values and ideals despite their fundamentally culturally arbitrary character. Such values and ideals, of course, can include perceptions about the relative importance of languages as well as the kinds of associations that different languages may have with notions of prestige, employability, ethnic identity and so on (see Chapter 2).

Because the Bourdieusian habitus is presented as reflecting an 'unconscious mastery' (Bourdieu, 1977: 79) of how actors are expected to respond in relation to a specific field and as a result, 'cannot be touched by voluntary, deliberate transformation' (Bourdieu, 1977: 94), this leads to a conceptual conundrum about the relationship between the unconscious nature of the habitus and the conscious deliberation associated with reflexive awareness. That is, it is not clear how the former can (ever) give rise to the latter, or how the two can even co-exist. This is a puzzle with far-reaching consequences, since unless the habitus can be reconceptualized so as to accommodate conscious deliberation or reflexive awareness, any potential for transformative agency would appear to remain muted.

One possible approach toward addressing this conundrum is to start with the general Bourdieusian picture of a fit between habitus and field, but to then argue that as actors move across fields, this degree of fit is likely to vary. As we noted above, this is the tack taken by McNay, who suggests that where the lack of fit is sufficiently strong, actors may then experience a sense of dissonance, which rudely forces them to become reflexively aware of their relations to their surrounding social structures. In this picture, the sufficiently wide disjuncture between field and habitus that might prompt the emergence of reflexive awareness is more the exception than the rule. However, McNay's proposal has been countered by the argument that such habitus-field disjunctures are in fact sufficiently common as to constitute a prevailing characteristic of actors' experiences – this is arguably the case in a highly mobile society or a society undergoing rapid social changes. But while it is conceded that this might mean that reflexive awareness is fairly widespread, any assertions concerning a rise in agency is mitigated by the suggestion that it is now appropriate to speak of reflexivity itself having become incorporated into the habitus (Adkins, 2003; Sweetman, 2003). Thus, Adkins makes the point that even the presence of reflexivity may not be sufficient to warrant any discussion of agency since it may be the case that 'reflexive practices are so habituated that they are part of the very norms, rules and expectations that govern gender in later modernity, even as they may ostensibly appear to challenge these very notions' (Adkins, 2003: 35).

At this point, it seems clear if any kind of agency is to be recovered from the concept of a habituated reflexivity, the understanding of the habitus has to be changed in a fundamental way. Skeggs (2004: 25, 29), in fact, makes this clear when she argues that the habitus (contra Bourdieu) is fundamentally characterized by ambivalence, since 'identities are a limited resource, a form of cultural capital that are worked and uncomfortably inhabited'. Skeggs thus points out that:

> Bourdieu cannot account for that ambivalence, as Adkins (2003) shows, because he places ambivalence outside of the realm of practice, he understands norms to be incorporated, ... he assumes that the field is a pre-condition of the habitus and the habitus will always submit to the field. (Skeggs, 2004: 25, 29)

The suggestion that ambivalence is a critical feature of the habitus goes directly to the very heart of Bourdieu's claims about how the dispositions of actors are really thoroughly informed by their socialization experiences. But while useful, it is still insufficient to address the issue of reflexivity since ambivalence and reflexivity are in principle independent properties. That is to say, it is possible for someone to be ambivalent without them being aware of being ambivalent (ambivalence without reflexivity). And conversely, one could adopt a meta-perspective on one's social situation without necessarily feeling any ambivalence (reflexivity without ambivalence). It is therefore necessary to arrive at an account of the relationship between ambivalence and reflexivity, and how these are bound up with the habitus – in other words, to understand in what way the habitus is always/already characterized by *both* ambivalence and reflexivity. The work of James Bohman proves useful in this regard.

Bohman and the Transformative Potential of Critical Reflexivity

Bohman acknowledges that a significant advantage afforded by Bourdieu's notion of habitus is that it provides 'a constitutive account of cultural constraint without the traditional conception of regulative rules or internalized norms' (Bohman, 1999: 130). This is because the habitus is fundamentally *formative* in nature: it is a set of dispositions and orientations that does not merely regulate the behavior of agents, but helps to define who they are. Thus, '(i)t is in virtue of being socialized into a common background of pre-reflective assumptions and orientations that agents have goals at all' (Bohman, 1999: 130).

However, Bohman argues that Bourdieu's account of a 'pre-reflective habitus' is too 'one-dimensional' and makes no place for 'deliberate processes and practices' (Bohman, 1999: 146). Consider, for example, Bourdieu's (1990: 59; see also Bourdieu & Passeron, 1979: 27) assertion that, with the habitus, '(t)he most improbable practices are therefore excluded, as unthinkable, by a kind of immediate submission to order that inclines agents to make a virtue of necessity, to refuse what is anyway denied and to will the inevitable.' Bourdieu's tendency to downplay the possibility of critical deliberation has the effect that his theory ends up being overly deterministic so that it is 'at its best, therefore, a theory of reproduction, and is at its weakest as a theory of transformation' (Calhoun, 1993: 72; see also Adkins, 2003; Collins, 1993; Lash, 1993).

To mitigate this determinism, Bohman suggests that what is required is a conception of agency that is both reflective and transformative, one that recognizes 'the capacities of socially and culturally situated agents to reflect upon their social conditions, criticize them, and articulate new interpretations of them' (Bohman, 1999: 145). To develop such a conception, Bohman finds the work of Frankfurt (1988: 11–25) particularly instructive. Frankfurt starts with the observation that even though human beings are not unique in having desires or in making choices, they are unique in being able to form second-order desires:

> Besides wanting and choosing and being moved *to do* this or that, men may also want to have (or not to have) certain desires and motives. They are capable of wanting to be different, in their preferences and purposes, from what they are. (Frankfurt, 1988: 12 italics in original)

Frankfurt therefore suggests that autonomy comes about when there are second-order desires, or the desire to have or not have a desire. Such second-order desires, as we shall see in the following chapters, are typically called upon when agents experience the need to resolve conflicting first-order desires regarding literacy practices.

Bohman expands on Frankfurt's ideas by situating them in relation to Bourdieu's sociological theorizing so as to open up a less deterministic conception of the habitus. Some second-order desires, Bohman acknowledges, are apparently constrained by cultural experiences, such as the hypercorrectness of Petit-Bourgeois speakers in France (Bohman, 1999: 146). However, there are other desires that are much more deliberate in character, such as the desire to be the sort of person who has particular sorts of desires or goals, or even the desire to be critically reflective. Bohman insists that far from being anomalous, there are in fact clear historical precedents where, in the context of particular communities or social movements, 'care for the self can open up a cultural space for greater self-interpretation and deliberate choice' (Bohman, 1999: 146). Some of the examples that he gives include the various aesthetic and moral disciplines pursued by the Greeks, Buddhists and the Jesuits. In a more modern context, Bohman points to institutionalized practices of legal review, scientific peer review and democratic debate, which are 'the institutional equivalent of practices of *character planning*, in which second-order beliefs and beliefs about the demands for justification lead people to reject certain sorts of widely accepted beliefs, such as those that depend on ignoring legitimate protests of others or that could not withstand free and open debate' (Bohman, 1999: 147, italics added).

The distinction between these two types of second-order desires highlights the fact that reflexive mechanisms can lead to the revision of beliefs, even where such mechanisms are institutionalized. In this way, the kinds of examples cited by Bohman speak directly to Adkins' concern that the habituation of reflexivity may be anathema to identity transformation or 'character planning'. For example, a scientific peer-review process is not simply a process that relevant agents in the field become accustomed to as they gain experience with the process of reviewing scientific articles or applications for grants. Precisely because the process requires/encourages an attitude of critical scrutiny – albeit of certain institutionalized objects (grant proposals, manuscripts) – there is always the potential for a 'spillover' where the actors may begin to question if the institutional status quo is adequate to the goals that it is supposed to serve. In such a situation, the reflexive practice acquires a second-order status. Actors no longer work within an established system of review, but can begin to question if the system itself needs to undergo a review of its own. Also, actors might even begin to ask about the kinds of individuals who might be best suited to undertake the reviewing responsibilities, that is, what kinds of attributes should such individuals possess and perhaps whether the incumbent actors themselves qualify as appropriate reviewers. Questions of this sort point inevitably to the presence of a reflexive engagement with the review system. More importantly, such a scenario does not require that actors weaken or renounce their commitment to the process in order to begin being reflexive [as might be the case with McNay's thesis of dissonance (see above)].

Moving from the narrow example of scientific review to broader societal phenomena, Bohman goes on to suggest that:

The more pluralistic a society is the less likely it is that its integration can be achieved pre-reflectively in common dispositions, even in sub-groups. ... the issue for practical reason in such a situation is the revision of beliefs and desires in explicit ways in accordance with more public and inclusive conceptions of legitimacy and authority. Reflexive agency in such societies requires not only changing beliefs and desires, but also the social conditions under which agents reflect, deliberate and cooperate with each other to widen their universes of discourse. By doing so, they may also change their existing relations of power. (Bohman, 1999: 147)

While Bohman's concluding remarks may seem to echo that of the modernization theorists, there are actually important differences that are worth remarking upon. Recall that for the modernization theorists, individuals are apparently compelled to fall back on themselves because institutional structures are no longer reliable.[4] This leads to an account of identity transformation that tends to eschew the possibility of institutional influence, and it has been criticized for creating unrealistic expectations about what the self is actually capable of achieving (Craib, 1994).

What is needed instead is a more nuanced and relational account of the self, one that allows for the possibility of reflexive awareness even if in the context of pervading institutional structures. Such an alternative account would have the advantage of acknowledging that it is in the '(e)xperience of the day-to-day limits of self-reliance and control, set by constraints of political economy on the one hand and family and intimate relations on the other' that creates a sense of reflexivity or 'self-awareness' (Webb, 2004: 735). It is precisely in the combination of Frankfurt's and Bohman's ideas that we get such an alternative account. As Frankfurt points out, individuals are always to some degree already reflective of their own goals as well as that of their surrounding institutions *regardless* of whether the latter are 'solid' or not. And as Bohman suggests, there are in fact institutions that even insist on reflexivity as part of their own institutional norms, so that individuals are required to be reflective not in spite of institutional failings but (*contra* the modernization theorists and their extended reflexivity thesis) *because of* institutional fiat.

Multiple Markets, Ambivalence and Reflexivity

But even if, as Bohman and Frankfurt suggest, individuals are always reflexive to some degree or other, it is still unclear how ambivalence can ever enter the picture, especially, if there are times when individuals are in fact encouraged to be reflexive by their institutional milieu. The answer, we suggest, is this: Individuals are always ambivalent about their relationship to a field or market for the simple reason that no single market ever completely exhausts the totality of any individual's social experiences. All actors are simultaneously embedded in multiple markets, and because of this, the potential for ambivalence is always present, since different markets will be characterized by different norms and values. As a consequence, individuals are always faced with the need to reconcile the potentially conflicting demands – including demands relating to identity work – which various markets may impose on them.

Bourdieu (1984, 1986, 1990) tells us that social life can be construed as a series of multiple, overlapping and even hierarchically embedded fields or markets. However, the greater autonomy a particular market enjoys (and this autonomy is always only ever a matter of degree), the more it is able to set its own logic governing, among other things, the kinds of capital considered relevant to the market, the convertability of different forms of capital, and the kinds of ends that actors in the market ought to be oriented toward. For example, the more autonomous a literary or artistic market is, the more possible it becomes for the actors in this market (artists, art dealers, art critics) to mask their concerns with money or power by appearing to be only interested in the 'disinterested' world of 'aesthetic purity' (Thompson, 1991: 16).

The assertion that interests in power and money are masked is intended to reflect Bourdieu's claim that multiple markets exist in relation to the more general 'field of power' where the latter is mainly characterized by the pursuit of economic capital more so than any other. This means that markets that are high in cultural capital, but low in economic capital are still often at a disadvantage in relation to, and thus open to influence from, other markets where economic capital is most valued. As Calhoun puts it:

> Directly economic capital operates in a money-based market that can be indefinitely extended. Cultural capital, by contrast, operates as a matter of status, which is often recognized only within specific fields. (Calhoun, 2003: 299)

From this, we can make a number of guiding assumptions. First, it is reasonable to treat the continuum from macro-institutions to micro-interactions, and any intermediate levels of analysis, as markets of varying sizes and influence. This means that the language policy of a state and the institutional arrangements marshaled in its support can be construed as forming a very large market while interactions in the home or among adolescents can be construed as forming smaller markets. As we will see later on, in Singapore, the language policy articulates a macro-market that includes the school system (where English is used as the medium of instruction and the official mother tongues are taught as second languages), the media (messages encouraging the use of 'good English' or Mandarin may be heard on television or radio) and other forms of mass communications (posters, banners and political speeches) (Bokhorst-Heng, 1999: 244). The huge reach of this macro-market means that it practically encompasses the entirety of Singaporean society. However, we hasten to point out that smaller markets (families, social cliques) should not automatically be treated as proper subsets of larger ones, since what counts as capital in the adolescent market, for example, can be informed by the activities of adolescents in other societies. Thus, the relationship between markets, regardless of their size, is better conceptualized as a dynamic multidimensional network of lattices rather than a rigidly defined strict hierarchical structure.

Second, since all actors participate in multiple markets, we have to recognize the potential for conflict as well as reinforcement between a given actor's different market-related activities. In this sense, ambivalence is more likely to be present when actors are confronted with conflicting market demands. However, the more autonomous a market is, the less pressure there will be for an actor to resolve any potential conflicts between his/her activities in *this* market and others, thus reducing (though not necessarily eliminating) the possibility of ambivalence.

The formation of identities on markets is therefore mediated by both reflexivity and ambivalence. By complementing the work of Bohman and Frankfurt with a sociological perspective involving multiple markets, we are able to insist on the potential for reflexivity and ambivalence as ever-present in any habitus. By extending this take on reflexivity and ambivalence to the semiotics of identity work in multiple, overlapping linguistic markets, we may then account for the multilingual dynamics in late-modern Singapore and how these are reworked into coherent narratives of self and other.

Performance and Identity

As actors negotiate their participation in multiple markets, they necessarily make decisions about whether or not some markets are better abandoned while others are further pursued. Such decisions are often informed by actors' own evaluations of their performances – including linguistic performances – in particular markets, including an appraisal of the kinds of receptions that these performances have received or are likely to receive. As Bauman and Briggs (1990: 66) point out, a performance approach necessarily views actors as having 'the ability to reflect meaningfully on their own communicative conduct', where 'audience evaluation of the communicative competence of performers forms a crucial dimension of performance.' Furthermore,

> ... performances are not simply artful uses of language that stand apart both from day-to-day life and from larger questions of meaning ... Performance rather provides a frame that invites critical reflection on communicative processes. A given performance is tied to a number of speech events that precede and succeed it (past performances, readings of texts, negotiations, rehearsals, gossip, reports, critiques, challenges, subsequent performances, and the like). (Bauman & Briggs, 1990: 60–61)

While most work on performance has focused on how it is 'anchored' in particular contexts of use (Bauman & Briggs, 1990: 72–73), it is also important to attend to how performances can be 'lifted out' of one context, and reinserted into new contexts, for it is in this way that actors may or may not attempt to extend the communicative strategies and skills acquired in one social encounter to other encounters. Especially relevant here is the notion of *contextualization*, which involves 'an active process of negotiation in which participants reflexively examine the discourse as it is emerging, embedding assessments of its structure and significance in the speech itself. Performers extend such assessments to include predictions about how the communicative competence, personal histories, and social identities of their interlocutors will shape the reception of what is said' (Bauman & Briggs, 1990: 69). In other words, the extension of past performances to newer social situations is not a simple process of replicating earlier uses of language. Rather, it requires constant monitoring of the ongoing social interaction, making careful adjustments that take into account audience feedback. This is because when an actor extracts stretches of discourse from an earlier interactional setting – in a process of *decontextualization* – the resulting discourse unit[4] may carry traces of its earlier history (Bauman & Briggs, 1990: 73), making it suitable to varying degrees (or not at all) for its subsequent insertion into newer contexts or *recontextualization*. The more skilful a performer is, the better s/he is at making judgments about what stretches of discourse to extract, and how to redeploy the extracted discourse units.

The implication of the foregoing is that the more reflexive an actor is, the greater the likelihood of the actor producing skilful performances. In other words, while all actors perform, not all are necessarily consciously viewing themselves or their interlocutors as performers. Those who do so are more likely to view past experiences *as performances*. By framing (Goffman, 1974, 1981) these experiences as performances, and thus by seeing themselves and others as performers, actors are more like to improve on future performances because they are able to treat their own earlier, less successful experiences as *rehearsals*, and to critically evaluate the behaviors of others by themselves taking on the role of an audience. Highly reflexive actors then are those who constantly modulate their behaviors by monitoring different audience reactions. As Bauman and Briggs observe, performance:

> puts the act of speaking on display – objectifies it, lifts it to a degree from its interactional setting and opens it to scrutiny by an audience. Performance heightens awareness of the act of speaking and licenses the audience to evaluate the skill and effectiveness of the performer's accomplishment. (Bauman & Briggs, 1990: 73)

The more reflexive the actor, the more heightened, then, his/her awareness of the demands involved in linguistic communication. And concomitantly, the more likely he/she will be aware of how 'people *use* or *enact* or *perform* social styles for a range of symbolic purposes' (Coupland, 2007: 3, italics in original). Such an approach to style treats styling as 'an interactional practice' and emphasizes its 'identity-making potential' (Coupland, 2007: 105), where individuals creatively make use of their available social (including linguistic) resources in the context of local interactions.

Style, Literacy and Identity

Given the foregoing discussion, it seems to us that one way in which we may gain an analytical foothold on how identity work can impact on language education is to therefore view literacy practices as manifestations of style. Such an extended notion of style is also in keeping with current developments in more mainstream sociolinguistic work. An important innovation in contemporary approaches to style involves exploring its use in expressions of identity. Here, we build on a recent treatment of identity construction in terms of *style* (Coupland, 2007; Eckert, 2000), and a 'broad conception of style as a social semiosis of distinctiveness' that 'crosscuts [...] communicative and behavioral modalities and integrates them thematically' (Hebdige, 1979). This allows us to construct an analysis of English literacy practices as stylistic practices, and to examine the extent to which the identities that adolescents perform through the styling of literacy are specific instantiations of a thematically integrated social semiosis of distinctiveness characteristic of a specific multilingual habitus.

Style has, of course, classically been conceived of as intra-speaker variation, where such variation is treated as a response to degrees of formality of a situation. The general hypothesis, within the variationist paradigm, is that as the formality of a situation increases, so, too, will the speaker's use of prestige linguistic features. More recently, however, the notion of style has been particularly productive in discussions of how the linguistic and nonlinguistic behaviors of speakers are specifically constrained by, and contribute to, identity construction, and the performance of personae. Eckert (2001), for example, has noted how adolescent use of language is enmeshed in constructions of self in symbolic markets of identity, and has developed the analysis of style in this regard. In so doing, Eckert includes attention to clothing, hair, physical gestures, facial expressions, along with prosody, morphosyntax and discourse, as being relevant to the analysis of style. In a similar vein, Coupland (2001; see also Coupland, 2007) has suggested that a sociolinguistics of style should treat it as the projection of the speaker's identity, arguing that style needs to be understood as an 'active, motivated, symbolic process' rather than one that is simply a 'situational correlate', as tends to be the case under the variationist paradigm (Coupland, 2001: 187).

This acknowledgement that the construction of style draws upon a variety of resources opens up the concept to be theorized as a form of bricolage (Hebdige, 1979; see also Bucholtz, 2002), where preexisting elements are appropriated and combined in new and different ways to create distinctive styles. Erickson (2001: 162) defines bricolage as 'making novel use of pre-existing forms to accomplish uniquely local functions,' stressing that bricolage is more than mere expropriation; rather, it crucially involves syncretism, where elements from differing sources are brought together:

> Considered as bricolage, innovation can be seen not as creation *ex nihilo* but as a novel re-use of pre-existing elements. What is 'new' in such innovations is only a tiny percentage of the whole. What makes for novelty is the new combination of forms, not the formal elements themselves. The new juxtaposition of elements makes for a change from the way in which each is seen separately. (Erickson, 2001: 163)

Viewing style as bricolage that is motivated by the desire to project personae of particular kinds is therefore consistent with our intention to see adolescents as cultural agents. And although other studies have approached literacy practices in terms of identity, few have investigated literacy practices from the perspective of a sociolinguistics of style. One advantage of such an approach is that it provides us with a conceptual framework that integrates adolescent activities and attitudes both outside and inside the classroom, thereby permitting insights into exactly how identity impacts on language education through practices of adolescent literacy. And given the importance that adolescents attach to the opinions of their peers (Eckert, 2000: 16), an added advantage is that we are able to take specific cognizance of how particular practices may be deeply influenced by the *anticipated* reactions of members of one's social cohort. In other words, just as choices concerning what kinds of music to listen to, or what kinds of clothes to wear, may be influenced by the opinions of one's peers, so, too, may classroom behaviors such as whether or not to seek the teacher's help or volunteering to read a text out loud. As Street reminds us:

> ... we have to start talking to people, listening to them and linking their immediate experience of reading and writing to other things that they do as well. ... because what might give *meaning* to literacy events may actually be something that is not, in the first instance, thought of in terms of literacy at all. (Street, 2000: 21, italics in original)

The concept of style therefore provides just such a unified perspective on students' behavior, allowing us to understand how identity work at home and among peers can impact on classroom-based language-learning practices.

Yet another advantage of this approach is that it allows us to view adolescent literacy practices as specific youth instantiations of more established, mainstream societal categorizations such as social, class, ethnicity and gender (cf. Eckert, 2001). After all, treating style as bricolage does not commit us to the view that the individual is completely free to combine elements in any way that he or she might wish. Certainly because it is a highly local phenomenon, any analysis of style must therefore be careful not to lose sight of the particularities of an individual's goals and desires. On the other hand, as Coupland notes, although style is specifically a highly situated phenomenon, individuals nevertheless draw upon broader sociocultural ideologies as resources for stylistic construction (Coupland, 2001: 196). This introduces an added dimension of importance to style because it means that identities are styled according to social class and gender and ethnic backgrounds, so that style plays a central role in the constitution of status and, ultimately, position in civil society. It is this conceptual symbiosis of insights from sociolinguistic theorizing and literacy studies that allows us to discuss issues of social reproduction and literacy in such a way as to suggest linkages between the social realities of our informants and their encounters with literacy.

Linguistic Markets

A number of scholars have recently emphasized the significance of identity for language learning (Hawkins, 2005; Norton, 2000; Pennycook, 2001), emphasizing the dynamic interplay between actors and their social environments. For example, in her ethnographic study of children in a fifth and sixth grade classroom, Lewis (2001: 51) draws attention to how identities serve to 'intersect and compete to complicate life in school and create the social drama that shapes the local scene of the classroom'. Drawing on the work of Bauman and Briggs (1990), Lewis (2001: 16, italics added) goes on to point out that 'An individual or group performance is created by context that is *re-created by the performance.*' And in an observation that anticipates much of what will be covered in the following chapters in this book, Lewis adds that 'literacy practices are enacted by readers who have been constructed through social codes that shape their relationship to peers and texts' (Lewis, 2001: 44–45). Hawkins describes the important relevance of identity work in more general terms:

> Individuals bring lived histories to activities and events in situated environments, and it is through communications and interactions with others in these environments that learners negotiate and co-construct their views of themselves and the world. The activities and contexts, however, are imbued with and represent specific values and ideologies (which privilege certain practices over others), and these shape the dynamics of the interactions. ... It is not enough to make a bid for a certain position or even to appropriately enact a desire identity within a discourse community – one must be recognized and acknowledged as that (kind of) person by others within the community. Additionally, one can be invited or summoned into a particular position within a given community, but that summons can be taken up, resisted, or denied. Thus individuals have agency but not autonomy; they do not choose a position outside of ongoing social negotiations. (Hawkins, 2005: 61–62)

And while the social attributes that go into identity work may include markers of gender, ethnic and class, some of these attributes can in fact be much more localized. For example, Varenne and McDermott describe what happens in the case of a student who hesitates while engaged in the task of reading aloud:

> And then, the child's delay is *noticed*. It is noticed by another human being, but not just any human being in a neutral setting. It is noticed by

a teacher (not a janitor), *in a school* (and not at home), *during classtime* (and not on the playground). Suddenly, the difference between performance and the teacher's expectation has been made into a difference that can make a difference in the biography of the child. The delay has become a 'failure' in need of explanation, evaluation and remediation ... The particular act is taken as exemplary of the kind of acts performed by this kind of person; it is now the child, rather than the act, that is identified as a success or failure ... This can be extended to characterize a group with whom the person is identified. (Varenne & McDermott, 1998: 5, italics in original, see also Rampton, 2006: 70–71)

Thus, particular instances of behavior in the language classroom, such as how a student manages the demands of reading a text out loud, can become definable of that student. That is, it can constitute the basis on which the student is classified as belonging to a type ('diligent', 'talkative', 'poor in English', 'troublemaker'). We will certainly encounter similar examples from the Singaporean context in the chapters that follow, but for now, what we wish to point out that is missing from Varenne and McDermott's account is the fact that the student is not inhabiting a single market. That is, even while the student is ostensibly reading in the classroom under the scrutiny of the teacher, the student is also likely to be highly aware of evaluations from his or her peers. And depending on how much importance the student places on peer evaluation, the teacher's own scrutiny of the student may be considered less critical. In this way, some students may even be willing to sacrifice the teacher's approval and deliberately read 'badly' in order that they gain credibility among their peers.

From a performance perspective, then, actors are therefore constantly negotiating the demands of many different markets, bearing in mind the fact that each market may privilege a different set of practices (for how else might one market distinguish itself from another?). However, performances in one market are not completely insulated from the potential repercussions of another market (for how else does capital get converted as a result of activities that are both intra- and inter-market?). Thus, actors are often obligated, in their performances, to be cognizant how an audience beyond the immediate market might view their behavior. For example, how a student behaves in the classroom may have repercussions on how he/she is viewed by peers once the class is over, or for how teachers may feedback to the student's parents details of his/her classroom behavior. And conversely, parental expectations about a student's ability may inform his/her classroom behavior. In addition, a performance perspective highlights the fact that identities are ultimately socially ratified via successful styling accomplishments. As Coupland points out:

> The issue here is how participants dynamically structure the very local business of their talk and position themselves relative to each other in their relational histories, short- and long-term. Personal and relational identities can be forged and refined linguistically in subtle ways within a consolidated genre and community of practice. A sociolinguistic feature that might otherwise bear, for example, a social class or a participant role significance might do personal identity work in the interpersonal frame. By using a particular feature, a speaker might style himself or herself as, for example, more or less powerful within a particular relationship, or style the relationship as being a more intimate or less intimate one. (Coupland, 2007: 113–114)

In the case of literacy practices, one's identity as a good student, or, more specifically, as someone who is proficient or competent in English, requires the display of the appropriate skills – where what counts as appropriate is relativized to different audiences located in different linguistic markets. Successfully styled performances and the consequent ratification that these bring allow actors to occupy particular positions or identities, and this in turn, contributes dialogically, to the actors' own sense of self. As Hawkins puts it:

> ... students entering school may negotiate an identity that enables them to be successful in school or one that marginalizes them as a student, based in part on how the experiences, behaviors, values and ways of engaging in language and literacy practices that they bring align with those privileged in schools (Heath, 1983; Lee, 1993; Michaels, 1981), but based also on what it is that they understand the place to be and who they imagine they can be there. Acquiring an identity as a *learner* is clearly a highly valued identity category within the institution of schooling, yet the identity work in which children are engaged may function to grant or deny them access to such an identity position. (Hawkins, 2005: 62–63, italics in original)

Our account of literacy as a reflexive performance of identity is therefore grounded in the appreciation that both the formulation of desires and the possibility of their actualization are always dependent on the affordances present in the different social environments. The deployment of linguistic resources for the styling of performances is not an individual's unilateral achievement, since the social meanings attributed to such resources also depend on their uptake by relevant others in the social environment. And in the following chapters, we aim to provide relevant illustrations through our descriptions and analyses of the identity work and literacy practices of our various informants.

Notes

(1) The discussion of reflexivity in this chapter is based on Brooks and Wee (2008), and Wee and Brooks (2010).

(2) For excellent and highly accessible discussions of Bourdieu, see Jenkins (1992), Lareau (2003, Appendix B) and Thompson (1991, Introduction).

(3) We emphasize that the distinction between these contrasting positions is a broad heuristic rather than a strict dichotomy. The work of Lash (1994), for example, on aesthetic reflexivity, while typically associated with the first position because it accepts the wide scope of reflexivity and its emancipatory/de-traditionalizing potential (Skeggs, 2002: 365), is arguably categorizable as also belonging to the second position since it does attempt to draw on the social theory of Bourdieu.

(4) Bauman and Briggs speak of 'texts' being entextualized rather than 'discourse units'. However, we prefer the latter because it is broader in meaning. Entextualizations can involve linguistic units of varying degrees of schematicity (Goldberg, 1995; Langacker, 1987) so that there may be units lacking in any formal features, but are instead fully functional in nature. We might call these discursive strategies. Be that as it may, the processes of de- and recontextualization are still relevant here.

4   Some Data About Our Data

The nature of one's data, including the circumstances under which they were gathered, is often one of the most controversial aspects of any piece of empirical research. It may be something of a truism to say that no methodology is ever completely flawless, no research design totally perfect. But, how one's sample was ultimately chosen, the kinds of practical constraints that arose and how one decided to deal with them, as well as the qualifications of the researchers themselves even, are all potentially subject to criticisms of various sorts. The methodologies one employs also offer themselves as objects of considered reflection, and may tell us something important about how an implicit understanding of lived reality determines our outlook on it. In the course of conducting our research, as well as in our subsequent presentations and discussions of our findings at various conferences and in various journals, we became acutely aware just how much our underlying beliefs about the type of community we were studying, its multilingual dynamics and its preferred genres of linguistic performance, styles of speech, and dominant modes of semiotic engagements, unconsciously influenced our leanings toward certain types of data collection and interpretation techniques. Reflecting on these issues now provides a wonderful posthoc opportunity to explore these tacit and seldom treated assumptions on the validity, credibility and reliability of data. In this chapter, then, we aim to explore the methodological difficulties and conceptual dilemmas we encountered and how we went about addressing them. As with our previous chapter, the core themes that we arrange the discussion around are those of reflexivity, narrativity and ambivalence.

Framing Parameters

As noted earlier, we wish to explore the reflexive and critical linguistic judgments about language and literacy represented in the voices of our student informants, and how these stances contributed to the constructions of their subjectivities as learners. Ultimately, we want to throw some light on how the different subjectivities and positions that learners took up vis-à-vis the English language literacy practices reflected or reproduced traditional modernist and stratificational organizations of multilingualism specifically. In the late-modern context of Singapore, this involves many considerations. For example, as late-modern subjects we are very much the selves we assemble rather than the products of constrained or scripted selves of a (pre) determined social categorization. As a consequence, we want to emphasize and be sensitive to how our informants are using literacy, and building an account of literacy artifacts and their uses of literacy artifacts, into a composite and varied, ever changing, narrative of selves – narrating, and performing through narrating, particular identities where literacy figures as an important semiotic and autobiographic artifact. We are not so much interested in the truth or falsity of *facticity* of our informants' literacy practices, as much in how, and in the ways in which, they represented these practices in relation to different languages, different activities and different semiotic artifacts (books, magazines,) in order to build 'temporary' life trajectories and construct a narrated subjectivity. As we will note below, 'individual stories' must lock into public narratives, and it is precisely in how these public narratives (many traditional, modernist understandings of literacy, taste and style), are incorporated, transposed and recycled in the service of momentary constructions of subjectivity that we come to understand the link between the macro and the micro.

The late-modern social condition of our informants also has methodological implications for the role played by sites, domains and fields generally. We noted in Chapter 2 how the modernist assumption of clear structural–functional divisions between institutions, sites and domains that exert unambiguous normative pressure on clearly definable segments of behavior, or areas of knowledge, is not a tenable assumption in late modernity. Instead, individuals move across multiple-sites and assemble selves out of a bricolage of different semiotic components from multiple sites. Therefore, what is of interest is how the narrative of self incorporates these different 'spheres, domains, and institutions' in talking about uses and understanding of literacy. This means that the motive for the choice of sites also shifts somewhat in relation to more conventional sociolinguistic studies. In this study, we have chosen students from a Singaporean neighborhood school (explained below). What is particularly interesting about these schools is how they are thought – in the minds and public discourses of the general public – to position their learners with respect to life-style options/opportunities more generally, ranging, as we shall see below, from the appropriate choice of partner, to what general demeanor is befitting of predicted life aspirations of their pupils.

In this chapter, we expand upon each of these points in slightly more detail, by detailing some core aspects of narratives in the research interview,

and moving over to a focus on the notions of stylization, style and performance and how this can be read off from the interview as an essential (late-
modern) tool. We then review the choice of school, procedures for engaging
interviewers, and practicalities around choice of topics and transcriptions.

Narratives in the Research Interview

Scholars working from both more discourse and more sociologically oriented perspectives have long recognized that 'The essence of humanness,
long characterized as the tendency to make sense of the world through rationality, has come increasingly to be described as the tendency to tell stories,
to make sense of the world through narrative' (Johnstone, 2001: 635; see also
Lawler, 2003). But narratives are certainly not 'free floating'; they are crucially dependent on and also contribute to social positioning and location (cf.
Lawler, 2003: 253). Thus, Lawler tells us that narratives are:

> *Social products* produced by people within the context of specific social,
> historical and cultural locations. They are related to the experience that
> people have of their lives, but they are not transparent carriers of that
> experience. Rather, they are interpretive devices, through which people
> represent themselves, both to themselves and to others. ... That is, sto-
> ries circulate culturally, providing a means of making sense of that world,
> and also providing the materials with which people construct personal
> narratives as a means of constructing personal identities. (Lawler, 2003:
> 242, italics in original)

We see some evidence of this in Johnstone's (1990) study of the American
Midwest, which shows that storytelling can shape a sense of community
and, importantly, that this is achieved by having references in the narratives
that are consistently anchored to specific locales, particular individuals or
culturally specific events and knowledge. And if the locales *from* which particular narratives originate are associated with certain kinds of attributes
(Johnstone, 2004: 69), then by implication, other locales are potentially asso-
ciable with yet other attributes. In this way, the 'local-foreign' distinction is
marked not just geographically but via the ascription of contrasting qualities
as well (Blommaert, 2005: 222).

In other words, the kinds of narratives that are produced depend very
much on the perspectives and values of the producers themselves. Rather
than being a drawback or disadvantage, this is precisely what makes
narratives invaluable into research on style and literacy; they provide us with
evidence (albeit of an indirect kind) of how participants are engaged in

identity work, and consequently of how this identity work impacts on their social practices. As Baynham puts it:

> ... what a narrative is 'about' can be read/interpreted as a kind of evidence of the way that the narrator constructs ideologies and values, for example, what counts as extraordinary, incomprehensible, unreasonable, or for that matter, typical. Narrative as a genre tends to be saturated with ideology and value. As Labov (1972) and Labov and Waletzky (1967) point out, narratives do not just report events but also evaluate them. From this perspective, narrative itself can serve indexically as a kind of evidence of the ideologies and values that drive it and by extension of the self-presentation or identity work being accomplished by the narrating subject. Narratives provide a way into the subjectivity of literacy practices, into understanding how participants construct what they do according to which ideologies and values, which historical trajectories, as well as what kind of self-presentation or identity work they are currently engaged in. (Baynham, 2000: 100)

In Singapore, identity work among adolescents, as we will see is tied up with, among other things, the kinds of schools they attend. Thus, one's school, one's home and the kinds of social practices one participates in (including literacy practices involving different languages) can all contribute to the construction of self-identity as well as that of others. In this way, the personal narratives constructed by our adolescent informants inevitably draw upon 'public narratives', which are narratives that are 'attached to cultural and institutional formations rather than the single individual' (Somers & Gibson, 1994: 62; see also Linde, 2001). These personal narratives therefore are not and indeed, cannot be completely divorced from the narratives of other individuals, nor from institutional narratives, especially those emanating from the state (Rappa & Wee, 2006; Wee & Bokhorst-Heng, 2005) because 'the narratives of individual lives must always incorporate other life narratives' (Lawler, 2003: 251).

Style, Stylization and the Interview

We chose to make use of interview data as opposed to observational data for the following reasons. Observations of classroom and other behaviors require that the analyst play a greater role in 'inscribing meaning' on the learners whereas we were much more interested in the learners' 'voices and opinions, along with information that would give us insight into their out-of-school histories and lives' (Hawkins, 2005: 67–68). We hasten to point out that we have nothing against observational data. We see such work as providing a complementary perspective, and we do draw upon such work in this book. However, we are also especially interested in approaching literacy and nonliteracy-based practices in terms of style. And as Rickford points out, because the issue of style is deeply intertwined with questions of agency and purpose, 'it seems important to arrive at interpretations that accord with or at least relate to those of local insiders and performers' (Rickford, 2001: 231). The use of interview data therefore cannot be dispensed with, though it must be acknowledged that analyzing such data is 'neither straightforward nor easy' (Rickford, 2001: 231).

In particular, we might ask whether in the course of the interviews our informants were projecting a persona specifically for the benefit of the interviewer. Such a possibility certainly cannot be ignored. But while we remain mindful of this, this possibility is mitigated by the following considerations. One, what emerges from the data may be reasonably taken as style rather than stylization. The distinction between the two is as follows. Coupland (2004: 250) suggests that the former is 'behavior', understood in relation to generalized normative expectations, whereas the latter is 'performance' in the sense of Bauman (1977). That is, 'stylized utterances are bounded moments when others' voices are, in a somewhat more literal sense, displayed and framed for local, creative, sociolinguistic effect' and 'the most clearly documented instances of stylization refer to specific utterance events or sequences *within* specific speech events' (Coupland, 2004: 249, italics added). Thus, a stylized performance takes place within the matrix of a styled behavior, and the actor cues this stylization to his/her audience, typically in an exaggerated or overtly emphatic manner (Coupland, 2004: 253; Rampton, 1991, 1995).

In this book, we want to be able to focus on style in relation to practices both inside and outside the classroom. We suggest that literacy practices can be treated as style rather than stylization precisely because, in the school, for example, they help to position students vis-à-vis generally accepted school-based norms. This is because, as noted above, stylization, in contrast to style, tends to occur as specific moments in the context of a larger ongoing interaction rather than constituting the entire interaction itself. And 'stylizers *intend* to be heard or seen as doing stylization' (Coupland, 2004: 257, italics added).

In the course of the interviews, there was little or no indication that our informants were hoping to be recognized as engaging in stylizations. There are, however, specific moments in the classroom when something close to stylization occurs, such as when students are asked to read aloud so as to have their pronunciation and word-recognition abilities evaluated. We say 'close to' because although students are clearly displaying or performing their language skills, it is not necessarily the case that they are adopting the voices of others for some exaggerated effect. However, our data do suggest that whether a student is comfortable with reading aloud appears to be correlated with whether or not stylized performances regularly occur outside the classroom amongst friends (e.g. Chapter 7).

This leads to our second consideration. As mentioned, the data were gathered during a series of interviews ranging over a number of months. Though not impossible, it is therefore unlikely that the personas presented in the interviews were completely disconnected from the informants' own behaviors with friends and in class, especially since the focus of the interviews was consistently on the informants' self-reports of their behaviors in those specific contexts. In saying this, we are not denying that our informants might still have been generating responses that they considered socially desirable in the specific context of the interview or, conversely, saying things that they hoped were controversial or rebellious. But this is precisely the point about styling – it always involves performances that are designed in anticipation of the possible responses. We would not and should not expect the interview to be an exception. Our informants, qua language users, are consistently styling themselves, both in 'real encounters' outside the interview situation as well as in the interview. In this book, we are interested in the reflexive and critical linguistic judgments about language and literacy represented in the voices of our student informants, and it is the case that our informants themselves often chose to construct their stances in terms of peer reactions. As these judgments are 'themselves both social facts and agents in the exercise of social power' (Jaffe, 1999: 15), careful attention to how our student informants talk about literacy promises, we believe, to reveal how the meanings attached to reading and writing are influenced by what they themselves consider stylistically appropriate.

Recent work on literacy has in fact begun paying attention to how the kinds of behaviors and activities learners consider stylistically appropriate outside the school may or may not conflict with the expectations of the classroom. For example, Moje (2000) demonstrates that the literacy practices of gang-connected youth, although unsanctioned by the school culture, are extremely important to these adolescents as means by which they are able to 'claim a space, construct an identity, and take a social position in their worlds' (Moje, 2000: 651). Moje (2000: 683) ends by observing that there is a crucial need for classroom pedagogies that can draw upon the use of 'graffiti or other unsanctioned codes' as sites for 'learning about and deconstructing language'. And Skilton-Sylvester (2002) examines the experiences of Nan, a Cambodian girl growing up in Philadelphia, and describes how Nan chooses popularity with her peers over academic success in the school. Skilton-Sylvester (2002: 88) points out that 'Nan was part of a peer culture in which being literate was not the pathway to popularity' and in fact, 'mastering "sanctioned literacies" was seen as the key to unpopularity'. One advantage of approaching literacy practices as style, then, is that it provides us with a conceptual framework that integrates activities and attitudes both outside and inside the classroom, since the teacher and classmates also constitute audiences, with the former usually occupying the role of addressee and the latter that of auditors.

Data Sets and Procedures: The Primary Data Sets

The Singapore data that we discuss are drawn from a variety of sources since there already exist a number of empirical studies that we feel are highly valuable. Quite naturally, we therefore wish to make use of them. Combined with our own data, we think these studies can provide valuable insights into different facets of the nature of literacy practices in multilingual Singapore.

We use the term 'primary data set' however, simply as a matter of expository convenience, to refer specifically to our own data, that is, to data that form the empirical and analytical focus of this book. Complementing our primary data set are the various sources that we have just mentioned, and we will refer to these as secondary data. As these secondary data become relevant to the specific discussion at hand, we will make the appropriate references. However, we want to point out that we will draw somewhat more extensively from two particular studies: Hing (2004) and Ong (2003) (see previous chapter for some reference to Hing, 2004). We therefore think it is useful to briefly describe the nature of these particular studies, that is, the samples involved in Hing's and Ong's work, and to explain how these samples mesh in with our own sample. We do this at the end of this chapter. For now, we focus on describing our primary data set. This data set[1] consists of a series of interviews conducted by four student research assistants between August 2003 and December 2004. The four student research assistants interviewed a total of 22 student informants, all adolescents ranging in age from 13 to 17 years.

The research assistants and the student informants were arrived at in the following manner. We made an announcement that we were interested in collecting data about language use, specifically English literacy practices among adolescents, and we asked if there were any students (particularly students pursuing an Honors or postgraduate degree) who were interested in getting involved. Since we had no access to specific student informants at that time, we also made it clear that it would be preferable if the student research assistants already had access to adolescents who might be willing to be interviewed. We anticipated that these adolescent informants would either be siblings, distant relatives or friends of our research assistants.

Since a number of our postgraduate students were also teachers, we anticipated that in these cases, the informants might then be students that the teachers were acquainted with in the course of their professional lives. As it turned out (see below), it was this latter case that provided us with the most useful data.

The profiles of the informants are as follows (we provide more detailed descriptions when we begin discussing them in the subsequent chapters). Fifteen of them were female informants (five Chinese, two Malays and eight Indians) and seven were male informants (four Chinese, one Malay and two Indians). The topics of the interviews covered their attitudes toward English language learning in school, their preferred leisure activities, and the kinds of literacy activities they engaged in. Whilst earlier interviews were rather more structured, subsequent ones became more conversational and open-ended as the subjects became more comfortable and familiar with the interviewers. The methodology is therefore based on that of interpretive sociolinguistics (Gumperz, 1982; see also Maschler, 1994: 329), where data gleaned from earlier interviews or conversations are transcribed, analyzed and followed-up in subsequent ones.

In this book, we draw mainly on our detailed analyses of interview data of six particular students, Edwin, Wen, Yan, Ping, Farid and Sha (the names are all pseudonyms). This is because access to these students was the most sustained of the lot, so that we were able to obtain much more details about their lives when compared to the rest of our interviewees. These six individuals were also chosen in order to represent a mix of different genders and ethnicities. Three of them are males (Edwin, Fandi and Sha), and three are females (Wen, Yan and Ping). Three of them are Chinese (Edwin, Wen and Ping), two are Malay (Yan and Fandi) and one is Indian (Sha).

In the case of Ping and Fandi, we were also able to interview their mothers. And with the exception of Sha (see below), our observations concerning the rest of our subjects suggest that Edwin, Wen, Yan, Ping and Fandi are by no means atypical in the values they espouse or the problems they face. All five are about 16 years old, all admit to having difficulties with English and all come from homes where English is not commonly spoken. Sha is an exception because, as we will see later, he seems to have little or no problems with English. In fact, unlike the others, Sha comes from a home where not just English, but 'standard English', as he rather proudly asserts, is spoken.

Choosing the School

Schools in Singapore can be broadly categorized as either 'neighborhood schools' or 'independent schools'. The latter are generally recognized as providing a higher quality of education, and generally tend to attract students who are academically stronger and who also come from relatively more affluent home environments, where English is more likely to be spoken. In contrast, the neighborhood schools are seen as attracting weaker and less affluent students, who come from homes where the mother tongues tend to be spoken.

In recent years, the distinction has become even more entrenched because the Ministry of Education has since 1992 instituted a system of school rankings, and in terms of academic achievements, it was fairly clear to most Singaporeans that students from the independent schools tended to consistently top the school exams. This is not to say that students from neighborhood schools are never among the top, but when this actually happens, it is often greeted with some surprise and reported in the media as 'proof' that the perception that neighborhood schools are academically weaker is wrong. But as Bourdieu and Passeron (1977) points out, it is precisely the existence of occasional exceptions that allow the status quo to be misrecognized and hence legitimized as being 'purely' meritocratic. As Jenkins puts it, 'the fact that some members of the cultural elite are not economically privileged, and vice versa – this is the argument about the functions of limited social mobility – is seen as proof positive of the inherent fairness of a meritocratic education system, through which *in theory* all can pass, irrespective of the economic capital' (Jenkins, 1992: 113, italics in original).

In any case, to their credit, the educational authorities in Singapore have recently taken steps to combat this negative perception of neighborhood schools. These have included expanding the components that go into the rankings so that academic achievement is just one of a number of determinants. These other components include 'value-added ranking' (which measures the difference between how well a school is expected to do in the examinations and how well it actually did) and 'ranking by physical fitness' (which looks at, among other things, the percentage of overweight students and the percentage of students who manage to pass the National Physical Fitness Award).[2]

The other is for state officials and representatives to simply argue that facilities and resources available in neighborhood schools compare reasonably well to those from the independent schools. Whether these measures will, at some point in time, eliminate the distinction between these two types of schools is unclear. But it is undeniable that in the public mindset, the neighborhood schools are generally felt to compare poorly in relation to the more prestigious independent schools.

An interesting but disturbing indication of how neighborhood schools are perceived can be gleaned from a recent internet debate that took place in

2004. The debate was sparked off when a girl from the elite Raffles Girls' School (RGS) was found to be dating a boy from a neighborhood school. In an article titled 'Schools shaping elitist mindset', Seah Chiang Nee (www. singapore-window.org, accessed April 15, 2006) notes that the 'Web debate stretched over a period of four months, attracting more than 400 postings in two chatsites.' Seah quotes from a number of postings, most of which point to a class division between those students from neighborhood schools and those from more prestigious ones:

Cynic, who suggested that the couple break up, said: 'It's not going to work out. She's going to be ashamed of introducing him to her friends and her family.'

'What about the future?' he asked. 'Will he be happy wallowing in her shadow when she starts earning three time more than him? Inferiority complex will soon kick in.' . . .

'Leave the RGS girl alone-lah! Leave her to other high-flying guys. It's good to know one's limits once in a while,' declared *Get Real*. . . .

Another 'elite' student, *Super-infector*, said he would never go out with a girl from a neighborhood school because of 'social and intellectual disparity'.

Cynic's remark that the RGS girl would at some point almost certainly be ashamed of her boyfriend from the neighborhood school, Get Real's suggestion that the boy 'leave her to other high-flying guys' and Super-infector's claim that there exists a 'social and intellectual disparity', are all indications that neighborhood schools and their associated students are perceived as being inferior to their more elite counterparts. What this means is that schools in Singapore are indexically marked for status and different individuals' associations with particular schools can often constitute elements of their 'narratable identities' so that '(t)he status-relevant asymmetrical structure of what is indicated as the interactants' pasts and presents thus remains a constant over the course of biographical time from the narrated past up to the present moment (and implicated future)' (Silverstein, 2004: 625).
    As Seah himself observes:

. . . if the debate is reflective of our best scholars and potential leaders, it doesn't offer much hope for optimism in the future. Many come across as arrogant and self-centered, looking down on others who are less academically capable. They seem to have a jaundiced view of life, believing that their distinctions somehow guarantee them success.

Students from neighborhood schools then are quite aware that they face a high degree of social discrimination, and this discrimination is in no small way tied to the fact that many of them do face significant problems with the English language. As we have already noted, English in Singapore is not socially neutral; it (i.e. the standard variety) is marked for high prestige, it is associated with higher incomes and better education, and its speakers are thus perceived to be more sophisticated and more affluent. So, because we were interested in the kinds of problems adolescents might face in attempting to learn English, we knew that it was important to gain access to students who were studying in a neighborhood secondary school. And while it might have been possible for us to gather the data ourselves, a significant practical problem made this difficult. As university professors from the Department of English Language and Literature, we would have had to overcome a major social distance in terms of status, power and competence in the English language, before getting to the point (assuming we ever would) where the students felt comfortable enough with us to speak 'naturalistically'.

We were therefore fortunate in that one of our graduate students, Serene Howe, was interested enough in our project to get involved. The data specifically discussed in this book were therefore all gathered by one and the same interviewer, Serene, who, at the time, was both completing her postgraduate work and also teaching in the same school as the students. As a teacher, Serene no doubt also had to overcome differences in status and power. But as Eckert (2000: 71) points out, the real aim for the researcher who is working with relatively young subjects is not to try to become an insider, but instead, to minimize differences by 'being or appearing young, presenting oneself as in roughly the same life stage' and so 'eliminating obvious reminders of status differences'. As a young teacher (certainly as someone who was much younger than either of us!), Serene was in a much better position than we were to do all this. And because she was teaching in the same school as the students, problems of scheduling regular interviews were minimized. Moreover, Serene specifically selected Edwin, Yan, Wen, Ping, Farid and Sha, because she already knew them fairly well even before embarking on this project, and she was confident that she was generally perceived by them to be a friendly teacher. These factors helped ensure that the interviews would have a good chance of starting off on a familiar and comfortable footing. There was every reason to hope that the students would be relatively at ease talking to her about their schoolwork, friends and home life.

All interviews were conducted in English and individually (with the exception of the home interviews, where the students were interviewed together with their mothers; see below). In the interviews that we present later on in this book, features of Singlish can occasionally be observed, such as the use of the discourse particle 'lah' (*I will go and borrow some books, lah*), subject pro-drop and the lack of verbal inflection ([I] *Just manage*[d] *to skip through*). We take the use of a highly colloquial variety of English, such as Singlish, in the context of conversations with an authority figure such as a teacher, as a sign that the students were indeed feeling quite relaxed about the interviews (see Chapter 8).

As the interviews were informal, they tended to vary in length, ranging from 30 minutes to over an hour, depending on whether the subjects had more to say and whether they had to leave because of some other obligations. In fact, although the initial interviews were about language use – this was not a problem because the students were told from the beginning that the interviews would be about language – our advice to Serene was to allow the interviews to move in whatever directions she and the interviewees felt were appropriate, even if these seemed unrelated to language. And as the interviewees grew more comfortable with the process, the discussions did indeed come to cover a range of topics, including interactions with siblings, leisure activities and personal aspirations.

Right from the start, we also asked Serene to keep in the mind the possibility of conducting home interviews with at least some students and their parents. This in fact proved to be a source of some frustration, since a number of parents were extremely reluctant to be interviewed.[3] The reasons for this remain unclear, but it seems reasonable to us that some parents felt rather shy being interviewed about English language literacy practices, especially when they did not consider themselves to be particularly good in the language. Despite Serene's attempts to assuage their concerns, in the end only the mothers of Ping and Fandi agreed to the home interviews. The fathers were either unavailable or excused themselves on the grounds that the interviews were about matters to which the mothers were likely to have more to contribute. Sha, who came from a home that spoke good English, was also supposed to have participated in the home interviews, but unfortunately, he had to withdraw at the very last minute due to a family tragedy.

Transcribing and Interpreting the Data

In presenting our data, we adopted a broad transcription, or what Johnstone (2000: 115) calls the 'play script', where information about conversational overlaps, latching or the timing of pauses has been omitted. This is because we were much more interested in the content of the talk rather than how it was actually conducted. That is to say, we were hoping to extract details about our informants' activities at home, amongst peers and in school, especially where these might shed some light on their language use. We were therefore looking out for, among other things, attitudes toward different linguistic varieties, self-reports of literacy practices, and descriptions of learning problems and coping strategies.

There were, of course, portions of the data where it was not clear what the person was saying. And in such cases, it was not always possible for the interviewer, Serene, to remember exactly what had been said. In those cases, we made use of brackets to indicate that the words and phrase within were guesses. In the really bad cases, the brackets were simply left blank. But these were relatively infrequent, and we were fortunate in that most of the time the conversations were readily intelligible.

We make use of the following simple notational system to refer to the various participants in our interviews. The letter 'I' refers to the interviewer. Any other letter than 'I' refers to the interviewee. For example, 'P' refers to Ping and 'E' refers to Edwin. When the interviewee is a mother of one of the informants, then the letter referring to the informant is followed by 'M', as in 'PM' for Ping's mother.

While we are interested in how literacy- and nonliteracy-based activities contributed to our informants' sense of identity, and furthermore, on how all these impacted on their learning of English, we have tried to avoid approaching the data in terms of any predetermined categories. We therefore have tried as far as possible to ensure that the categories we adopt are 'local' (Eckert, 2000: 69) in the sense that they are categories that our informants themselves were oriented to.

Ultimately, despite the wide-ranging nature of the data, they did seem to cluster into 'natural' categories. There were two reasons for this. One, as adolescents attending the same school in Singapore, our informants did inevitably share some similar orientations and values. The recurrence of these similarities across individual informants meant that the data was to a significant extent already structured. Two, as we pointed out in the first chapter, Singapore is something of a 'nanny state' with very strong language policies that aim to authoritatively define valued linguistic practices from nonlinguistic ones. Furthermore, the state is often very explicit in prescribing how individual Singaporeans ought to behave, so that Singaporeans are tend to be extremely clear about how language use at the local level can be seen to accord (or not) with the different linguistic valuations at the macro level. What this means is that individual Singaporeans

– and our informants are no exceptions – are keenly aware of how their own linguistic practices might be viewed at the macro level by the state in general and by the school authorities in particular. It is this highly conscious awareness of how the micro-sociolinguistic can be construed macro-sociolinguistically that often leads our informants to themselves articulate the links between their own negotiations of language use and the kinds of social indexicalities that may be said to transcend any immediate context. As a result, quite aside from any analytical impositions of our own, our informants readily offer their own meta-framings of their language practices, highlighting the ways in which these are attempts at conforming to or reacting against authoritatively defined ideologies of language.

Secondary Data Sets (Engaging with the Narrative Voice of Voices): Hing (2004) and Ong (2003)

Hing's study was conducted as part of his Honors degree. Hing was particularly interested in how the Chinese dialects were still able to find a place in Singapore despite the state's attempts to eliminate them in favor of Mandarin as the official mother tongue of the Chinese community. Hing interviewed four young Chinese adults (two females and two males) in their early 20s. Their ages ranged from 22 to 24 years.

Hing chose these particular subjects because he wanted to focus on 'one of the first generations of students who have grown up in the wake of the bilingual education system and also the Speak Mandarin Campaign' (Hing, 2004: 30). He also felt that by focusing on young adults, he would be able to gain access to their home and school experiences as well as their use of language in other domains. There are a number of reasons for this. One, many young Singaporean adults continue living with their parents often until they reach their late 20s or early 30s, moving out only when they get married. This is partly due to the high cost of housing in Singapore. By interviewing these young adults, Hing reasonably expected to be able to gather data about their patterns of language use in the home. Two, the school experiences of these adults would also still be relatively fresh in their minds. And three, some of the subjects were already working, and the men would have undergone National Service. These other experiences would have provided Hing with comparative data on language use in a variety of domains.

The subjects in Hing's study were obviously much older than our own subjects. Furthermore, because Hing's subjects were all either studying in the university, working or had undergone National Service, they had a series of experiences that our own adolescent informants lacked, even though we might expect them to live through such experiences themselves in due course. Despite these differences, Hing's study is useful precisely because his subjects represent 'the future of Chinese dialect speakers in Singapore. Their attitudes and perspectives on dialect use, as dialect speakers themselves, may help determine the factors affecting the likelihood of language transmission' (Hing, 2004: 31). Thus, we will draw upon Hing's work when we specifically discuss the issue of dialect maintenance vis-à-vis the Chinese community in Singapore. And while we want to be careful in how we extrapolate, we think that the factors that influence the status of the dialects could well be relevant also to any discussion on the maintenance or elimination of the officially maligned variety of English known as Singlish.

The other study that we also draw on is that of Ong's, which was conducted as part of her Masters degree.[4] Ong's informants were three secondary school students, two males and one female, whom their teachers felt had problems with their English language writing. Ong's data, too, came from students studying in a neighborhood secondary school.

All three students in Ong's study were Chinese and came from non-English-speaking homes. Ong observed eight English classroom lessons over a period of four weeks to understand the literacy practices surrounding the students' writing. Her data comprised transcriptions of audio-recorded interactions, participant observations and interviews with teachers and students. As Ong (2003: viii) points out, these students 'hardly read or enjoy reading, and do not see how the writing done in school is connected to what goes on in their lives.' And in school, 'they find themselves positioned negatively. The teacher focuses on their mistakes in grammar and vocabulary, emphasizes on what they lack, and discourages their use of Chinese, the language of their identity' (Ong, 2003: viii).

The study by Ong thus provides information concerning on-floor interactions. That is, student–teacher interactions that take place in the classroom's 'public' arena, and thus potentially involve the entire class. In contrast, our primary data set provides information pertaining to off-site interactions in the sense that it contains self-reports about students' classroom behavior that take place in small groups outside the purview of the teacher. When taken together, then, both the primary data set and Ong's work provide complementary perspectives on the English language and literacy experiences of Singaporean teenagers, a complementarity that is enhanced by the fact that both studies were conducted in similar institutional and cultural contexts.

Closing Remarks

The study that is presented in this book aims to provide details about the problems faced by adolescents in learning English in Singapore. It tries to do this by focusing on the micro-interactional identity work performed by our adolescent informants. The study is therefore qualitative in orientation. And furthermore, because it makes use of a nonrandom sample, the conclusions we draw cannot be easily generalized to the broader population.

The qualitative orientation of this study is important because, with few exceptions, much of the empirical work done on the sociology of language in Singapore has tended to take the form of large-scale surveys. These large-scale surveys have been often used to inform language policy and planning. It is only in more recent times, however, that greater attention is being paid to the qualitative aspects of language use. And while it is undoubtedly the case that policy and planning will still give greater weight to quantitative data, we think it is important to continue the case for qualitative approaches to be taken into account as well. Precisely because of this, we will aim, in this book, to also suggest how our work may point to emerging trends, as well as how our observations may fit in with studies that involve much larger samples, in particularly large-scale survey data.

Notes

(1) Funding for this study was provided by the National University of Singapore (Research project R-103-000-041-112).
(2) School Ranking and Appraisal System – Singapore (www.logos-net.net/ilo/195, accessed April 17, 2006).
(3) Skepticism about the willingness of families to get involved in research appears fairly widespread, as observed by Lareau (2003: 265).
(4) We thank Dinah Ong for permission to quote freely examples from her work. Please note that the interpretations we provide, and the use we make, of Ong's data are ours alone, for which we take full responsibility. Given constraints of space, not all of the data collected by Ong appears in her completed thesis. Thus, in presenting Ong's data, we will refer to examples from the thesis by citing the relevant page; and we will refer to her other examples simply as 'Ong, unpublished'.

5 Fandi and Ping: Literacy Practices and the Performance of Identities on Ambivalent Markets

In order to better comprehend how the literacy practices of our informants can be seen as manifestations of particular social and ethnic identities, in this chapter we draw upon data concerning two student informants, Fandi and Ping. We leave our discussion of the others for the next two chapters. Our data here include self-reports by Fandi and Ping of leisure and school-based activities. Additionally, however, we also have access to interviews with their parents, in particular, their mothers. These interviews were conducted in the presence of our informants, who occasionally also contributed to the exchange, and they give us a greater sense of how the peer orientations of Fandi and Ping intersect with the kinds of literacy practices encouraged in the home and school environments.

Aligning the Home with the Dominant Market

Fandi is a Malay male, 15 years old, who generally scores a low to mid-level B in English. Ping is a Chinese female, also 15 years old. While she also usually scores a low to mid-level B in English, she seems to project much greater confidence than Fandi in her command of the language. However, as we will see later, it is not clear if Ping's confidence is actually justified. Her choice of reading material tends to be more appropriate for someone much younger than her 15 years; and as she herself admits, her choice is limited by her own desire for 'simple' material.

(1)

I: Ok. Now what is the main language that you speak at home?

FM: English and Malay.

I: English and Malay but mostly will be in …

FM: Both..I should say fifty and fifty.

I: So you and your husband what language do you speak?

FM: Both.

I: Both. You speak to the children also..both.

FM: Both.

I: Your husband to them?

FM: To there … also both. He speaks both.

Fandi's home comprises his elder brother, their baby sister and their parents. In (1), Fandi's mother indicates that they use both English and Malay equally at home (*I should say fifty and fifty*).

(2)

I: So there is English and Malay.

FM: Hm.

I: Even to the little girl?

FM: Yes. Because one time I forget that she is still in the beginning of learning part so keep concentrating on Malay. Then she speaks more Malay. Then my husband notices say "look, she don't understand". She don't understand. Now I speak to her in English and I make her see this show central all in English right. Then as I sit I will sit down with her and say "you see this baby bird, this is baby penguin". She does this wrong in nursery. She told this thing to parents. It is very wrong. That's bad. Then she likes it. That is why she sticks to this show central.

(2) demonstrates that the presence of both English and Malay results from a deliberate attempt by the parents help their children be bilingual in the two languages. Thus, when the father begins to feel that the baby daughter is not speaking enough English, he points this out to the mother, who then attempts to use more English with her. This is clearly an attempt to align the language practices of the household with that of Singapore's language policy.

Ping comes from a home that comprises her father, mother and a twin sister. Although her parents do regret that neither Ping nor her sister speak much Hokkien, which is the Chinese dialect of the parents, they had made an early decision to avoid using Hokkien with their children (3). Ping's home therefore clearly supports the rationale behind the state's bilingual policy.

(3)

PM: So maybe I am too *ganjiong* [Cantonese: over-reacting] in English and Mandarin only. I forget to tell them they are Hokkien. ... You know my girls they don't know Hokkien ... It is because from young I didn't tell them Hokkien. I never speak to them in Hokkien.

There is great encouragement from her parents to improve her English in order to do well educationally, and ultimately, economically. Also, as Chinese Singaporeans, Ping and her parents accept Mandarin as their official mother tongue. But in Ping's case, the attempt to align language use in the home with the larger language policy is even clearer because, unlike Fandi's home where both languages spoken are officially recognized, Ping's family had to consciously *avoid* using an officially devalued variety, namely, the Chinese dialect Hokkien.

The state's efforts to institute Mandarin as the official mother tongue of Chinese Singaporeans include a long-term Speak Mandarin Campaign that called for the elimination of other Chinese dialects such as Hokkien and Teochew (Bokhorst-Heng, 1998). Parents were told that it was their responsibility, if they wished to increase their children's chances of academic success, to use only Mandarin and not the other dialects. Ping's parents have obviously taken this message to heart and so the most common language in the home is Mandarin, with occasional switches into English. Hokkien is still used in private conversations between the parents. But as far as possible, it is avoided in conversations with Ping or her sister. This decision to eliminate Hokkien from the home, so that only English and Mandarin are spoken, is therefore an attempt by Ping's parents to align language use in the household with the state's bilingual policy. As figures of authority, Ping's parents obviously are in a position to make and implement decisions about language use within the household.

Orders of Indexicality

Despite the presence of both Malay and English in his household, it is clear that Fandi considers English to be the more important language of the two. Not surprisingly, the reason he gives for this valuation is socioeconomic in nature.

(4)

I: I mean for example in your case in Singapore, why is it that we need to learn English?

F: For English, I think it's important for getting jobs now. Because now if you are English literate, you will tend to get more chances of getting jobs lah.

I: Than if you only know how to speak your mother tongue?

F: Yes.

Similarly, in Ping's case, while she appears to accept the rationale behind the bilingual policy, in (5), she explicitly compares the relative importance of English with that of Mandarin/Chinese.[1]

(5)

P: Everyone is saying that English is more important in Singapore than Chinese. They came up with the syllabus B for Chinese. ... Easier. Then they are like English is what you have to study, Chinese never mind. Don't care about your Chinese. We will make it easier for you.

Notice how she points to the simplified syllabus 'B' that 'they' (i.e. the Ministry of Education) recently implemented as evidence for the lesser importance of Chinese. The simplification of the Chinese syllabus, for Ping, is a clear indication that even the state considers English to be more important than Mandarin.

(6)

P: I think we being Chinese should speak Chinese better.

I: Better than English?

P: Yeah. But since they emphasize so much in English, might as well study English also.

Ping is not asserting that Chinese has no value at all; it is simply of lesser value than English. In (6), the justification she gives for knowing Chinese is that it is part of one's ethnic identity as a Chinese.

(7)

I: But if you only know English and don't know Chinese?

P: I think it's OK, lah. I think it's a disgrace to Chinese.

I: It's a disgrace, but it's fine.

P: Yeah, I think it's fine . . . . Because English everyone else also understands. Then those, this language, right, for everyone the most important thing is to communicate and to understand each other. So Chinese is, I would say it's only the minority.

This ethnic-based justification is, of course, an echo of the Singapore government's division of labor between English, on the one hand, as the language of socioeconomic mobility and the mother tongues, and on the other, as repositories of cultural history and values. So, even if one does not know one's mother tongue (*I think it's a disgrace to Chinese*), this becomes understandable because it is really English that serves the larger function of allowing a person wider participation in society (7).

For Ping, languages other than English, then, appear to either have little or no particular value in Singapore. Thus, even when Ping's household aligns itself in support of the state's language policy, English is already given a higher value than Mandarin. Here, we can see the signs that speak to ambivalence and reflexivity. Acceptance of Singapore's official language policy in both Fandi's and Ping's households is modulated by an indexical ordering that is at odds with the government's official stance of treating English and the mother tongue as being equally important. The ambivalence that results from the need to straddle the relationship between the dominated market of the home and the dominant market imposed by the state is accompanied by a reflexive awareness of this distance between their own valuations of language and the stance officially prescribed by the state.

Parental Help with English Language Proficiency

Fandi's mother considers English an important subject in Singapore, and as a parent, she expresses the opinion that reading is key to doing well in English, particularly as a means of increasing one's vocabulary (this is an opinion shared by the adolescents themselves) (8).

(8)
FM: So I told him if he can't get through his English, I got no choice but to get a tutor for him, for his Malay also. We don't mind to spend but as long as he gets through. What we want is a good support for his future like that.
I: That's true, that's true. Now why do you think some students do better in English whereas others don't do well?
FM: Because they like to read, they like . . . spend reading and they do some research, research and then they discuss with friends. From

there, their volume of vocabs and their ideas are growing very rapidly. That is what my son, elder son is. He score A1 for English, he scored because he spent more time reading. Until now he reads, even though the book this thick he reads already. He keeps reading reading reading.

Fandi's mother starts by expressing the concern that she may have to hire a private tutor to help him with both his English and Malay. She goes on to compare Fandi with his elder brother (19 years old), who is doing better than Fandi in English, and she attributes this to the fact that the elder brother reads a lot more than Fandi.

(9)
I: Now what do you think of her English ability?
PM: Because I myself, my English is not very good, so for me, I feel that not bad, loh.
I: Not bad. OK, I mean how about her result? Do you think it is OK?
PM: OK, but maybe she can do better, lah. As what you can say, maybe she can do better but then, frankly speaking, I am quite proud already, lah. Because I am not very good at English and second language [Mandarin] as well, but she can do that, result not bad without a tuition teacher.

Similarly, in (9), Ping's mother also believes in the importance of reading, but unlike Fandi's mother, Ping's mother seems quite satisfied with and proud of her daughter's accomplishments, and this possibly contributes to Ping's sense of confidence in her command of English. Note, however, that the mother's pride in Ping's achievements stems from the fact that her expectations are not particularly high to begin with. Because Ping's mother is generally satisfied with her daughter's achievements, she is quite happy to leave her alone, fully confident that her daughter has the self-discipline to work on her English without parental supervision.

(10)
PM: I don't really need to worry about her. OK, she always knows when to start doing homework, when to sleep, when to talk on phone. She is quite OK, lah. Disciplined in . . . at home.

In contrast, Fandi's mother thinks his English needs more work, but she also feels that she should take some responsibility for the situation (11).

(11)

FM: I … I agree by early learning, early learning, OK. I think, example, my elder son and Fandi. My elder son when he is around 1 year plus, I was retrenched. That is where I spent most of my time at that time at the time he was 1 year plus that is where they begin to pick up you see. So, as I fit in, I will try to taught and sing along whatever. I join in the game then I will read books and then I will just go through reading, reading, reading. And I notice my elder son that is why he likes books. That is where my error is. Whereas Fandi … I am very sad. It is my error. Because I don't got the time. At the time when I was retrenched, I spent lot of my time. But he was being babysitted. So I don't blame the babysitter. It is my fault because I don't have the time. Because by the time I go home, I have to prepare the housework. So I don't really sit down with him to taught or to teach. So when he go through in primary one, I find he is in a deep … his result was very bad. He failed the primary 1 and then the teacher called.

Fandi's mother was working when he was born, and because of this, she feels that she did not spend enough encouraging him to read when he was young. This sense of guilt is compounded by the comparison with Fandi's elder brother, with whom she was able to spend more time because she had been retrenched and was therefore not working when the elder brother was born. Thus, Fandi's mother frets because she feels he does not read enough to improve his English (12–13). Consequently, she is generally happy if he reads at all (14).

(12)

I: So basically when he … what do you think of his language ability, English?

FM: Language … and the English, is it? I should say he … a lot of improvement … he must put efforts in but I don't know how to help him. … His reading … he reads too little, under the normal standard, I should say.

(13)

FM: The main problem I could find is, he is lazy. Lazy to read, lazy to read.

(14)

I: OK, so what are some of the books that Fandi would ask you to buy?

FM: Mostly ghost stories. Magazines like cartoon all that. His, his favorite, lah.

I: But ...

FM: I don't really restrict on him, lah. For me if my child likes whatever he likes to do, I will leave him. I don't encourage him, but behind sometimes, I try to help him by sitting down. He doesn't like I don't know maybe he is too ... too old already.

Both parents are of course keen to help their children with their English. And below we see that there may in fact be an additional reason why Ping's mother tends to leave her alone to do her own work. Ping's mother was able to play an active role when her daughters (Ping and her twin sister) were younger.

(15)

PM: Her English. For my side, I don't really can do anything, but it all depends on her, loh. As what I say, from young, maybe ... in primary school, sec 1 that time, I really do a lot like I really go back to study, you know. I buy a lot of books. Everyday I go Popular [a local bookstore], every time I go Popular, I search books for their two [Ping and her sister], you know. Then teach them. Let them do assessment books all these. Now they are so big already. I can't do that. Because it is out of my limit also. I don't understand what the book. So it depends on them, loh.

(16)

I: OK, now, so basically where her English is concerned, when she is young, you did try to read, teach a little bit of reading and all. Then once she started primary school, you try to do homework with her, right? OK, then secondary school, it is on her own?

PM: After sec 1, I already, sec 1 or sec 2, I already give up because I don't know how to teach already.

As the extracts above indicate, she used to select and buy specific books for them, and also tried to help them with their homework. But by the time they reached the secondary level, she felt that she had no choice but to stop doing this because the material was beyond her capabilities.

(17)

I: Ok, how about, do you think it is possible for you to, like, sit down when [...] teach him?

FM: Oh, he doesn't like. He says 'Mom, your English is ... so terrible pronunciation. My other son says 'Mom, you pronounce ...' [Laughing]. I say during my old time, my pronunciation is this way.

Because what I notice, the English during my time and this time is
really a big gap.

I: OK.

FM: Totally a big gap. I can't teach him.

Like Ping's mother, Fandi's mother, too, finds the level of English demanded
at the secondary level beyond her (17). But in Fandi's case, the mother still
tries to play an active role in her children's learning of English. And unfortunately, this results in Fandi and his brother actually denigrating her attempts
to help them with English, criticizing particularly her pronunciation
of English words.

So, neither Fandi's nor Ping's mother possesses much symbolic capital
when it comes to providing advice, even though both mothers are greatly
interested in helping their children improve their English. Ping's mother is
forced to abdicate her involvement since she finds the schoolwork totally
beyond her. Fandi's mother finds her attempts rejected and ridiculed. This
situation contrasts greatly with that of Sha, our Punjabi adolescent informant,
whom we discuss in Chapter 7. We will see then that Sha's father's advice on
what to read is taken very seriously by Sha, who understands that the recom-
mended material would have already been read by the father himself. Sha's
father represents a familial role model, not only as someone who wants Sha
to improve his English, but also as someone who has taken effective steps to
improve his own English – that is, Sha's father speaks with the authority of a
person whose proficiency in English Sha respects. This is the kind of respect
that neither Fandi's nor Ping's mother is accorded. In this regard, perhaps the
final word on this matter should be left to Ping, who bluntly underscores the
lack of symbolic capital that her parents have for her (18).

(18)

I: So you think that you can do without parents' help?

P: Yah.

I: Why?

P: Even if we need help after school right, we will seek for tuition
teachers. . . . They are more professional. They can, they can teach us
the right things. Instead of parents, you know, pretending to know
and then just trying to help but teach you the wrong thing.

There is almost a note of resentment in Ping's remark that parents mask their
ignorance and simply 'pretend to know' even when they don't, so that they
end up teaching their children 'the wrong thing'. Thus, the parents' attempts

to match the linguistic capital in the home with that prescribed by the state are undermined by their own lack of symbolic capital in English. That is, any suggestions they may make regarding the use of English lacks credibility to their own children. This serves to further reinforce the disparity between the linguistic markets inside and outside the home, contributing further to a sense of ambivalence. The microcosms of Ping's and Fandi's homes can recreate the state's prescribed bilingual policy only so far. Even though the same named variety called 'English' is being used in both homes, the linguistic practices that actually realize the use of English are, in the eyes of Ping and Fandi, far from satisfactory.

Multilingualism in Fandi's and Ping's Households

We have noted that though both of Ping's parents grew up speaking Hokkien, this dialect is rarely used in the household. Recall that one of the key messages of the Speak Mandarin Campaign was that other Chinese dialects should be eliminated from the household as far as possible; parents were told that it was their responsibility, if they wished to increase their children's chances of academic success, to avoid using other dialects such as Hokkien, Cantonese, Teochew, among others. Ping's parents have obviously taken this message to heart and so the most common language in the home is Mandarin, with occasional switches into English (19).

(19)
I: OK, then what language do he [Ping's father] use to speak to the twins?
PM: Mandarin, loh. Most of them, most of the time.

Hokkien is used in private conversations between Ping's father and mother, and with their relatives. But as far as possible, it is avoided in conversations with Ping or her sister.

For Fandi, we already saw that Fandi's mother claims that both Malay and English tend to be spoken at home in roughly equal amounts (1).

(20)
I: OK, how about when you are at home?
F: At home with my father and all . . . I will speak to them in Malay, ah.
I: Your mom also, is it?
F: Yes, unless sometimes, lah, when I angry or something like that, I will speak to them in English, lah.

I: Why?

F: I don't know, not so comfortable speaking Malay, ah. Some vocabulary in the English, some are lack in vocab ... vocabulary in Malay can't be spoken in ... Malay.

While Fandi's mother gives no indication of the particular circumstances in which one language might be used over the other, it is interesting to note that, according to Fandi, switching to English tends to take place particularly when he and his family members are arguing with each other (20). Fandi's mention of a 'lack in vocabulary' suggests that the switching is mainly lexical, substituting English words for Malay ones probably because English words lack the same emotive force as their Malay counterparts, and are probably perceived to be far less intense or not as taboo.

This connection between English and scolding is also mentioned by Ping.

(21)

I: Does he speak to them in English?

PM: Sometimes but not so.

I: Oh, OK. What sort of topics usually?

P: Fear, loh. When he fears us. Like 'You everyday so late. Don't need to study, ah?' Like that, lah.

(22)

P: At home, it depends. Ah ... father, when he asked about my studies or else, I would speak in English. Then normally it's Chinese with my mother and sister. Then during quarrels or arguments, then I will use English. Can express myself better. ...

I: How about your mom?

P: Yeah if we have to quarrel, I will also use English.

I: Then how about you and your sister?

P: Sister, ah ... also the same. When I am scolding her, I will use English. It seems to be more serious. Then when I am just chatting with her, I will use Chinese.

In (21–22), Ping explains that her father uses English when he is asking her about her schoolwork, but also when he is scolding her and her sister. And in interactions between Ping and her sister, English is also used when they are arguing with each other. Ping's mother, on the other hand, suggests that she just tends to switch between English and Mandarin without any specific reason (23).

(23)

I: When do you use English?

PM: Both, lah. Happy or not happy. This kind of . . . sometimes scold them also use Chinese, sometimes scold them also use English. That depends on what like like what she and her sister like that.

I: OK, so there is no specific reason. Just sometimes you just want to use it.

PM: Sometimes, I am just like 'Girl, you better pack your room!' so I also speak English to them. That is all. Sometimes I will call and tell them *'Ni Chi Bao Le Meiyou'* [Mandarin: Have you eaten yet?]. Sometimes, so happen have to use Mandarin.

However, in the light of Ping's and Fandi's comments about the use of English for scolding, we might hypothesize that for these households, English tends to be associated with notions such as social distance, seriousness, authority or power. And whether or not Ping's mother is conscious of this, it is plausibly the case that for her, too, the choice between English or Mandarin is motivated by the level of seriousness or social distance that she wishes to project on a given occasion. This is further evidence of the attempted alignment between the dominated market of Ping's and Fandi's homes and the dominating market of Singapore's language policy. That is, it is not just the choice of languages that is being replicated, but also the officially prescribed indexical associations in the sense that English, the inter-ethnic lingua franca and prestige variety in Singapore, is associated with notions of seriousness and distance, and the mother tongues (Mandarin for Ping, Malay for Fandi) with relative solidarity or intimacy. (Recall that the official prescription is not perfectly replicated since English is allocated a higher value than Mandarin by these adolescents.)

We will see more evidence of the differential associations of English, on the one hand, and the mother tongues, and on the other, when we consider Fandi's and Ping's interaction with their friends. For now, we note that switching between the lingua franca and the mother tongue in order to convey relative seriousness and distance is not at all surprising in multilingual societies. In such cases, the home language is often used to signal greater intimacy and solidarity, whilst a switch to a more prestigious variety signals greater distance and seriousness. Romaine (2001: 524) provides a similar example in her discussion of a conversation between a brother and a sister in Kenya. The conversation takes place in the brother's store and involves two codes, Lwidakho and Swahili. Their shared mother tongue is Lwidakho, whilst Swahili constitutes the 'ethnically neutral choice in this speech community'. Romaine points out that whereas the greetings take place in

Lwidakho, the language of solidarity, the brother switches to Swahili as soon as he starts asking the sister what she wants. In contrast, the sister persists in using Lwidakho throughout the entire conversation. We can understand the code choice in this exchange in the following manner. The sister's switch to the shared mother tongue, Lwidakho, is intended to remind her brother of their kinship ties, and on this basis, she hopes (in vain, ultimately) that he will grant her special treatment, such as giving her goods free of charge. However, her switch to Lwidakho is not reciprocated by her brother. His continued use of Swahili indicates that he is treating the exchange as a commercial one (the relevant roles, for him, are proprietor–customer rather than brother–sister). And since she is has no money, he will not give her any goods.

Both the Singapore and Kenya cases graphically illustrate how, in multilingual societies, a crucial component of the kind of competence that speakers must acquire is the ability to manage different linguistic systems. Here, it is useful to recall the distinction between literacy events and literacy practices. Particular literacy events in Singapore and Kenya will call upon the use of different linguistic codes. But pervading across specific events are broader ideologies that associate particular codes with particular social meanings, and being literate enough to operate in such multilingual societies requires an appreciation of the different social meanings attached to different codes. Most speakers acquire the ability to manage different codes as part of a 'practical sense' or 'feel for the game' (Bourdieu, 1977, 1990). This is undoubtedly the case with Ping, Fandi, the various members of their respective households, and the Kenyan siblings as well. This is performance, albeit not in a self-conscious manner since there is, after all, a continuum running from what might be termed 'mundane performance' to 'high performance', with the latter involving greater metalinguistic focus on form, meaning, audience attention and reception, and the achievement of specific perlocutionary effects (Coupland, 2007: 147).

And from an educational perspective, what needs to be cultivated is this meta-awareness of how codes are being used or can be used. Such meta-awareness provides learners with a greater degree of reflective (and hence, strategic) control over the different connections between particular codes and their social meanings (cf. Vygotsky, 1987). The educational strategy of double-crossing that we propose in Chapter 8 contains just such an element of meta-awareness. It encourages both teacher and students to focus overtly on language use, on the kinds of social meanings attached to different forms of language, and consequently, it has a strong likelihood of leading students to reorganize or reevaluate their own perceptions of how language functions in the world around them (Gee, 2001: 663).

Entertainment at Home

The multilingual nature of Fandi's home is underscored by the fact that, in addition to using English and Malay, he and his family enjoy watching Chinese television programs (24).

(24)
F: Cause they are ... I mean compared to Malay and some English sitcoms, lah, I find it Chinese ... Chinese sitcoms or [VCDs], lah, quite better cause there are better actor, actresses, actors all sometimes like that. Then the scripts they do then the jokes they make, the comedy all, I think Chinese are better, lah. .....
Actually the whole family watch, lah. Then the volume is up then I will understand some of the Chinese words. Then I will bring them to school, talk to the Chinese friends in Chinese, like that, lah.

Fandi's reference to picking up some Chinese words and using them with his Chinese friends in school indicates that he is quite willing to try out his limited proficiency in the Chinese language. There is no apparent fear of being ridiculed by his friends since Chinese is not expected to be part of Fandi's linguistic repertoire at all. As a Singaporean studying in the English-medium educational system, Fandi is all too aware that competence in English carries great symbolic value as a marker of prestige. And as a Malay, Fandi knows that there is a social expectation that he speak Malay since it is supposed to mark his ethnic identity. But because Chinese has no bearing at all on either his identity as a Singaporean or as a Malay, Fandi can afford to 'dabble' in Chinese without worrying about being marked as an 'unsophisticated' Singaporean or as a Malay who has lost touch with his ethnic roots. This, of course, is deeply reminiscent of Rampton's work on crossing, where much of the entertainment generated by adolescent interaction in a foreign language is due precisely to the fact that the speakers are not expected to be proficient in the language (Rampton, 1998). In other words, the speakers face no threats to any identities that they are deeply vested in. This is an observation that we think can and should be exploited in order to develop pedagogical strategies that address the issue of identity-based anxiety. As we show in Chapter 8, while there is growing appreciation of the fact that identity work can significantly affect language learning, it still remains far less clear exactly what kinds of strategies teachers can adopt in the classroom so as to assuage student concerns in cases where language learning appears to threaten the kinds of identity that they hold dear.

(25)

F: I won't listen to Malay song, lah.

I: Why?

F: How to say? I mean the Malay songs are not so attractive as the English songs. The English songs they are quite ... they got rock whatever. But Malay, they only have pop songs, very small. ...

I: Very limited, is it?

F: Hmm, very limited.

It is not just television watching that takes place in a non-Malay language. Fandi's preferred music entertainment is in English rather than Malay (25).

(26)

I: Are you able to catch their lyrics when they sing?

F: No, actually I only care about the rhythm and how the lyrics go with the rhythm. That is what I am interested.

I: So you don't bother, don't really bother the lyrics.

F: No, unless I am so into the song, lah, I will read the lyrics, maybe memorize it, lah.

However, before we get too optimistic in assuming that listening to English songs might help Fandi improve his English, note that, by his own admission, he does not really bother listening to the lyrics (26).

(27)

P: I often write about love stories, which my teacher doesn't recommend ... I just imagine what kind ... what kind of relationship I will be in when I grow up. Then what problems will arise, then how am I going to solve it. Those love ... those complicated love relationship, ah.

Like most other Singaporean girls of her age group, Ping is not very keen on sports or computer games. She, however, does have a strong interest in 'celebrity gossip' and romance, with the latter often figuring as a prominent theme in her English language compositions, even though she is aware of the need to show more diversity (27).

(28)

PM: So newspaper until now, until now my house got not English newspaper.

(29)

I: So basically when you come to TV programs and all, it will just be basically Cantonese [on DVD], sometimes Chinese.

PM: Chinese, hmm.

I: So you like ... sometimes on TV they have like English movies or English shows like *Phua Chu Kang* [a local English sitcom] and all these, you don't watch also? Because no interest or what?

PM: No interest, maybe.

(30)

P: Then at home, then reach home, then I will read television, the subtitle.

I: OK, when you watch Chinese movies?

P: Erm, when I watch English drama, I also read the Chinese subtitles.

Overall, it would seem that while both English and Chinese are used in Ping's home, it is Chinese that plays a greater role than English. For example, there is no English newspaper at all in her home (28). And while Ping watches both English and Chinese programs, the shows that her parents watch are mainly in Chinese, specifically, they are either in Mandarin or Cantonese. We should also note, that when watching English programs, Ping needs to refer to the Chinese subtitles in order to understand what is going on (30).

We will see below that neither Ping nor Fandi has a sufficiently strong command of either English or Mandarin/Malay which would allow them to interact and articulate fully in just one language alone. There is considerable appeal to both languages in most of their social interactions. Let us be clear here that we are not falling back onto any notion of language deficit. Language deficits are usually understood in cognitive terms, such that an apparent lack of 'complete linguistic proficiency' (whatever this would mean) in a given language is taken to point to some kind of cognitive deficiency. In a multilingual society, no one would be expected to be equally fluent or proficient in the various languages, since the level of proficiency is highly dependent on the kinds of social situations that a speaker tends to find himself/herself in (Romaine, 2001: 517ff). However, different linguistic repertoires are accorded different values in different markets (Bourdieu, 1991) and here, we have to be realistic and acknowledge that the (socially acquired) inability to fully interact in a single language, especially English, does put Ping and Fandi at a social disadvantage in Singapore society, since it has potentially serious consequences for the social trajectories of adolescents like them. In the case of Ping and Fandi, their levels of proficiency in English and Mandarin/Malay are undoubtedly functions of their patterns of social interaction so that the 'deficit' resides not in the individual, but in the interactions themselves (Gee, 2001: 647). We see further evidence of this in the next section.

Interaction with Peers

Like many young male Singaporeans, Fandi enjoys soccer and has friends of different ethnicities, mainly Malay and Chinese, and he speaks to them in either English or Malay. He points out that he usually uses English when speaking with his Chinese friends (because he does not expect them to know Malay), or when speaking with other Malays that he does not know well. With Malays that he knows well, Fandi is uncomfortable using any language other than Malay. As we saw above, for both Fandi and for Ping, there is a suggestion that English is associated with seriousness and greater social distance. In contrast, Malay (for Fandi) and Mandarin (for Ping) are languages that are associated with intimacy and solidarity.

(31)
I: OK, now. When you are with your friends, what language do you use to speak to them? OK, lets start with your band friends.
F: To Chinese I speak English but to the Malays that I know well, I will speak in Malay. But if Malays, right, if I see them for the first time, I will speak in English because I don't feel quite comfortable if I don't get to know him well that I speak with him in Malay.
I: Ok, then for Chinese, why is it natural you will use...?
F: They can't understand Malay.

(32)
I: How about when you are with your classmates?
F: Speak them, to them ... I will speak to them in English for Chinese and other people, lah. But for Malays I will speak to them in Malay, ah.
I: So that means you are quite close with your Malay friend in class.
F: Yes, yeah.

(33)
I: How about in the band? I know there are girls. You speak Malay to the Malay girls as well?

F: Yes, because usually Malays are Malays, lah. So ... So you tend to speak Malay, lah. Cause if you are speak ... for me, lah ... if I speak English to a Malay friends or what, it will feel unusual.

In (31–33), we see further evidence that for Fandi, Malay is a marker of ethnic solidarity, since he indicates that he uses the language with other Malays that he feels close to, while English serves to mark greater social distance.

(34)
I: How do you decide when to use what language, I mean for the ... for your friends?
P: Depending on whom I am talking to. If I talk to teachers whom I am very familiar with, I speak in Chinese. Then if I am talking to like discipline master or the principal, then I will use English, lah. More formal.
I: Why?
P: Because English seem to be more formal in school.
I: But teachers you are close with, you will tend to speak?
P: Mixed.

Likewise, (34) provides further indication that Ping, too, tends to use English when she wants to project formality. Notice that even in the course of speaking Chinese, Ping mixes it with English. This is also the case for Fandi, whose use of Malay often involves some appeal to English. Thus, even the Malay being used by Fandi is not 'pure' Malay since it is interspersed with English words.

(35)
F: Sometimes I speak with my Malay friends also mixed right. English and Malay, so it's quite natural.

The fact that there is mixing of languages would appear to be part of the norms of interaction for Ping and Fandi when they are with their peers. In other words, the predominant use of Mandarin or Malay with switches into English constitutes a form of 'social language' (Gee, 2001: 652), that is, a set of 'lexical and grammatical resources (whether in speech or writing) that a recognizable group of people uses to carry out its characteristic social practices'. And because language systems are porous, it is no surprise to find that in multilingual societies, social languages often draw, to varying degrees, upon the resources associated with different named languages such as

'English', 'Mandarin' or 'Malay'. However, if we are at all concerned about the fact that students do enter schools from different kinds of backgrounds, and that this can detrimentally influence their ability to succeed in the formal school environment, we cannot simply romanticize such language mixing. We have to acknowledge that while there is nothing inherently bad or wrong with mixing, it can become socially disadvantageous if it means that speakers are unable to (in other contexts) interact without having to resort to such mixing.

(36)
P: Vocab? I don't think I am so good at it. I just ... my English is good because I lose a little bit of marks only, not because I gain marks.
I: So if you think your English, but not fantastic. Then why is it that you think your English is not fantastic?
P: Erm, some, some English vocabs they have ... the same words can mean two different things. Then the same words can mean a noun and a verb at the same time. Then it is very confusing.

(37)
P: Yeah. I am not sure about my answers. The comprehension is kind of hard.
I: OK, why do you think that the comprehension is hard?
P: The story very hard to understand.

One key contributing factor to Ping's and Fandi's language mixing is that their English vocabulary is clearly limited. And Ping acknowledges that this does affect her grades in English.

(38)
I: What are some of the things that you talk about for public speaking?
P: Relationship between teachers and friends. I did an article and then I present it to the whole school.
I: Were you nervous?
P: Nervous? No.
I: Why not?
P: Errr ... It ... it wasn't the first time I go up on stage to do public speaking. Then I have got the article in front of me, so I can read it well.
I: Ok. So you are all right with public speaking. I mean, in English.
P: Yeah.
I: As long as you think you are well-prepared, you are ok.

Ping's limited English vocabulary means that even when she does express confidence in her English, we need to take this vote of self-confidence with a pinch of salt. For example, Ping indicates that she is quite good at public speaking. But in this case, we have to realize that she is referring specifically to school events where she reads from a prepared script).

(39)
P: Yeah. As long as I am well-prepared. But if they were to ask me a question suddenly, then if I am not prepared, I will be dramatically errored.
I: So that means … let's say after your public speaking, and then somebody asks you a question?
P: Yeah, yeah, I wouldn't be able to answer well. I … I am not able to speak well dramatically, you know, use the correct vocabs and adjectives all, but if writing down … better in writing down.
I: So that means basically you need to prepare first.
P: I need to prepare. I..
I: So impromptu speech?
P: Can not.

Notice in (39) that when a more spontaneous kind of exchange is called for, Ping's difficulties come to the fore.

As will become clear momentarily, Ping is under some pressure (more so than Fandi) to style herself as someone who is reasonably good in English. But the problem she faces is that her available English language resource is not adequate enough for her to comfortably assume this persona. Her ongoing styling practices therefore involve attempts to participate in activities that can help legitimize her claim to the identity of someone who is 'good at English' whilst being careful to balance these with strategies that avoid putting her in situations where she might not be able to live up to social expectations.

In fact, realizing that this might be the best way for her to improve her command of the language, Ping wants to have more opportunities to interact in English. And quite naturally, one good way might be to use English when interacting with her friends. But unfortunately, because of peer pressure, she is resigned to interacting mainly in Chinese instead. She points out below (40–42) that she used to have a friend, Jestina, with whom she interacted mainly in English. It is not clear why she and Jestina stopped seeing each other. However, nowadays, her friends are mainly Chinese speaking and as she points out, if she tries using English with them, she is likely to be accused of putting on airs. Recall that Yan (Chapter 1) faced a similar dilemma among her Malay-speaking friends, fearing that she would be seen as a snob.[2]

(40)

P: There was once I had a friend, Jestina, ah. She speaks English. Then
I enjoy speaking to her very much, because I find myself expressing
better in English. Then it's like if I speak English with my Chinese
other friends, lah, they will say you are acting, acting like you are very
educated. . . . . Majority they are Chinese, what. Then outside you
speak English to them, they will think that . . . what are you trying to
say . . . my English is bad? Trying . . . me over English?

(41)

I: When you are with your friends, what language do you use to speak to
them?

P: Ahhh . . . my friends, majority they are Chinese. I speak Chinese to them.

(42)

P: So far, I haven't got any friends who will speak to me in English all the
times, so every time in Chinese, lah.

Interestingly, Ping reveals that there were times in the past when she actually tried to use English with her Chinese-speaking friends.

(43)

P: Because I speak Chinese most of the time . . . with my friends, lah.
Although I love to speak in English more, but they speak in Chinese,
so I reply back in Chinese, lah.

(44)

I: What language do you feel most comfortable in speaking?

P: Actually, everywhere I feel like speaking in English, but then people
will say acting, or just they cannot understand.

I: So eventually what do you do?

P: Eventually, ah, speak in Chinese, loh. Go with them.

I: Then why? Why do you choose to like follow them and not like, you
know, hopefully one day they will . . . ?

P: Because it is the whole group of them influencing me. I don't think me
one person speak in English can make the rest of them reply back in
English.

I: Have you tried?

P: Yes.

I: Oh, OK, you failed.

P: Yes.

But after a while, she gave up since she was the only one in the entire group that wanted to interact in English. To remain an active and accepted participant in the symbolic market of her peers, Ping therefore has little choice but to abandon her attempts to use English. Ping appears to be an exception amongst her friends, probably because of her attempts to style herself as someone who does well and is expected to continue doing well in English. Her use of Mandarin amongst her friends creates a conflict with this identity, which, as we have seen, she attempted to resolve (in vain) by persuading them to use English more. It does not seem to be the case that her friends have similar conflicts that need resolving, since they do not appear to see themselves as being good in English in the first place. Recall in (40) that they accused Ping of trying to show them up when she tried using English with them. The differences in attitudes are probably traceable to the fact that Ping and her friends see themselves in very different ways vis-à-vis their English language proficiency. Recall that in her home environment, her mother supports the view that Ping is doing well. This may have contributed to Ping's desire to use more English with her peers, as a way of behaviorally manifesting her self-image as someone who is comfortable with English. But the informal market of her home environment, where she enjoys great symbolic capital as someone who is doing well in English is not transferred to the informal market of her interaction with her peers. Thus, opportunities to use English, and the concomitant opportunity to display and improve her proficiency are frustrated by the fact that her peers prefer to interact using Chinese.

In this particular adolescent market then, interaction is defined in terms of the use of Mandarin. Unlike Ping's home, there is no attempt to adopt a bilingual orientation, especially if the reason for this change is couched in terms of alignment with a more dominant adult market. This is perhaps understandable. Unlike children, adolescents are expected to be responsible for their own actions. But unlike adults, they lack true independence. As Eckert notes, adolescents resolve this tension by being highly preoccupied with distinguishing themselves so that adolescent markets are typically strongly motivated by a desire to maintain their autonomy:

The very status of adolescence, with its institutional supports, separates the age group from childhood once and for all. At the same time, the focus on autonomy sets up a new kind of opposition between adolescence and adulthood. Since institutional requirements prevent adolescents from affirming independence from their parents through engagement with the adult world, they must do so through engagement in the adolescent world. (Eckert, 2000: 15)

This is not to say that Ping's friends do not acknowledge the value of English, but it appears to be a value that *others* may pursue, not *them*. It is not unreasonable to suggest that Ping's friends may have experienced early difficulties in learning English. These experiences of relative struggle would lead to them to naturalize what they might consider to be 'realistic' levels of English language proficiency as well as the extent to which the language is acceptable as a manifestation of their identities. This, in fact, is one of Bourdieu's crucial insights. As Calhoun points out:

> The confidence that defines greatness is largely learned, Bourdieu suggested. . . . One of the most important points Bourdieu made is that this is precisely how our very experience of struggling to do well teaches us to accept inequality in our societies. We learn and incorporate into our habitus a sense of what we can 'reasonably' expect. I, for example, would *like* to be a great tennis player, but have accepted that I am not. More basically, I have come to regard tennis as a mere recreation. I play it for fun, and sometimes play aggressively, but I do not play it for serious stakes. The games I play more seriously are ones I early learned I was better at, games involving words instead of balls, requiring more speed of thought and less of foot. . . . It is our desire for the stakes of the game that ensures our commitment to it. (Calhoun, 2003: 276)

Like Ping, Fandi, too, has problems with English comprehension stemming from his limited vocabulary. And unsurprisingly, this makes English his least favorite school subject (45–46).

(45)
I: Now what is the subject that you like least in school?
F: Should be English.
I: English? Why?
F: I can't seem to understand it and I would surely score badly in English usually . . . yeah.
I: What is it that you don't understand?
F: The comprehension part. It's very hard to score.

(46)
I: Ok, now. How about comprehension? You say comprehension. Why is it that you find it so difficult? You say you can't score, why?
F: I think because I don't understand the passage. Because some of the passages given during exams are quite tough, so when I don't understand the passage then the questions are more . . . harder for me to answer.

I: Now if you imagine the passages, those passages you have seen, what makes the passage difficult for you to understand?

F: Some hard words lah. Then I read the passages, when there are some hard words, I don't understand, I would need to refer the dictionary. But in the exam, I ... we can not use the dictionary so ... so when I don't understand the particular word, I don't understand the sentence, so that doesn't ... that makes me don't understand the whole passage.

I: So it is basically the difficult vocabulary that you think is difficult?

F: Yeah.

But unlike Ping, Fandi is under no pressure to style himself as being good at English (47).

(47)

I: Ok, now. Do you do public speaking?

F: No.

I: No.

F: Yes.

I: I mean do you speak to a group of people?

F: For like small groups or friends, yeah. Like 10–15 like that, can ah. Then sometimes in band practice during CCA, I will like speak to the whole band sometimes but usually like other people who are more public speaking they will speak to the band lah. Only sometimes when they are not here or what, I will speak to the band lah.

I: = What do you usually = ...?

F: = But that's very seldom = ...

I: What do you usually speak to them about, I mean when you do speak?

F: For ... in the band it's like ... tell teachers something, or any announcement that the teacher asks me to do ah. Then I will speak to them ah.

The default expectation for Fandi, both among his friends and family, is that English will always prove to be a challenge that requires a fair amount of effort to overcome. Hence, Fandi makes no claims about being good at public speaking and in fact, initially denies that he does any such speaking at all. Later, when he does give an example, his idea of public speaking is clearly on a much smaller scale than Ping's. Fandi's public speaking takes the form of briefing his fellow members of the school band.

(48)
I: Ok. Do you feel comfortable? [about public speaking]
F: First ... like ..in the first ... first time I meet them one time I will
not ... I will not feel comfortable because I do not know them, right.
Then if I know like ... each of them, I know them well already enough
or know their name, I am quite comfortable lah. But still the shyness
is still there. Quite ...
I: So how do you think you can improve then? Do you think ... you will
be better if you ... by given more practices?
F: Maybe if I get closer to the members lah. Maybe I will get more
comfortable with it lah. Then like my Malay friends lah, first time I
will speak to them like shy shy. First time I will speak very little
sentences to them, talk very little, but when I get to know them better
then I will speak more to them lah.

Furthermore, notice Fandi emphasizes that what would help him with his
'public speaking' is if he gets to know his audience personally so that the
interaction becomes more like communicating with his Malay friends (48).

Unlike Ping, who displayed a greater degree of metalinguistic awareness
when she noted the distinction between prepared and impromptu communication, Fandi's remarks take no cognizance of the sociolinguistic dimensions of public speaking at all. In particular, he seems unaware that the
interpersonal dimensions of public speaking are often quite different from
those that relate to his own interactions with personal friends. Thus, Fandi
merely tries to extend the competencies associated with the latter to the
demands of the former, instead of attempting to acquire distinct sociolinguistic competencies. But like Ping, Fandi's interactions in English tend to
also be quite limited. While he will use English if he happens to be addressing
a group of Chinese and Malay friends simultaneously, he usually uses Malay
if he is just talking to Malay friends, even in the presence of other Chinese.
But unlike Ping, who chafed at the fact that most of her interactions with
friends did not allow her the opportunity to use English, Fandi seems a lot
less concerned. This is consistent with the earlier observation that Fandi is
less metalinguistically aware about language issues, and as a consequence,
less fretful of whether his informal peer interactions provide him with the
opportunities he needs in order to improve his English.

The differences in attitudes are probably traceable to the fact that Ping
and Fandi see themselves in very different ways vis-à-vis their English language proficiency. Recall that Ping does express greater confidence in her
English, and that in her home environment, her mother also supports the

view that Ping is doing well. This may have contributed to Ping's desire to use more English with her peers, as a way of behaviorally manifesting her self-image as someone who is comfortable with English. But the informal market of her home environment, where she enjoys great symbolic capital, as someone who is doing well in English is not transferred to the informal market of her interaction with her peers. Thus, opportunities to use English, and the concomitant opportunity to display and improve her proficiency are frustrated by the fact that her peers prefer to interact using Chinese.

(49)
F: Depends on whom I am talking to lah. With Malay I will speak Malay, very odd very seldom I will speak to my Malay friends in English.
I: Why?
F: Not used to it lah. Because I usually speak to them in Malay so when suddenly this kind of thing happen, I won't like speak to them in Malay although I know there are the Chinese peoples playing with me.
I: Oh, even though there are Chinese people around, you still won't speak to your Malay friends in English?
F: Yeah, it is quite hard lah.
I: But when you talk to . . .
F: It's unusual.
I: But when you are talking to . . . rather than you are talking to one-to-one, one to one Malay.
F: Yes.
I: But you talk to like a group of them where there are Chinese and Malays, do you still?
F: Yeah, if it is a group, if they are listening to me, of course all of them are listening, I will speak in English. But if I am talking one to one, I will Malay to a Malay friends.

In contrast, Fandi does not enjoy the same kind of symbolic capital in his own home; both he and his mother agree that his English needs a lot more work. In such circumstances, it would require an unusually motivated and individualistic person to try to change the language of interaction with his/her friends, something that we recall Ping already attempted without any success. For Fandi, there is less dissonance between his self-image vis-à-vis the English language in both markets: home and peer interaction. In neither case is English language proficiency recognized or expected.

Reading for Leisure: Choice of Language and Material

Thus far we have seen that both Ping and Fandi face problems with their English, in particular, their vocabulary is highly limited. This leads to both of them having difficulties in English comprehension. Furthermore, in the case of public speaking, Ping's confidence is limited to cases where she reads from a prepared script to the entire school; any kind of discourse requiring her to improvise or show spontaneity is deeply problematic. For Fandi, public speaking takes on a much smaller scope, comprising briefings to his band members. Here, he relies less on language proficiency and more on goodwill and solidarity in helping him to communicate. The latter is something that he hopes will accrue as the people he speaks to move, over time, from being mere acquaintances to friends. It is clear that these are avoidance strategies that Ping and Fandi have evolved in order to help them compensate for their problems with English. In Ping's case, the strategy is to avoid events where she may have to ad lib. Ping's self-image as someone who is (supposed to be) good in English does not allow her to completely avoid public speaking. Events where she reads to the entire school allow her to sustain this self-image. In Fandi's case, no such self-image exists and his strategy is to avoid as far as possible all forms of public speaking. Where this is not possible, Fandi then relies on the hope that even if you do not speak well, provided the audience is made up of personal friends, he is less likely to be judged harshly.

Having seen how specific literacy events such as public speaking or comprehension tests are informed by more generalized notions of identity and peer interaction, let us now consider the practice of reading. In the following, Ping indicates that she hardly ever reads – which is perhaps not surprising.

(50)

I: Do you read?

P: Er, seldom.

I: OK, when you do read, what sort of things do you read?

P: Ha ... I read, I read stories, stories.

I: What sort of story books?

P: Enid Blyton.

I: Huh? At this age?

P: Until now.

I: Why? You like it?

P: Yeah. He ... he like tell ... he writes the story very simple. His stories are very simple. Then he uses simple English.[3]

(51)

I: OK, besides Enid Blyton, are there anythings that you read?

P: Newspapers … Emm, when there are news about celebrities, then I will read them in the *Straits Times* or what newspapers.

When pressed for examples of books that she does read, she mentions books by Enid Blyton, a well-known *children's* author. For Ping, Blyton's books are enjoyable because the language is 'simple'. Aside from books by Blyton, Ping also tends to read entertainment news, especially celebrity gossip. Ping's choice of relatively simple and unchallenging reading material is, again, part of a larger avoidance strategy.

(52)

P: But learning new vocabs, I don't think so because I am lazy to check the dictionary whenever I come across hard words, words which I don't understand.

(53)

P: Because normally I read the story, right. Then as long as a story line, a word or two which I don't understand, I don't think it will hinder my understanding.

I: But how about when it becomes to … when you read comprehension passages or when you read textbook?

P: Then I am dead, lah.

She does not like having to consult a dictionary for words she does not understand, and staying away from more challenging material means that she does not have to. Unfortunately, as Ping herself is aware, this means that she will probably have major problems with her schoolwork (*Then I am dead, lah*).

Ping understandably has some anxiety about her ability to maintain an image (to herself, her family and possibly her friends) as someone who is good in English. This avoidance strategy is Ping's way of maintaining this image. Her occasional acknowledgements that she does in fact face difficulties in school, her recount of failed attempts to get her friends to speak English, these are all further indications that she is trying hard to reconcile what she sees as conflicts between her participation in the markets of her home, her peers and her school.

(54)

I: Do you think your reading is good?

P: Still OK, lah.

I: Which one is better? English or mother tongue?
P: Mother tongue.

Having admitted that she avoids reading challenging English material, Ping goes on to suggest that she reads better in Mandarin (54).

(55)
I: What are some of the Chinese materials that you read?
P: Er, reading. If it comes to speaking, I would like to speak in English more. But when it comes to reading, I like to read Chinese more. . . . Because there are a lot of ancient stories about China. Then Chinese stories, they often have morals behind. . . . Because of the idiom stories behind and the stories behind the idioms that we use. And stories . . . there are a lot a lot of stories about morals and some long long phrases of Chinese. There are stories behind every phrases. Then it is very . . . very cute. It is very fun to know how to come up with that phrase with that particular story.

Her Mandarin reading material consists of parables that provide a historical background for the use of Chinese idioms. Again, Ping's interest in the history of Chinese idioms is consistent with her awareness of and sensitivity to metalinguistic issues. Thus in (55), she indicates that she enjoys reading about how particular turns of phrase come to be. However, note that even in the case of Mandarin, she finds her vocabulary to be limited (56).

(56)
I: How about if you write in Chinese? Is there a difference?
K: Chinese? Forgot lah. I cannot express myself in Chinese. I find Chinese.
I: So you write to your sis, and to your parents and =to your teacher = .
K: English.
I: You always write in English, =even you = ..
K: To my Chinese teacher, I also write in English.
. . .
K: In Chinese I will have it as simple as possible, because I don't know much Chinese characters.

Ping points out that when it comes to written communication with others, including her parents and Chinese language teacher, she prefers to use English.

(57)

P: No one ... I can not improve myself lah. No one will be there to listen to my pronuncation; no one will be teaching me. Then I don't think any teacher will have the free time to just teach a student ... how to pronounce better in Chinese. Every one is saying that English is more important in Singapore than Chinese.

Ping seems less concerned about her Mandarin than her English, probably because she considers Mandarin less important (57). However, regardless of which language she ranks more highly, it is crucial to note that she does not have a sufficiently strong command of either English or Mandarin, which would allow her to interact and articulate fully in just one language alone. As we have noted earlier, there is considerable appeal to both languages in most of her social interactions. Ping's inability to interact fully and comfortably in either English or Mandarin means that her code-switches are more likely the result of gaps in her vocabulary rather than the strategic manipulation of codes to achieve interpersonal goals. This is a potentially serious problem because Singapore's bilingual policy is based on the belief that 'properly' bilingual individuals are those in complete control of two separate sets of monolingual proficiencies. The mixing of elements is construed as a form of linguistic contamination, and the linguistic repertoires of individuals like Ping will be judged as linguistic deficiencies (Bhatia & Ritchie, 2004: 516).

The problem is compounded because Ping is not an isolated case; there are many others like her, including Fandi (as well as Edwin, Yan, Wen, whom we will meet in the next chapter).

(58)

F: Because I am not so interested in reading. Only when I really like the book, I will buy it and I will read it.

Fandi makes it clear that reading does not figure as a significant leisure activity for either him or his friends (58). However, he will read if it happens to be about something of strong personal interest. At the time of the interview, he expressed interest in soccer and rearing fish, as well as wrestling, so these constitute the topics that he would not mind reading about (59).

(59)

I: What sort of books would you like to receive then?
F: Biography about things that I am interested in.
I: Like what?
F: Soccer, fish.

...

F: For me now I am reading read about wrestlers, lah

I: So you like wrestling as well.

F: Yes, So when I read about them, it tells about how ... what they went through during the wrestling years, what they went through. It's quite brutal what they go through.

Aside from interest, Fandi's willingness to read is also shaped, unsurprisingly by what he considers relevant to his age group or appropriate to his gender.

(60)

I: Ok now, how about something like that, *Seventeen?* Will you read something like that?

F: No, I mean magazines like this are for girls only.

(61)

I: Now, lets look at *Reader's Digest*. OK, will you pick up something like this to read? No? Why not?

F: Cause it focuses on adult life. That is what I think, adult life, how they feel of what life. So what ... sometimes some of the things, the topics inside ... my friends say they are quite interesting, lah. But my mindset of *Reader's Digest* is adult stuff, lah, I won't like touch it.

(62)

I: Lets see what do they have in *Fortune*, ok? Samsung Digital, stocks and bonds, ... recession ... Things are looking up unless you want a job. This economic recovery really is different. You read something like that?

F: No. Cause this is, like what I said just now, still targets at business man or these adults who want to get a job or interested in stock market, paying for shares or what. But for me, I don't even have CPF, no need to read this kind.

(63)

I: So because you think National Geographic the target reader is adults.

F: Yes.

I: Not for teenagers.

F: Because you don't see in any teenagers reading National Geographic also.

...

I: So you think ... is this difficult to read?

F: Yeah.
I: Will you pick it up to read? No?
F: No.

He will not read *Seventeen* because he thinks it is suitable only for girls. He will not read *Reader's Digest, Fortune* or *National Geographic* because he considers them to cater mainly to adults.

(64)
I: Which do you enjoy reading more? English or in Malay?
F: I think it should be in Malay, because in Malay I can understand some of the words well. But sometimes I do prefer reading English books, English newspapers.
I: When do you prefer Malay and when do you prefer English?
F: Me like ... English for me is just when you see just read it, lah. Then when I see English newspaper I will read it, lah. Then sometimes if I see the first page, if the first page of English newspaper or the Malay newspaper is better, lah, then I read the interesting one first, lah. But I read both, I will read both.

Initially, Fandi indicates that he prefers reading in Malay more than English, but notice how he vacillates between the two (64). Unfortunately, like Ping, rather than showing facility with either language, Fandi's vacillation points to inadequate proficiency in each.

(65)
F: I tend to understand easier in English. Even when I watch Malay shows, I will read the subtitle rather than listening to them, because I am more comfortable in English, lah, when I listen or read. But when I speak to people, like my friends or what, I will speak in Malay, ah, unless there are other races, lah.

For example, even though he claims to prefer reading in Malay, he points out that he reads the English subtitles when watching Malay shows, because he feels more comfortable with English (65).

(66)
I: How about..are there anything that you read and you find difficult to understand?
F: Books lah. Some novels that I buy, I lend from the library I would not understand, because there are so many hard words inside the passage

or that certain page that I don't understand. Then I tend not [. . .]
borrowing the novels lah.

This is a significant point because here we have an indication that the home
language (Malay) is not necessarily the language he feels most comfortable
using (66).

(67)
I: What happens if you come across a . . . some words . . . ok, your own
     leisure reading, if you find some words you don't understand, what
     will you do? Will you check the dictionary?
F: No, ah. Because I think what I want to read, just read, lah. No need to
     check the dictionary or be so formal like that, lah. If you like the thing,
     you just read it and you should be able to understand. So far I haven't
     encounter this kind of situation. When I read something I like, I don't
     think I have any problem reading them, lah. Because the language they
     use are not so hard, lah.

(68)
F: Some hard words lah. Then I read the passages, when there are some
     hard words, I don't understand, I would need to refer the dictionary.
     But in the exam, I . . . we can not use the dictionary so..so when I don't
     understand the particular word, I don't understand the sentence, so
     that doesn't..that makes me don't understand the whole passage.
I: So it is basically the difficult vocabulary that you think is difficult?
F: Yeah.

But despite his professed comfort with English, Fandi in fact regularly faces
problems in understanding English, so much so that he ends up not buying
or borrowing books from the library at all – yet another manifestation of
avoidance (67–68).

Fandi's problem with English is unlikely to be easily resolved, in part
because, like Ping, he too has a strong aversion to dictionaries and will avoid
consulting them even if he is faced with words he does not understand. This
affects both the reading that he does in his leisure as well as his reading of
school-based materials.

Concluding Remarks

We began by noting that Singapore's bilingual language policy encourages proficiency in both English and the official mother tongue. In the case

of Ping and Fandi, this means English–Mandarin proficiency and English–Malay proficiency, respectively. However, we also noted that at the macro-level, there tends to be two rather problematic assumptions being made: that the home language is either the mother tongue or English; and that the language that a person is most proficient in is the home language.

Our study of Ping and Fandi demonstrates that these assumptions over-simplify the nature of actual linguistic practices. Both Ping and Fandi represent individuals who are struggling with both English and their mother tongues. This is despite the fact that Mandarin–Malay predominates in their respective homes. Ping's situation in particular indicates that a conflict can arise if the language that the speaker prioritizes (English) is not also the language that the speaker uses most often (Mandarin). This conflict may lead to various attempts at conflict resolution, some unsuccessful (changing the language of interaction with her peers) and some more successful (avoidance strategies at school).

We have suggested that ambivalence arises when actors have to manage the conflicting expectations and demands of different markets. In Ping's and Fandi's cases, such ambivalence is attested to the fact that both these individuals tend to engage in extensive code-switching despite being aware that this conflicts with the norms prescribed by the dominant market of Singapore's language policy. Even at the relatively more micro-levels of interaction, for Ping in particular, the need to manage varying expectations about English and mother-tongue usage in the markets of her home, school and peers makes it impossible for her to fully inhabit either the role of a competent English or Mandarin speaker. The stories of Ping and Fandi are in fact all too common in Singapore. This means that language (including educational) policies that are predicated on a clear division of social domains and concomitant officially expected monolingual competencies are more likely than not to create significant problems for adolescents regarding the acquisition of literacy practices. And given the high value placed on English language literacy in this society, understanding and appreciating how their literacy practices are related to the kinds of identity work they are engaged in when at home or with peers is not enough. We need to also see how identity work can impact on classroom behaviors, and in the next two chapters, we will focus on just this issue – the connections between practices inside and outside the classroom.

Notes

(1) Ping and her parents use 'Chinese' and 'Mandarin' interchangeably, again reflecting their acceptance of the state's assertion that Mandarin is their mother tongue as Chinese Singaporeans.

(2) See Goldstein (2003: 255) for a similar example of Cantonese-speaking students (originally from Hong Kong) in Canada. Goldstein notes that when these students used English with other Cantonese-speaking students, they 'could be seen as showing off their linguistic capital and flexing their linguistic power.'

(3) Ping seems unaware that Blyton was female.

6 Edwin, Wen and Yan: Styling Literacy Practices Inside and Outside the Classroom

Our discussion of Fandi and Ping in the previous chapter took the home environment as a point of departure. There, we focused in detail on how literacy events and practices in the home are ultimately mediated by peer-oriented identity work. We saw that Fandi and Ping provided interesting contrasts in terms of their self-images. Ping felt the need, specifically an obligation arising from parental expectations, to project an identity that involves being good at English. And we saw that this led Ping to adopt various avoidance strategies in order to help sustain her desired identity. It also led Ping to try persuading her peers to start using English as the language of interaction, and although this attempt proved to be ultimately unsuccessful, it underscored the important role that peers can play in either undermining or reinforcing strategies for learning English. Fandi, in contrast, did not feel the same pressures or needs as Ping because his own parental expectations were relatively low and easy to meet.

In this chapter, we center on the classroom, and our focus is on understanding the relationship between literacy-related activities that take place inside the classroom and those that occur outside it. To do this, we highlight the notion of style, which refers to a socially distinctive way of being, which is why 'people *use* or *enact* or *perform* social styles for a range of symbolic purposes' (Coupland, 2007: 3). We draw extensively on our detailed analyses of interview data of three other adolescents, Edwin, Wen and Yan. Like Fandi and Ping, these three also come from homes where English tends not to be spoken. But as we shall see, as far as their self-conceptions regarding English are concerned, all three are more like Fandi than Ping: they all consider themselves to not be particularly good in English and they do not feel any strong obligation to project an identity that has competence in English as a significant component. This kind of identity and its concomitant identity work inform the processes by which Edwin, Wen and Yan style themselves. Again, in appreciating the connection between activities that occur inside the classroom and those that take place outside it, we will have occasion to note the mediating influence of peer interaction.

Introducing Edwin, Wen and Yan

Edwin is a Chinese male. He is about 16 years old, and he usually scores a C or D ('D' is considered a fail) in English. His friends include Malay and Chinese boys, with whom he plays soccer. In interacting with them, he uses Mandarin (with his Chinese friends) and English (with both Chinese and Malay friends). Edwin expresses bewilderment as to what he can do about improving his English (*I also don't know what to study*). And even though he thinks that reading might be helpful, we shall see later that there are problems with his conception of what reading as a form of literacy activity actually entails. These are problems that ultimately undermine the effectiveness of reading as a strategy for English language improvement.

Wen is a Chinese female. She is also about 16 years old. Even though she does fairly well in most of her other subjects, her English is only slightly better than Edwin's. She usually scores a C. Her friends are mainly other Chinese teenagers, and the language that Wen uses when interacting with them is mainly Mandarin. Like Edwin, Wen also faces problems with English, especially in the area of comprehension tests. Also like Edwin, Wen considers reading important for improving one's English. And here, we will also see problems with Wen's conception of what the activity of reading involves.

Our third subject is Yan, whom we first encountered at the very beginning of Chapter 1. Yan agrees with the other two on the importance of reading. Yan is Malay and female. She is also about 16 years old. Her English is probably the best of the three, since she normally gets a B grade even though she is still not satisfied with this. Her circle of friends tends to be mainly other Malays.

One example of a shared stance toward literacy is that these three students all express a lack of proficiency in English, which they perceive to be related to their lack of 'reading'. At the same time, they all firmly appreciate the importance of learning 'legitimate' English for utilitarian purposes. For example, Edwin aspires to be an aircraft engineer, and he acknowledges that English is important in this regard.

(1)
I: OK, now do you think English language is important in what you want to do, in aircraft engineer?
E: Yes.

On the other hand, for both Wen and Yan, the need to do well in English is given a more immediate justification. They want to continue moving up the education system and they understand that to do so requires passing the English exams (2 and 3).

(2)
W: I mean you take this is a very important subject. Like if you fail your English, you cannot go to JC [junior college] ... If you fail your English then you can't get your cert.

(3)
I: In what situation do you think English is important?
Y: To, to promote you from Sec 3 to Sec 4, you need English. I mean, you need to get a grade in English. If not, then it is either you repeat or you have to channel down. So I think it's very important. It's embarrassing if you have to stay back.

It is clear, then, that all three subjects recognize the legitimacy and capital value of English. It is also clear that all three have fairly similar ideas about what needs to be done in order to improve their level of English; in particular, they all believe in the importance of reading, although as we see below, exactly what they understand by 'reading' is a matter of some complexity.

Informal Literacy Practices

How then does reading actually fit into the lives of these students?

(4)
I: Ok, would you be happy if you receive books for your birthday?
E: Nope.
I: No?
E: I don't read.
. . .
I: Where do you get your sources of books from? I mean, when you read, where do you get your books from?
E: Library.

I: Library. School library? National Library?

E: National Library. Sometimes like for NCC purpose or camp, I will go and borrow some books, lah.

I: What sort of books?

E: Like survival training. About NS one. I will read see whether [. . .] some can be useful, lah.

While Edwin recognizes reading as relevant to improving one's English, it is, for him, an activity that one does *specifically* for this purpose of language improvement. In other words, for Edwin, reading is *work* and there appears to be no conception on his part that reading could ever be a pleasurable or fulfilling activity in its own right. He makes it clear that he is not interested in receiving books as presents (4). And as he goes on to point out, on the occasions when he actually does read, it is to obtain information that might be relevant to his school's extracurricular activities. In the particular case being discussed here, the National Cadet Corps (NCC) is a student-based military organization, and Edwin mentions that he sometimes reads up on survival training in the hope of getting tips when preparing for his stints in the NCC camps.

(5)

E: Like some people say what everyday write out five vocas, one day you have a lot. Then when it comes to the exam, those words you have come across will be useful. All these I don't do it.

Edwin's view of reading as work is further highlighted by the fact that he seems to think that the main purpose of reading for English is simply to expand one's vocabulary. According to him, the goal is one of accumulating five lexical items on a daily basis (5). For Edwin, then, reading is a solitary activity, to be conducted either to extract information vis-à-vis some non-linguistic activity, or to be done in order to acquire newer words so that he may pass his English exams. Needless to say, this is a view of reading as a dreary and mechanical activity, one that precludes the possibility of reading as being an intrinsically pleasurable activity. We shall see later (Chapter 7) that such a conception of reading contrasts radically with that of another adolescent, Sha. For this other person, reading is fun. Moreover, although Sha, too, is conscious of the importance of vocabulary expansion, this is an activity that he does as a form of informal interaction with his friends. The result is that, unlike Edwin, for whom vocabulary acquisition emerges as a passive activity involving word recognition, Sha and his friends treat vocabulary acquisition as an enjoyable activity of performing among one's peers. Where English language competence is concerned, Sha's familiarity with words extends far beyond recognition to include the creative ability to extemporaneously use these words in extended discourses *of their own making*. Edwin's attitude toward reading as a chore seems traceable to his sense of what he and his friends, *qua* a community of practice, would consider appropriate leisure activities. These activities include playing soccer and computer games; reading is most certainly not one of them.[1] Instead, reading is treated as a highly pragmatic activity. Edwin thus exemplifies a perspective on literacy emanating from a sense of *necessity* (Bourdieu, 1984).

(6)
I: Do you do anything to improve your English?
W: Yeah, I have been reading these few days, lah.
I: You have been reading these few day after exams, activities.
W: There is nothing I can do, I just read and read and read. I just borrow some books from the library. I mean it doesn't cost. I mean you just borrow. If you borrow already, you don't want to read that is it, lah. I mean at least if you have free time, you don't sit there to bore then you just take out a book and read.

Like Edwin, Wen also recognizes the value of reading, although unlike Edwin, she seems to have a somewhat more positive attitude toward reading. Reading is something that she does in her 'free time' since the alternative would be utter boredom (6).

(7)
I: Now will you be happy if you receive books for your birthday?
W: Ok, lah.
I: What sort of books?
W: Stories, novels. . . . Books relating to teenage. . . . Like those like those romance stories, sometimes like at this age, then what they do, that kind of things.
I: Then what sort of books would you not want to receive?
W: Those scientific books. That means those like what . . . what outer space, you got what thing what thing what thing. Then not interested.

When it comes to justifying her choice of preferred reading, notice (7) that Wen invokes the category of *teenager*. Her preference is for 'romance stories' rather than 'scientific books', with the latter apparently holding no interest for her. In the same way that Edwin's reading of military information is relatable to his own gendered subjectivity concerning what he would consider appropriate reading material for a young adolescent male, so too, we see that Wen's preference for reading romance stories is part of what she feels would be appropriate to her particular gendered conception of a female teenage identity.

(8)

Y: I am a teenager, I won't read this section. [Of a newspaper]
I: OK, how about this¿
Y: Yes, movies.
. . .
I: OK, how about something like that¿ [Picks up Seventeen, a teen magazine]
Y: Yes.
I: Yes, Seventeen. What do you think it is about inside¿ Do you read it all, Seventeen¿ What is inside¿
Y: Teenage stuff, especially for girls.

Like Wen and Edwin, Yan makes it clear that her choice of reading material is very much tied to her own sense of what is appropriate to her notion of a teenager. She enjoys *Seventeen* and *Teens*, magazines which specifically target a readership of her age group and gender (8).

While both Wen and Yan display a more positive attitude toward reading than Edwin, the kinds of things that all three do read are clearly informed by what they each consider appropriate for themselves as (gendered) teenagers. This is point of some significance and we can conceptualize this by referring to Bell's (1984) provenance hypothesis, which argues that stylistic meanings do not arise *ex nihilo*. Rather, they are deployable in local contexts only because they are already meaningful by virtue of the fact that they index norms and values associated with social groups. Even though Bell was speaking more generally about the social distribution of linguistic features and their group-level indexical meanings, the line of argument can be extended to cultural categories such as 'teenager' and 'gender', and the distribution of literacy practices. Thus, in the case of Edwin, Wen and Yan, the elements that constitute their separate literacy practices appear to be deeply influenced by their particular interpretations of what it means to be a teenager of a particular gender. 'Teenager' then constitutes 'an absent reference group' or 'referee' (Bell, 1997: 248) that intersects with broader conceptions about appropriate gendered behavior to influence the style of these individuals.

(9)
I: Now do you think do your parents help you English at home?
E: No.
I: No? Not at all?
E: Cause my father can't really speak English. Then my mother also not good at English.

Again, anticipating our discussion of Sha in the next chapter, none of these three adolescents are seriously challenged to read materials that go beyond a stereotypical notion of what would be appropriate for teenagers. In contrast, Sha is motivated by his father, who assiduously selects relatively sophisticated articles from the internet for him to read. Thus, unlike Sha, for Edwin, Wen and Yan, the home does not seem to provide a strong influence with regard to English language literacy. For example, Edwin indicates that his parents are unable to provide any help with English because their own command of the language is almost nonexistent.

(10)
Y: Sometimes my dad will come over and he will just leave the papers he took from the mailbox on the dining table. I just read those I can read.

Likewise, Yan's parents' involvement in cultivating her reading habits appears to be minimal. Yan reports that they provide occasional and incidental access to English language newspapers by leaving such materials lying around the home. This is understandable given that Yan's parents' proficiency in English is limited. Thus, they neither select specific articles as material to be read nor do they talk to her about the content of the newspapers. As a result, Yan is not really pushed at home to improve on her reading. Her home environment can be characterized as one that is pervaded by a general awareness and appreciation of the importance of English, but which is unsupported by any specific literacy practices that would actually help cultivate competence in the language.

The kind of identity work that Edwin, Wen and Yan engage in informally, then, clearly does not involve competence in English. In fact, it would not be putting the point too strongly by suggesting that this identity work involves just the opposite: the absence of any claim to such a competence.

In the next section, we see that this identity work – one that actively eschews any claim to English language competence – is also highly present in the classroom. We will also see that this has particular implications for the organization of classroom interaction, and for the types of strategies that the students have access to when acquiring English language literacy.

Literacy Practices in the Classroom

The notion of style is conceptually significant because it helps to open a window on how social interaction outside the classroom can impact on learning inside the classroom. This is because although the classroom consti- tutes a distinct community of practice, the fact that students interact with their classmates during and after school means there are linkages between the classroom and beyond that cannot be disconnected (Eckert, 2000: 40). This is a point worth dwelling on here, even though we will revisit it in Chapter 8, since both the management of classroom activities and the ratio- nale for particular language pedagogical devices are usually predicated on the assumption that it not only is possible but in fact desirable to expect students to leave behind their nonclassroom identities and language practices once they enter the classroom (cf. Siegel, 1999).

The fact remains, though, that such an expectation is sociolinguistically unrealistic. It simply insists by pedagogical fiat what the educational authori- ties expect of student without taking into account the students' own abilities and constraints in responding to these expectations. Consider, as an example, Heller's ethnographic study of Champlain, a minority high school in Toronto. Champlain is an educational institution dedicated to preserving and protecting the francophone identity, and because of this, it aims to create within itself a monolingual environment where Canadian French, as part of the school's heri- tage, is officially the only French tolerated (Heller, 1999b). However, the stu- dents of Champlain try to find different ways of subverting aspects of the school's ideologies that they are unhappy with. Even those students who are academically successful and ambitious may appear to cooperate by publicly keeping to monolingual French, but they still find the need to use English (forbidden because of school's championing of a francophone identity) in 'backstage' or more private interactions, even while on school grounds.

(11)
I: OK, do you like to read aloud in class?
W: Read aloud, not really.
I: Why not?
W: Very shameful.
I: Why?
W: I mean you read in front of the crowd then not everybody seems to
       listen to you. Then if you read something wrong, then you think 'Aiya'
       [Expression of concern]

I: So it is a face thing, is it?
W: Yeah.

It is therefore undeniable that the kinds of behaviors and activities that the students might consider to be stylistically appropriate given their concern with situated local identity orientations are also found in abundance in the English class. Returning to our own informants, we found that Wen, for example, expresses concern over the activity of reading aloud in class (discussed below) because she finds it 'very shameful' (11). As she points out, it is the reaction of her peers that worries her most rather than that of the teacher. What this suggests is that even though Wen would prefer the teacher to evaluate her reading as 'correct' or 'acceptable', she is more worried about whether her peers evaluate it as 'embarrassing' or not.

Peer group orientation is therefore also clearly highly influential in determining what goes on in the classroom. We noted above that style is designed with different audiences in mind. In the case of classroom interaction, the impact of *auditors*, that is, socially ratified third persons (Bell, 1997: 246) on the identity work of students is paramount. In a student–teacher interaction, auditors will include classmates who are present in the classroom but are not directly involved in the interaction, which is typically some version of the familiar Initiation–Response–Feedback sequence (cf. Sinclair & Coulthard, 1975). In his own study of classroom interactions, Rampton suggests, following Foucault, that students try in various ways to oppose the sequence (which he refers to as Initiation–Response–Evaluation) because it is a 'disciplinary technique' that 'would give the teacher a good deal of control over students' conduct' (Rampton, 2006: 72). The students, according to Rampton, are in the first instance reacting to their own desire for self-determination and 'an objection to the insidious disciplinary techniques that try to stop people from being individuals in the way that they want, and that seek to turn them into the types of person desired within the regimes of expert knowledge' (Rampton, 2006: 71). Rampton himself observes that different groups of students utilize different strategies of opposition, some of which are more aligned with, or putting the same matter differently, less explicitly opposed than others to the teacher's desire to implement the IRF/E sequence.

Our own observations are entirely consistent with Rampton's, although we are keen to emphasize that the students' attempts to react to the IRF/E sequence and hence to prioritize a sense of self-determination are to a significant extent colored by the kinds of determinations that are acceptable to their peers. Thus, while we do not have observational data on how the students themselves behave as auditors, it is worth noting, from Wen's own statement, that it is how *she thinks* her peers will react that most concerns her. In

Bourdieuan terms, Wen is mainly concerned about how her act of reading out loud will convert into any symbolic profits or penalties from her peers.

In the next section, we see that this same concern is also expressed by Edwin and Yan, with similar consequences for their own attitudes toward the activity of reading aloud.

Reading Aloud

One common activity the English language teacher does in the classroom is to get individual students to read aloud portions of a text. Because the selected texts are read out loud, the teacher typically uses this activity to gauge students' ability to recognize and pronounce particular words. In performance terms, reading out loud comes close to stylization in that the students are called upon to consciously display their language skills for evaluation by the teacher, and to a more implicit extent, by the rest of the class as well. However, unlike a more stereotypical case of stylization, the students are obviously expected neither to adopt the voices of others nor to frame this adoption in relation to the classroom context. Rather, the students are expected to offer up a persona that is specific to the classroom itself: that of an obedient or diligent student who engages in a language performance in the hopes of garnering praise from the teacher. Needless to say, not all students are comfortable when they have to inhabit such a persona. And it therefore comes as no surprise when we find that none of our subjects welcome this activity.

(12)
I: Do you like to read aloud in class?
E: Ok, lah.
I: Why 'OK' only?
E: A bit shy, embarrassed.
I: Why are you shy and embarrassed?
E: I mean not used to speaking aloud … When you stand and read, lah, a lot of eyes are looking at you. Quite … I am quite those shy one, lah.
. . .
I: As if like let's say you read wrongly and oh, everybody is looking at you. Everybody knows your mistake.
E: And laugh.
I: And they laugh at you.
E: Yes.

We have already seen that Wen is concerned about embarrassing herself. Similarly, Edwin describes himself as being shy and embarrassed (12). He is particularly concerned therefore about drawing the attention of his class-mates and being laughed at. In other words, like Wen, it is less the reaction of the teacher than the reaction of his peers that most concerns him and affects his attitude toward this particular pedagogical activity. And as a con-sequence, he is extremely uncomfortable with the idea of being called upon to display or perform his language skills.

(13)

I: Is there any time that you read aloud?
Y: When I am alone in the room.
I: When you are alone you read aloud, why?
Y: It's for oral and saves my face if I don't know the word.
I: Really? Seriously, you read alone when you are in the room?
Y: Yeah.
...
I: You like reading aloud.
Y: When there is no one around.
I: Oh. When there is someone around?
Y: I don't like.
I: Why?
Y: Some words, like I say, are very alien to me. So it's like when I try to pronounce I find it so funny. I am afraid a lot of person will laugh.
I: And then you will be
Y: Embarrassed.

It is this same desire to avoid embarrassment that, in Yan's case, leads her to practice reading aloud only when she is alone in her room (13). Like Wen and Edwin, Yan's concern is with the reaction of her peers rather than that of her teacher.

As we can see, for our three subjects, it is the evaluation of their peers *qua* auditors that is highly important to them, even in a setting such as the class-room and even where the activity is one ostensibly addressed toward the teacher so that we might expect the teacher's evaluation to override every-thing else. This observation highlights the interactional dimension of style (Coupland, 2007: 11), where speakers attempt to act and speak in ways (and these may include withdrawal or avoidance strategies) that would allow them to manage various kinds of social relationships. And where the differ-ent relationships, such as the student's relationship with his/her teacher and that with his/her peers, may lead to conflicting expectations, a speaker will have no choice but to prioritize.

This observation also has significant implications for language peda-gogy. It indicates that pedagogical strategies that are developed on the basis that the teacher is the sole or even primary arbiter and controller of the students' responses are likely to be ineffective. It ignores the possibility of placing students in socially awkward, if not difficult, positions of having to choose between conflicting styles and identities. Instead, the development of such strategies, we suggest, needs to also take into serious and careful consideration the effects of anticipated peer orientation, rather than presumed for the very outset their apparent irrelevance. We return to this point in Chapter 8.

For the moment, we continue, in the next section, to investigate how peer-oriented identity work also underlies the very strategies whereby students acquire literacy skills and take meaning from texts.

(Not) Asking the Teacher for Help[2]

(14)
I: If you don't understand, do you ask⸮
E: Maybe I will ask my friend.
I: You ask your friends first. Why not ask the teacher⸮
E: That is the mentality with our class, lah. We will ask our friends then if ask a teacher maybe after a lesson or after school.

In (14), Edwin indicates that he is generally reluctant to ask his teacher for clarification if there is anything that he has difficulty understanding. Instead, he prefers to ask his friends in the class. Interestingly, Edwin also indicates that this is a fairly common attitude; it is not one that is peculiar to him and his friends only (*That is the mentality with our class*).

(15)
I: But why don't you ask the teacher first if the teacher is in class⸮ ... Why don't you put up your hands and wait for the teacher to come to you⸮
E: OK, the class is very quiet. And if like you stand up, you are like, it is almost like an atmosphere. Then you speak very awkward. Everybody will see you stand up and ask the teacher.
I: So it is still shy. That means you don't want people to have attention to you. Why not⸮
E: Shy. If you purposely do this, some people will say you are attention-seeker all these nonsense.

And echoing once more the concern with being embarrassed that was discussed above in connection with reading aloud, Edwin explains that this reluctance is motivated by a desire to avoid derision from his peers (15). Thus, it is the constraining influence of his peers – specifically the fear that he might be labeled an 'attention-seeker' by them – that prevents him from asking his teacher for help. Needless to say, this desire to not seek help from the teacher but to instead rely on his friends has a serious impact on Edwin's success with English language literacy in the classroom since he is not only avoiding an authoritative source of information, but he is also opening himself to the possibility of getting misinformation.

(16)
I: If you have questions you don't understand, who will you ask?
W: I will ask my friend to ask.
I: Why? Will you ask your friends first?
W: Yeah, lah. That means I will ask my friends first. If my friends also don't know, then I say 'OK' you ask the teacher.
I: Why?
W: OK, I will ask my friends because my friends know then you don't trouble the teacher to come forward to your group and then to ... So ask my friends first, lah. If my friends knows already then no need to trouble the teacher to come.

In Wen's case, her reluctance to ask the teacher for help is dealt with in a slightly different manner. Like Edwin, her first impulse is to approach her friends. But should this fail, that is, if it turns out that none of her friends can help her, then Wen's next strategy is to get one of them to ask the teacher (16). Under such circumstances, the act of asking the teacher is no longer open to derision. But this is only because the act of asking has now been socially ratified by Wen and her group of friends: it is one that has been requested by members of the group themselves rather than initiated individually. The student who actually asks the teacher for help thus avoids being labeled an 'attention-seeker' by her peers, which as we just saw, was a major concern for Edwin.

(17)
I: Do you read anything and you realize, you know your level of English is not up to it, you don't understand what you read or what people say?
Y: Yeah.
I: When?

Y: For example, Vincent Clark [One of the teachers]. I mean I can understand his English but sometimes he uses funny funny words, I also
don't know what he is talking about.

I: So does that cause embarrassment? Do you clarify?

Y: No.

I: Why not?

Y: Embarrassment. . . . I will go home and check . . . [the dictionary]

Like Wen and Edwin, Yan, too, is reluctant to seek clarification or help from
her teacher. But here, we have an example of yet another strategy for coping:
when there are words that she does not understand; she consults the dictionary at home. By working on what she does not understand in the privacy of
her home, Yan avoids embarrassing herself in front of her peers (17). This
means that as far as Yan is concerned, the classroom is not a site for learning.
Rather, it has become reconstituted as the site where problems and questions
arise, and it is only away from the classroom that learning for Yan actually
takes place. This state of affairs is obviously far from ideal, but it does point
out the importance of developing language pedagogical strategies that are
sensitive to the identity concerns of adolescents.

Of the three strategies exemplified by our subjects thus far, Wen's might
be considered the least damaging, at least where language pedagogy is concerned. Wen's group has established a strategy where teacher consultation is
acceptable, even if only under specific circumstances. Edwin's and Yan's
strategies, in contrast, do not seem open to the possibility engaging the
teacher for help at all. We might perhaps be charitable here and suggest that
Yan's strategy of working at home on her own at least has the benefit of
helping her to cultivate a sense of independence or self-reliance. However,
this perspective would, we think, be too optimistic for two reasons. First, it
is clear that Yan's own motivation for working at home stems less from any
sense of independence than from a fear of being embarrassed. We do not
discount the possibility that Yan may have a healthy desire to be independent, of course. But by her own admission, in the specific case of English
language lessons at least, Yan's actions are clearly the result of wanting to
avoid being made fun of by her peers. Second, this is a point that will emerge
with greater clarity when we encounter the case of Sha in the following
chapter; effective language learning requires an interactive social environment rather than self-imposed isolation. This means that Yan's strategy of
working at home prevents her from actually using English in the context of
actively engaging with others. Any competence she may have with regard to
English is subsequently highly passive in nature, amounting to some knowledge about the meanings of words and their pronunciations. Recall that

Edwin, too, faces a similar disadvantage given that he tends to construe the act of vocabulary expansion as a matter of word recognition rather than the practiced ability to creatively use new words in unfamiliar contexts. Crucially, this means that for students like Yan and Edwin, there will tend to be a sense of unease when it comes to the performance of language as an online, interactive activity.

To summarize the key points of the discussion thus far, our adoption of an extended audience-oriented and situational perspective on style reveals the formal classroom to be a highly textured and complex environment, where, for example, the officially sanctioned role of learner is displaced in favor of multiple manifestations of the social identity of 'teenager'. Furthermore, although Bell does not discuss in detail what it actually means to be socially ratified, it is obvious that even more important than the mere physical presence of the auditors is the issue of what specific social identities are being ascribed to them. A teacher would quite reasonably ascribe to the auditors the identity of other *students*. However, a student would not necessarily view the auditors as other *students*. Rather, from his or her perspective, the more salient identity might be that of *attention-seekers, friends, bullies* or perhaps more generally, other *teenagers*. And reciprocally, this same student would be only too aware of the social sanctions that could accrue should he or she himself/herself be so labeled. In this kind of scenario, both teacher and student are ascribing different social identities to what is apparently the same body of auditors, with potential conflicts between how the teacher expects the student to behave and how the student himself/herself feels he/she ought to behave.

The jockeying for social position in small groups is, of course, a common enough activity. And participants often compete and collude, forming alliances and cliques where possible, to maximize the various statuses available. This can involve not only attempting to claim particular positions for oneself, but also involve positioning others in socially devalued or stigmatized positions (Goodwin, 2006). Here, we are reminded of Eckert's remarks concerning the phenomenon of stylistic objectification:

> ... social development involves a process of objectification, as one comes to see oneself as having value in a marketplace ... at this point, speakers can point to social meaning – they can identify others as jocks or burnouts [group labels that young people use to mark their pro-school or anti-school orientations], as elite or working-class, educated or not, prissy or tough. (Eckert, 2000: 14, 43, cited in Coupland, 2007: 23)

The result of such stylistic objectification, then, is that socially attributable categories such as 'attention-seekers' or 'bullies' become reified as labels that attach to individuals. The consequence of such labeling is that an individual's behavior and qualities tend to then be interpreted via the lens of these labels. So, while it is certainly always possible for any individual to renegotiate or perhaps even resist those labels that he or she finds undesirable, the success of these attempts is ultimately intersubjectively determined, rather than unilaterally decided by either speaker or hearer alone.

Off-Floor Interaction in a Singapore Classroom

To better understand what is going on, it is important to appreciate that in the course of peer group activities, multilingual practices and vernacular forms of literacy typically used by Edwin, Wen and Yan create their own off-floor spaces in the classroom. The off-site nature of such interaction is underscored by their reluctance to involve the teacher (discussed above) so that even if they have difficulties with the lesson, they try hard to avoid asking the teacher for clarification. For example, we just saw that Edwin, Wen and Yan are not really at ease about asking the teacher for help, and this state of affairs is traceable to their concerns about what their peers might think of them were they to do so. Thus, the classroom needs to be recognized as a set of variegated social spaces, some of them in dynamic tension if not outright conflict with the social space officially sanctioned by the teacher.

Once this recognition is in place, we can understand why it is that despite the fact that English is the one and only sanctioned official language of on-floor instruction, particularly in the English language class (cf. Heller & Martin-Jones, 2001), these students regularly still use other languages such as Mandarin and Malay as well. This is because these other languages are marking social interaction that is occurring in off-site spaces. These students are well aware that this would not be considered appropriate by the teacher, but the fear of being labeled an 'attention-seeker' or 'snob' is part of the complex series of equations that teenagers need to juggle so as to conform to peer pressure. Edwin, for example, switches between English and Mandarin, especially when interacting with his peers. For him, this language switching is 'natural' or 'automatic' (*It's very natural. You talk to your . . . yeah . . . Mandarin Chinese friends, very auto one, lah. Automatically you switch to Mandarin*). Thus, even in a situation where English is expected to be the only language used, and where the teacher is attempting to reinforce this expectation at least as far as on-floor activities are concerned, the pattern of language use in off-site interaction is dictated not by institutional norms, but by far more local peer-oriented considerations. The off-site nature of this interaction is made clear from Edwin's remark that he will only stick to using English if he happens to be under direct scrutiny from the teacher (*Unless the teacher is staring at you. Then no chance, lah. Converse in English.*).

At this point, we think it is worth mentioning that there is no contradiction in noting that English is supposed to be the only language used in the classroom and observing (as we do below) that even the teachers themselves engage in code-switching. After all, the exclusive use of English is an idealization that actual classroom practices cannot always afford to realize (Cook, 2001). What this means is that teachers often find themselves code-switching for a variety of reasons. Such reasons may include the need to clarify materials, to compliment or scold students, or to joke with them in order to establish some kind of rapport (Martin-Jones, 1995).[3] Our view of code-switching, therefore, treats it as one of many possible communicative resources, specifically, as a contextualization cue, that a speaker can draw upon in constructing meanings (Gumperz, 1982). As a contextualization cue, the acting of code-switching in and of itself carries no specific meaning; it is only in occurrence with other verbal cues in the course of a particular interaction that the localized pragmatic meaning emerges as inferences along the lines of Gricean implicatures are invited (Auer, 1995; Irvine, 1985; Martin-Jones, 1995; Stroud, 1998). And because outside the classroom, the individual codes are already typically associated with particular social and cultural values (Blommaert, 2005; Heller, 1995), code-switching, when it takes place in the classroom, can be creatively and strategically used to either reinforce these preexisting values or subvert them. In the case of the students' off-floor spaces, code-switching serves to index or draw upon peer-oriented social norms that exist outside the classroom.

(18)

I: OK, you say you like to play soccer. When you play soccer, I mean I am sure you talk to your friends. Who do you play with?

E: My friends, most of them are Malays.

I: All from other classes?

E: Yes. Sometimes I can converse with them in a bit of Malay, lah.

I: So you speak to them in Malay. But most of the time what do you speak in?

E: English.

I: Are there any Chinese boys there?

E: Yes.

I: So do you speak Mandarin together? I mean, among yourselves, Chinese boys?

E: Yes.

In Edwin's case, for example, his use of Mandarin with his Chinese class-mates and English with his non-Chinese classmates *in the classroom* is a reflec-tion of his interaction with them *outside the classroom*, when playing soccer or computer games. Thus, consider (18), which shows that Edwin's interaction with his friends is resolutely multilingual. The linguistic resources drawn upon include Mandarin, English as well as Malay. Such multilingualism, while a normal enough pattern of behavior for Edwin when interacting out-side the classroom, is, however, prohibited in relation to the on-floor class-room activity. The latter is expected to be conducted using English only.

(19)
I:　Then when you talk to your friends, you speak in?
W:　Both languages.
I:　Both languages. What sort of friends do you speak to in Mandarin and what sort of friends do you speak to in English?
W:　Mixed. That means to friend A or friend B all the same, lah. That means if during the conversation there will be a lot of English used inside, lah.

This pattern of switching between Mandarin and English in the English language classroom also applies to Wen (19). Wen admits to using both English and Mandarin when she is engaging in off-floor activities, such as group work with her friends. She is aware that the use of Mandarin is not desirable since it may affect her learning of English. However, this awareness is clearly insufficient to motivate Wen to avoid code-switching. This is because the use of both Mandarin and English is a reflection of Wen's lan-guage use outside the classroom among her friends, and it would be sociolin-guistically unnatural for Wen and her friends to suddenly use only English, even if this is the official prescription.

(20)
Y:　It is like because now is like I have more Malay friends compare last time. So it is like the common language is Malay. Then I shouldn't be talking like one clever person, superior. If then they will think I am such a snob.

In the case of Yan and her friends, the languages involved are Malay and English, rather than Mandarin and English. Again, we see that this pattern is carried over from norms of interaction outside the classroom. As Yan explains, Malay is the language of interaction with her friends, and any attempt to use English might lead to accusations of snobbery (20).

As Canagarajah (2004a: 123) points out, such off-floor spaces or 'safe houses' allow students to adopt identities 'deriving from the heterogeneous discourses they were competent in', identities that are otherwise marginalized or disparaged in the on-floor activities of the classroom. It is important at this point to take note that there is an issue of directionality involved here, one that will be significant when we start considering the development of effective language education pedagogies. The directionality is this: Students are importing language practices outside the classroom into the classroom, rather than vice versa. This is not to deny that the reverse trajectory never occurs. For example, in Rampton's (1999; see also Rampton, 2006) discussion of language use outside the classroom, he observes that the students make use of German, which is a language they encounter in the foreign language classes. These students use German 'in breaktime, in corridors, in English, Maths or Humanities lessons' (Rampton, 2006: 144). However, as Rampton himself points out, while the students' use of German is clearly based on their classroom experiences with the language, it is highly stylized, being associated with self-dramatization and playfulness. In any event, this use of German was a 'passing fad' that also seemed not to really have any significant influence on the students' interest in German as a language worth learning (Rampton, 2006: 137). The use of German outside the classroom, in other words, is highly marked by the students themselves as not being their natural way of communicating. Rather, these highly stylized uses of German constituted for the interactants a means for 'showing off' in the sense that these uses pointed to 'the voluntary "performance" of exuberant students intent on embellishing the curriculum discourse in whatever ways they could' (Rampton, 2006: 163). In contrast, when students are importing their external language practices into the classroom, they do so because they find this to be a more natural way for them to communicate among themselves.

There is therefore a useful generalization that deserves to be captured here. Bearing in mind that styling involves a continuum of practices from the highly stylized to the more naturalistic, we might suggest as a heuristic that the directionality involved when language practices outside the classroom are imported into the classroom is more likely to fall on the naturalistic end of the scale. In contrast, language practices that are imported from the classroom are more likely to fall on the highly stylized end of the scale.

And because of this subjective sense of naturalness that accompanies the importation of language practices into the classroom, when these practices are held up by the teacher as the objects of disparagement, the effects can be all the more damaging. All this is relevant to the issue of language teaching because it makes good pedagogical practice to begin with what the students themselves know or are familiar with, rather than to simply disparage this prior knowledge and experience as irrelevant or worthless. In the next section, we discuss examples of such disparagement.

On-Floor Interaction

Although standard English is officially the main language of education, the diverse language backgrounds of the students frequently force the teacher to acknowledge and refer to other languages and varieties in concrete classroom contexts. In the course of making such references, the teacher often positions these languages and their associated identities negatively with respect to standard English. In this section, we wish to focus on two occasions when the teacher's use of code-switching is part of a larger interaction where the student's work is being disparaged.

(21)
T: Elvan, this time ah you wrote a very very crappy piece of thing.
There's so much grammatical and spelling errors in the compo I begin to wonder whether I teach English or are you – Because compared to the previous compo, it's like two different persons writing.
E: Which compo?
T: The teenagers. You ask your *ah ma* to write for you one, right?

Consider (21). In this example (Ong, 2003: 57), we see how the teacher's reference to the Chinese identity of a student, Elvan, is made in somewhat derogatory terms through the use of the Hokkien word for 'grandmother' *ah ma*. Here, the teacher makes it clear that he is criticizing Elvan's essay and when the reference to *ah ma* is juxtaposed with the topic of the essay, *Teenagers*, both the grandmother's (assumed) lack of ability in English and Elvan's having to solicit her help with writing this topic is ridiculed publicly in the context of the teacher's on-floor commentary. The macrosocial message to come across is that (old) Chinese culture has little or no social capital and most certainly no place in the modern English language classroom.[4]

(22)
T: I can say it in two Chinese phrases, *Yi2 cun4guan1 yin1 yi2 cun4 jin1.*
Cun4 jin1 mai3 cun4 guan1 yin1.
[This is a Mandarin proverb that literally translates into 'An inch of time an inch of gold. The inch of gold cannot buy the inch of time.' Some students recite along with the teacher. Students cheer after the teacher has completed reciting the Chinese phrases.]

T: That phrase can be used to describe yours. Alright now.

T: Frankly speaking, ah, how much content is there? You basically beat around the bush you know – around the bush, but you still talk about time is money, money is time and that's it. Never waste time, and that's it.

Ok this is what we call a very rhetorical topic. Actually, you have chosen to write what we call the very didactic, the very dead type of topic whereby people look at it, they *hai yah* (sigh). Very philosophical. You deserve to have a tablet next to Confucius. Ok, well done.

S: Cher,[5] but we made a dead topic come alive!

A similar interaction can be observed in (22) (Ong, 2003: 73). Here, the teacher refers to the Chinese proverb 'An inch of time, an inch of gold' to summarize the topic of another student essay, which he finds unsatisfactory (*how much content is there? You basically beat around the bush*). He then proceeds to characterize rather sarcastically (to the general and concerted amusement and applause of the rest of the class) as a 'dead type of topic'. That is, as a topic which elicits *hai yah* (sighs of resignation or expressions of tedium) from people when they read it. The teacher then concludes, by way of parody, that the student's attempt is deserving of a memorial stone tablet that deserves to be laid next to the grave of the Chinese philosopher Confucius. The student recognizes this parodic intent on the part of the teacher and protests that credit should actually be given for having made a 'dead topic come alive'. Once again, as with (21), when reference to Chinese is made by the teacher and when Chinese/Mandarin fragments are actually used by the teacher in the English lesson, it is in a context of derision that underscores the marginal role accorded to the Chinese language and its associated identifications.

Elsewhere, in an interview with the teacher, Ong (2003: 94) points out that the teacher is resigned to the fact that he is unable to completely eliminate what he describes as 'the Chinese problem'. In referring to one of the male students in the study, the teacher states: 'Even in class, out of ten sentences, for example, that sprouts from his mouth, I think probably about six would be either Chinese or Hokkien. What can we do?' And in discussing another male student (Ong, 2003: 37), the teacher points to the influence of Chinese as having a detrimental effect on English proficiency. The teacher specifically laments the students' tendency to first think in Chinese before translating the Chinese sentences into English: 'A lot of broken English here and there. At the same time, once in a while, if you think in Chinese, you can almost hear him speaking in Chinese in the English format. So the trans-lation wise, we can see for ourselves.'

In the context of such disparagement by an authority such as the teacher, it is no wonder that as a consequence, standard English, by default, comes across as linked to mainstream identities and academic accomplishments when compared to the other languages.

Conclusion

In the preceding discussion, we have noted how deeply embedded the linguistic mediation of literacy learning is in the pupils' discursive construc-tion of peer-oriented identities. The discussion in this chapter illuminates the observation made earlier (Chapter 1) that multilingual language practices and their associated ideologies of sociolinguistic indexicality are deeply implicated here in the data on classroom practices. For the ELT professional in the second or foreign language classrooms, this poses potentially massive pedagogical challenges, which require renewed attention to the role played by multilingualism in identity work and resource distribution.

We close this chapter by sketching some outlines of the kinds of con-straints that ELT professionals might have to bear in mind as they strive to respond to such challenges, leaving detailed discussion till after we have seen a case of a more successful language learner (Chapter 7). We noted earlier in this chapter that the choice of preferred reading materials appears to be inflected for both age group (teenager) and gender. Recall, for example, that Edwin's reading included military survival strategies while Wen's included romances. However, such simple gender associations disappeared once we went on to consider strategies of interaction within the classroom. Edwin's group preferred to avoid consulting the teacher as much as possible, while Wen's group was prepared to have one member ratified as the indi-vidual responsible for approaching the teacher for clarification, and finally, Yan's approach was not group based but rather involved her working at home by herself.

All the three strategies share a common motivation: they all result from each individual's lack of confidence in his or her English language ability and also from the desire to avoid the derision of his or her peers. But despite this commonality, the diversity of the actual strategies being employed signals an important point of caution. Even when attention is given in language teach-ing to identity work, it is necessary to avoid developing pedagogies that are grounded in stereotypical and perhaps even simplistic typologies, gendered or otherwise.

If we consider the issue of gender, for example, it is clear, given a moment's reflection, that gendered expectations are abstract ideals, so that not only individual females but individual males as well may feel the need to justify any disparities between their own actual situations and these ideals. Thus, while it may be the case that all the three individuals discussed here are responding in ways that still allow them to cleave to relatively established ideas about gender, even within the same gender category, there are indisputable differences about what counts as appropriate and acceptable behavior. This will become especially clear when we encounter our final subject, Sha, a Punjabi male adolescent, in the following chapter. There, we will see that while some of Sha's activities clearly overlap with those of Edwin's, there are also important differences that, we suggest, are traceable to the intersection between gender and social class. The interest that Sha and his friends have in language performances might, from the vantage point of Edwin and his peers, seem somewhat less than properly masculine.[6]

What all this means is that any proposal for language teaching must necessarily be broad enough to take into consideration the situated responses of specific individuals. It is, in other words, necessary that the language teacher be specifically encouraged to pay close attention to the localized practices of his or her classroom cohort, rather than enter the classroom with broad generalizations. And if this kind of localized attention leads students to critique established notions about appropriate language behavior as well as their inevitable indexical links to ideologies governing gender, then this is all the better since it may be said that individual autonomy and capacity for critical thinking only truly arises when there is 'the relinquishment by both men and women of their investments in conventional notions of masculinity and femininity' (McNay, 2008: 53), as well as other 'ethical regimes' (Ong, 2006: 21) such as those pertaining to class or ethnicity.

Notes

(1) Computer games clearly do involve a kind of literacy. But for Edwin, the kinds of texts he encounters while playing these games are clearly not what he considers 'reading'. The focus, rather, is on the rapid hand–eye coordination needed to play these games proficiently. Any act of reading is therefore incidental, and like his perusal of library books for NCC survival training tips [see (4) in text], it is done only in order to extract the information necessary to partake of the activity – in this case, to play computer games.

(2) We see no reason why 'not asking for help' should not be treated as a literacy practice, since learning *how* to use language also means learning *when* to use it and consequently, when to refrain from speaking ('silence') and their associated symbolic values (cf. Heath, 1994: 77). In any case, regardless of whether we treat 'not asking

for help' as a literacy practice or a general learning strategy, it is an unavoidable fact that 'not asking for help' is a school behavior that does have a detrimental impact on our subjects' acquisition of English. Whether this behavior also manifests itself in other classes (e.g. mathematics) does not, we think, reduce its relevance with regard to English language literacy.

(3) We are grateful to Suresh Canagarajah (p.c.) for bringing to our attention that clarification was needed on this point.

(4) In the context of Singapore's political culture, there is no reason to assume at all that the teacher is being racist. For one, the teacher is also of Chinese ethnicity. But even if he were a non-Chinese, a racist interpretation is still implausible. This is because Singapore's political culture strongly emphasizes the importance of multiracialism (see Chapter 2), and even though this multiracial discourse increases Singaporeans' awareness of ethnic identity, it also reduces the tendency to attribute racist readings to each other's utterances unless the evidence to the contrary is incontrovertible.

(5) This is a truncated form of *teacher*, a common way of addressing teachers among Singaporean students.

(6) See Thompson (1991: 17–18) as well as Chapter 8.

7   Sha: A Comparison

We now provide a comparison with Sha, a 16-year-old Indian male, in order to demonstrate a set of literacy practices that is significantly different from that of our previous five adolescents. Like our other informants, Sha has friends of different ethnicities, mixing around with Malay, Chinese and other Indian boys. While he occasionally uses Malay in speaking with his Malay friends, Sha is quite clear about his preference for using English. Unlike them, Sha comes from an English-speaking home and he generally feels quite comfortable with his level of English. This general sense of confidence is substantiated by the fact that he usually scores a distinction in his English tests at school (again, unlike the other five).

Sha's circumstances make him a relative rarity in the neighborhood school. Not only does he come from a home where, in his own description, 'Standard' English is spoken, his father is a professional, which puts Sha's family in a different socioeconomic class than that of the others. And Sha is clearly impressed by the fact that his father's professional success is due in no small part to his (the father's) proficiency in English. This, as we shall see, strongly influences Sha's attitudes about the importance of English vis-à-vis his mother tongue.

English at Home and among Friends

Sha is interested in soccer and computers. But note that unlike Edwin, who we also observed to be interested in computers, Sha's interest is somewhat more 'geeky' in nature. That is, rather than simply playing computer games (which seems to be the extent of Edwin's interest), Sha is fascinated with computers from a more technological perspective, which therefore makes it imperative that he read computer magazines in order to learn about new developments. Thus, Sha tends to read relatively voraciously about whatever interests him, including soccer and computer (1).

(1)

S:　Soccer, I read everything about it.

I:　How about things like that? Computer . . .

S:　This one I read cause I have to know about this.

I:　Why?

S:　Because I don't like to have an outdated computer. Of course I mean if I read about this then I don't have to actually go and buy computers. I will see what parts I need to upgrade on this model. Then I can go and buy those.

This is in contrast with Edwin (see Chapter 6), who reads reluctantly at most. For example, recall that Edwin will read about survival training in order to prepare himself for his camping experiences as part of his involvement in the National Cadet Corps, the student-based military organization. Other than that, Edwin concedes that reading is important if he is to improve his English, but sees this as a rather laborious activity of trying to acquire five new vocabulary items per day. The idea that reading might be pleasurable seems quite distant to Edwin. And this is very much unlike Sha, for whom reading seems part and parcel of how he enjoys his soccer and computer hobbies. (And as we shall see below, Sha can sometimes be so caught up in his reading that he tries to continue reading even in class, and then gets his books confiscated by the teacher.)

(2)

S:　Because all his [= Sha's father] life he has been around people who only speak English. So he knows what is the importance of it. Because he used to be in Singapore until he left for Norway and all that. He told me he had a very hard time, his first one or two years there. Because he kept speaking in Singlish. He didn't understand them. So he asks he wants me to have a good command of English so I can go overseas and all.

Unlike the other students, Sha comes from an English-speaking home and one that in comparison with the others is far more affluent. In fact, before coming to Singapore, Sha spent seven years in the United States, where his father used to work (Sha's father worked in Norway prior to moving to the States). His father, in fact, is a very strong influence on Sha's attitudes toward English. Below, we see clearly that Sha's father has impressed upon him the instrumental value of speaking good English. The father managed to improve his own English, from Singlish to 'Standard English' and this obviously means that the father represents a highly influential role model to Sha. To Sha, he represents someone who has (i) personally experienced the disadvantages of not being able to speak Standard English and who has (ii) through his own efforts, improved his English substantially and in so doing (iii) improved the socioeconomic status of himself and his family.

There is therefore a highly significant difference between Sha's home circumstances and those of the other five adolescents discussed in the preceding two chapters. While all these adolescents come from homes that are generally supportive of the need to acquire competence in the English language, in Sha's case, the link between English and socioeconomic rewards is much more concrete. Sha's own material comforts (his home, the fact that he has lived abroad) are very clearly connected to his father's (based on his father's own narrative) efforts at successfully learning the English language. This presents Sha with a counterfactual scenario that is also extremely concrete: Sha is aware that his living circumstances would have been very different *if* his father had not managed to acquire a good command of English. There is therefore (at the very least) an implicit of class difference between Sha and the other adolescents, a difference that Sha himself cannot but help be appreciative of.

(3)
S: Now there is some of my friends are … Hari is a very good … class for English, he is also … he can also speak very good, Haron … they can speak very well in English so now I don't have to speak Malay so often with them.

Because Sha feels that he already speaks 'Standard English' at home with his parents,[1] it is therefore no surprise that, in contrast to Edwin, Wen and Yan, for example, Sha generally feels quite comfortable with and proud of his level of English. Sha's friends – he mentions two Malay friends, Hari and Haron – too, tend to be relatively fluent in English (3). This is another major point of difference. Recall that among our other five informants, Ping was the one who expressed greatest confidence in her English. But even she was left to rue the fact that her interaction with peers was conducted in Mandarin, thus leaving her with very little opportunities to improve on her English language proficiency.

(4)
S: Most of my friends are, I have a lot of mixed friends, lah, Chinese, Malay, I also got Indian friends. So normally I try and speak English

with them. But sometimes if the situation calls for it then with my Malay friends I got to speak Malay.

(5)

S: I have friends from E6, they normally speak Malay. So over the years, I pick up, lah, how they, what they spoke. Then sometimes I ask them, but then other like Sec 4 some of the Malay people they speak good English, lah. So with those I speak English, lah.

On occasion, though, Sha switches to Malay if he has other Malay friends who are more comfortable using the Malay language, but it is clear that Sha himself would prefer to speak only using English (4 and 5).

(6)

S: Because most of our parents also speak primarily English with us, lah. They don't really focus on Punjabi so much, maybe food or something when they talk in Punjabi. Normally they speak English with us so it is like the first language to us.

(7)

S: Normally I just play with my brother. Sometimes Nazirin ... he comes over, lah.

I: So when you guys play, what do you converse in?

S: Normally we speak English because Nazi also he can speak English quite well.

I: And your brother as well?

S: My brother is always speaking English.

This preference for English stems from his home background where, as we already noted, English is the main language used. Sha indicates that the use of English (rather than Punjabi) as the home language is not unique to his family, but is actually a common feature of the Sikh community in Singapore (6 and 7). Thus, among the Sikh families in Singapore, especially where younger speakers are concerned, Punjabi appears to be ceding ground to English.

The Relative Values of English and Punjabi

(8)

S: Cause I never ... I was never brought up in the way like ... my parents never stress to learn Punjabi. I only started learning Punjabi when I came back to Singapore and even ...

I: Which is how old?
S: Primary four.
I: Primary four is twelve right?
S: Twelve.
I: You started learning Punjabi only at the age of twelve.
S: Yeah. I mean in American I can greet my grandparents when they came over or aunties. But normally even my aunties they also speak English with me and some of them speak very well. My father used to tutor them in English mainly cause he wants them to be able to speak very good English so that they could get good jobs and all. Since he has been spending so much time overseas, he always stresses on English first then my mother tongue.

Not surprisingly, Sha clearly considers English to be more important than Punjabi. Notice in the final part of (8) that Sha's father, once again, is a major influence on Sha's attitudes toward English. It turns out that the father not only advises Sha, but he also tutors Sha's aunts. Thus, like our other informants, English, for Sha and his family, is inextricably linked to better socioeconomic prospects, and because of this, knowledge of English is considered far more valuable and important than knowledge of Punjabi.

(9)
I: But I don't understand. You seem to like don't like don't like don't like Punjabi. What is this thing that is making you like I hate Punjabi? What is this thing, what is this thing that is making you dislike Punjabi?
S: Because for 7 years of my life in America, I never have to speak Punjabi, I never ever have to you know in school never ever have to say anything in Punjabi or have to learn to read something in Punjabi or learn to write in Punjabi. So I was very used to just using English as a way of communicating people. Then when I came back also it is still ok. But then after a while I have to go to Punjabi class. Then again the whole world like I have to speak Punjabi in the school I can not. I have to learn and write in the new language then. The kids I was with they for them it is nothing for they are in K2. So they are like we are learning Punjabi for the first time. But primary 4, 5 kids I am sitting. Primary 6, I was sitting, I understand I actually have to learn this. It depends if I can not learn, I can not get anywhere this kind of things. I am very angry with it.

What is quite surprising about Sha, though, is how vehemently negative he is toward his mother tongue, unlike our other informants. Sha started learning

Punjabi mainly after he returned to Singapore at the age of 12. Prior to that, while growing up in America, he only spoke English. Sha's disdain for Punjabi is undoubtedly linked to his difficulties with the language, a disdain exacerbated by his comparative ease with English (9).

(10)

S: I hate writing in Punjabi. It's so like why ... why do I have to learn Punjabi. I never going to go to Punjab. And Punjabi is such a funny language. Ok, if I learn how to speak it, I learn how to speak. But then if I have to learn how to write, I am never going to write a story in Punjabi, I never go to Punjab and write a story for some girl in Punjabi. I still don't still see a point in it.

I: What happens if you fall in love with a girl who knows only Punjabi?

S: Then I have to find another girl, lah.

Unlike our other informants, who struggle to accommodate both English and their associated mother tongue, Sha is very clear that Punjabi holds little or no value for him. In other words, despite our other informants' struggles with English, they do not view English negatively because they see it as a language that confers specific socioeconomic privileges on its speakers. This makes it a language *worth* learning despite the difficulties involved. In contrast (10), Sha does not see any role at all for Punjabi in his life (*I never going to go to Punjab; I am never going to write a story in Punjabi; I still don't still see a point in it*). Thus, his much greater sense of frustration results from the feeling that he is putting in a lot of effort in an endeavor that he finds pointless. It is worth noting at this point that Sha's critical attitude toward the value of his historically inherited mother tongue, Punjabi, is not at all atypical. Instead, it presents significant challenges for educators, parents and communities that steadfastly adopt an uncritical stance toward the idea of language and cultural preservation, and refuse to take into consideration the changing life experiences of younger genera-tions of learners/speakers. Thus, Blackledge and Creese (2008), in their study of Bengali schools in Birmingham, show that the students resist the idea that Bengalis need to speak Bengali. These students have grown up in a linguistically different environment, where English clearly has greater value and relevance. This leads Blackledge and Creese to point that 'These young people were discursively negotiating paths for themselves which were in some ways contrary to the ideologies of the complementary schools, where teachers and administrators held the view that they ought to learn Bengali because to do so was a practice which carried with it knowledge of Bangladeshi history, nationalism and identity' (Blackledge &

Creese, 2008: 552). Therefore, as Süssmuth (2007) points out, one of the key challenges in engaging youths about their cultural heritage is that educators should be careful not to force them into accepting identities that may not have the same kind of meaning or social significance as these might have had for the educators themselves. Otherwise, these young people are at risk of adopting an 'ascribed identity', one projected on them from the outside based on their ethnic or religious affiliation (Süssmuth, 2007: 207). Returning to the case of Sha, it is clear that he vehemently rejects any attempt to impose on him an obligation to learn or even embrace Punjabi, especially if the basis for any such imposition is his attributed ethnic identity.

(11)
I: What is it about Punjabi that you don't like. I mean you are …
S: What is the point of studying it? I hate … Punjabi is a language I don't know 300 years old. Then where we speak Punjabi?
I: Your Punjabi community?
S: Punjabi community also is … how all of them speak Punjabi? All of them only speak Punjabi when other mothers are around and their kids are there their kids can not speak Punjabi, all must speak Punjabi just to …

Sha sees Punjabi as a language of the past and one that has little or no current relevance (11). Even within the Punjabi community, Sha characterizes it as a language being used between children and their mothers, and only because of a desire to retain some historical connection with the Punjabi ethnic identity. This is a desire that Sha does not identify with since he is more interested in what Punjabi might have to offer him in his current and imagined future identities.

In a sense, Sha's attitude is understandable. He is extremely confident of his proficiency in a language, English, that he knows is highly valued. He sees no such comparable value in Punjabi at all. Because of this, he is ready to commit himself fully to linguistic markets where English is the medium of communication. In contrast, our other informants are far less confident. Even Ping, who professes to be fairly good at English, we saw, struggles to find opportunities to use and improve her English, and consciously avoids English texts that she knows are beyond her reading capabilities. Thus, for the others, hedging between English and the mother tongue is a rational strategy; there is no point in committing to particular linguistic markets when one does not have (and may not ever have) the kind of linguistic capital needed to succeed in those markets.

Pride in 'Standard' English

Interestingly, Sha is quite clear that the kind of colloquial English he uses with his friends is 'broken English'.[2]

(12)
S: Most of them [i.e. Sha's friends] ... most of them when we are together we also speak broken English like we will speak half English half Malay, but most of them they can actually speak English so now I will just go and speak pure English with them.
I: Broken or standard?
S: Broken.

Notice that while Sha's initially uses 'broken English' to refer to a mixture of English and Malay (*half English half Malay*), he also uses the same phrase even when there is no mixing (*pure English*) (12).

(13)
I: When d yoou speak standard English?
S: Standard English when I speak with my teachers, when I speak with my dad and my mom.
I: To your parents? Why?
S: Because my father if I speak broken English he will always ask me to repeat or he becomes sarcastic ... he will say 'What did you say? I don't understand, can you repeat?' Then I will have to repeat. Then my mom because she will ... start questioning why I am speaking like that.
S: From a young age I have been taught you know my father.

And he contrasts this 'broken English' with the 'Standard English' that he uses on other occasions (13). These other occasions include not just talking with his teacher but with his parents also. Sha makes it clear that his attention to 'proper' English is very much due to both his parents' influence, though it is clear by now that his father seems to play a more significant role in this regard (e.g. *Because my father if I speak broken English he will always ask me to repeat or he becomes sarcastic*). In fact, Sha comes across as being extremely confident in his command of English (14).

(14)
I: Ok, then how do you feel about the English language?
S: English language is the best.

I: Er¿

S: The best. I like English language.

I: You like it¿ Why¿

S: Because the … I always like English, lah, because with English I always can understand what is going on, lah. Even if I don't understand the subject at all, if you write it all down for me, write it all down for me legibly that I can read it, most probably I can understand.

(15)

S: My father will … every article he thinks I should read in the newspaper, he will ask me to read. Sometimes he will just leave it on the table then I know it must be important, lah. I have to read it. My mom, I don't think she is not concerned or anything, but she doesn't stress English so much for me. But she also, she only speaks English to me. But it is my father, my father always show me things to read. Internet he see some, he prints it out and asks me to read all.

Interestingly, Sha's father not only takes an active interest in encouraging him to read, but actually selects the materials as well (15). Contrast this with Yan's home environment, where, as we noted, her parents play a much more passive role in simply making available the occasional English language newspaper, or with Ping's almost bitter comment that parents who do not really know English should not try to help otherwise they risk giving their children the wrong answers.

Thus, unlike all our other adolescent informants, whose parents do not speak much English, Sha's father's encouragement is underscored by the fact – a fact that Sha is very much conscious of – that these materials would have already been read by the father himself. That is, in Sha's case, the father can be considered an adult familial role model, who provides support not only on the activity of reading, but specific advice on the choice of reading material as well.

The contrast between Sha's experiences of reading, on the one hand, and those of the other adolescents we encountered in the preceding chapters, on the other hand, is analogous to Heath's (1994) observations concerning the social distribution of the literacy event commonly known as the 'bedtime story'. Heath points out in the socialization of literacy events, 'participants follow socially established rules for verbalizing what they know from and about the written material' and '(e)ach community has rules for socially interacting and sharing knowledge in literacy events' (Heath, 1994: 74). In her own study, Heath suggests that 'the bedtime story is a major literacy event which helps set patterns of behavior that recur repeatedly through the life of mainstream children and adults' (Heath, 1994: 75), and outside the mainstream, children may learn different ways of interacting with texts that might prepare them less well for participation in the educational system, or that might even be in serious conflict with the interactional patterns expected in the system (Heath, 1994: 73).

In Sha's case, his father constitutes the primary 'literacy caregiver' in the home, that is, the individual most responsible for and most influential in shaping Sha's early English language literacy experiences. And as the foregoing extracts demonstrate, Sha's father consistently emphasizes not only the ability to read English texts, but also the ability to adapt one's spoken English, especially in response to the presence of an adult evaluator. Such experiences collectively provide Sha with the necessary performance skills of language reflexivity. For example, he is able to check his use of English and style shift 'upwards' toward the more standard variety. He is able to do this, initially perhaps, *in response to* his father's sarcastic remarks about his language, but later on, *in anticipation of* how his father might react. These kinds of experiences with 'incipient literacy' (Scollon & Scollon, 1979), as we will see shortly, provide Sha with a greater sense of ease and confidence when asked to perform similar tasks in the context of the classroom.

Reading for Pleasure

In fact, Sha's interest in reading, ironically, sometimes gets him into trouble in the classroom because he will continue reading a book even if it has no relation to the lesson being taught. For Sha, then, reading is unequivocally a pleasurable activity.

(16)
S: If I got a good book, something I want to read, sometimes I try and read during lessons and all. . . . Normally the teacher will give me a warning, lah. Sometimes the book will be confiscated then.

(17)
I: Do you read a lot?
S: Yes.
I: What sort of materials do you usually read?

S: I like to read the science fiction books, stories, novels. That is what I like to read.

...

S: I used to read about four books a week. Four to five books a week. But now I read about three, two books cause I read normally books that are quite thick and it takes me about two days to finish one book.

And Sha enjoys reading to the point where he can be said to be a voracious reader (17). Even though he says he is reading fewer books per week nowadays, he is quick to point out that it is only because the books he reads are much lengthier than they used to be.

The difference in attitudes toward reading and confidence in English between Sha and the others is significant. The home environment, as we just saw, no doubt makes a major contribution to this. Neither of the others has a role model approaching anything like Sha's father. That is, a parental figure who speaks good English and transmits *on the basis of personal experience* the sense of possibility, pride and enjoyment of the language. But it is also worth noting that the influence of Sha's father is reinforced by that of his peers (below).

In contrast with, say, Edwin's, Yan's and Wen's experiences, the kinds of activities that Sha and his friends enjoy emerge as extremely unusual. For example, recall that Edwin, Yan and Wen all expressed concern about being asked by the teacher to read aloud in class, fearing that they would embarrass themselves. They all also preferred not to initiate any exchanges with the teacher even if this meant not understanding the lesson. If we bear in mind the attitudes of Edwin, Yan and Wen toward these all activities, we find that Sha presents an almost diametrically opposite case.

Language Performances as Peer Activity

For example, Sha and his friends actually enjoy learning and practicing new English words (18).

(18)
S: I ask Hari, does he speak English at home? He says 'Yes'. Harun also. Most of time they speak English so ... and they also ... I don't think they actually have an interest in the English language but they like to learn words. If we say we don't know a word, we normally go and look it up then we continuously use it in sentences while we are talking then ... until we can actually know how to use the words, lah.

On encountering an unfamiliar English word, Sha and his friends make it a point to look up its meaning in a dictionary, and to consciously practice using the word until it becomes a naturalized part of their linguistic repertoire.

(19)
I: How about reading to your friends?
S: Yeah, to them I am not afraid of reading anything.
I: Does anybody read to you now during English class, beyond English class, your friends?
S: My friends sometimes Hari will bring materials he downloads from the Internet or some jokes or stories or things like that. He does read to us cause he knows how to read jokes.
I: Do you like it?
S: Sometimes it's very very funny the jokes he reads.

They also enjoy reading out loud to each other, and this, together with their conscious attempts to make use of newly acquired words in the utterances, mean that their peer-oriented use of language incorporates elements of conscious performance. To put the matter rather paradoxically, self-conscious language performances become 'naturalized' for Sha and his friends, and a means by which the successful performer acquires symbolic capital. For example, in (19), Sha states that he has no problems reading to his friends, and he also comments positively on his friend's (Hari) ability to read jokes well. This naturalization of language performances among Sha and his friends amounts to the development of an interactional ritual (Rampton, 2002). Crucially, according to Rampton:

While it [ritual: CS & LW] is being performed, there is 'time-out from normal social roles, responsibilities, rules, orders, and even modes of thoughts' (Rothenbuhler 1998: 15), and the mood is often what Turner calls 'subjunctive' rather than 'indicative', characterized by an orientation to feeling, willing, desiring, fantasizing, and playfulness rather than by an interest in applying 'reason to human action and systematis[ing] the relationship between means and ends' (Turner 1987: 123; cf. Sperber 1975). Rituals tend to generate an increased feeling of collectivity in PERFORMANCE, 'an aesthetically marked and heightened mode of communication, framed in a special way and put on display for an audience' (Bauman 1989: 262, cited in Rothenbuhler 1998: 8–9). (Rampton, 2002: 492, small capitals in original)

That is, such stylized performances of language use, where particular attention is paid to language form and where the actor's use of the forms is opened up for evaluation (Bauman & Briggs, 1990), appear to constitute a routinized aspect of how Sha and his friends interact. In Sha's case, then, distinct communities of practice (Lave & Wenger, 1991) such as his home, his circle of friends and even his English language classes, all appear to be mutually reinforcing vis-à-vis the learning of English. The connection with Heath's (1983, 1994; see above) remarks about how the literacy practices acquired outside the classroom might better prepare (or not) students as they move into the school environment is clear.

There are degrees of ritualization (Rampton, 2002: 493), of course, but what is particularly relevant to us here is that these kinds of interactions involve Sha and his friends in performances of English language display, where the participants are engaged in mutually evaluating one another's use of the language. Significantly, then, the interactions do not constitute a zero-sum gain, where the symbolic capital accrued by recognizing one member's linguistic prowess necessarily comes only from depriving some other member of the same kind of recognition. Rather, these interactions encourage the feeling that, together, Sha and his friends are pursuing activities that allow members to derive pleasure and admiration from each other. This contributes to the feeling of 'collectivity' that Rampton (see above) comments on. In this regard, it is of particular significance that much like the London-based adolescents observed by Rampton (2002), who are learning German as foreign language, these ritualized exchanges that occur outside the classroom are less threatening to the interactants themselves because 'it is their peers rather than the teacher who evaluate the product; *the interaction is conducted in a spirit of levity, not seriousness*' (Rampton, 2002: 505, italics added).

(20)
I: Is there any time that you read aloud?
Y: When I am alone in the room. . . . It's for oral and saves my face if I don't know the word. . . . Some words, like I say, are very alien to me. So it's like when I try to pronounce I find it so funny. I am afraid a lot of person will laugh

And in relatively stark contrast to Sha and his friends, the orientation toward English language performances – even those that might conceivably be 'conducted in a spirit of levity, not seriousness' – appears to be completely absent from the home and social activities of Fandi, Ping, Edwin, Yan and Wen. For example, recall that Yan prefers to go home and look up her dictionary rather than risk asking questions in class. As (20) shows, Yan also prefers to practice reading aloud when she is alone at home. Yan's fear of the derision that may greet her language performance provides a significant contrast to Sha's interaction with his friends.

Thus, unlike Sha, who, in concert with his friends, can pursue their English language displays in a light-hearted and unthreatening environment of mutual support, Yan's attempt to improve her own use of English is marked by the imposition of self-isolation. Yan's worry that she may be mocked not only points to the absence of anything like a peer support group that might encourage displays of English language use; perhaps more poignantly, it indicates that even if such a group were to be somehow made available to her, she might view it with too much trepidation for her to be able to take sufficient advantage of the opportunities it would present. For Yan, the fear of derision may have become too deeply entrenched for her to feel any ease with the fairly impromptu and improvisational modes of interaction that otherwise work so well for Sha in his own informal peer interactions. Where language pedagogy is concerned, these observations suggest that for weaker and less socially secure students such as Yan, it is important to be able to find ways of accommodating and encouraging language improvisation and play *within* the context of the classroom (see Chapter 8).

Reading Aloud

(21)
S: Like it ... I guess so. I am not scared of speaking aloud.
I: OK. Why? I mean why it is like you are OK reading to your friend aloud?
S: Because ... I don't know. I have never been shy to speak aloud or read aloud. Because in America they used the body system then what my English ... I don't know if it is English, lah. But they say I could read well so used to ask me to tu ... not tutor, lah, but read to the younger kids and all. So from there I got a good start of speaking.

We can therefore expect that Sha's own classroom behavior will be markedly different from that of the others. And indeed, this is confirmed by (21). Sha enjoys reading aloud when called upon to do so by the teacher.

(22)
S: In primary school when I used to read I used to read for the sake of ... when I was read to, I listen more for the sake of listening to the story. Now when I am read to, I am listening more to the way the teacher

stress and I try and learn reading skills from the teacher. I don't listen just to hear the story anymore.

In fact, he takes reading aloud as an opportunity for him to practice his delivery (22). Notice that Sha talks about the activity in symmetrical terms, where he feels there are opportunities for him to improve his English *both* when he is doing the reading as well as when he is listening to someone else read. The awareness of the performance aspects of language use and the desire to be able to perform language well, already a key feature of Sha's peer-oriented activities outside the classroom, recurs inside the classroom as well (*I am listening more to the way the teacher stress and I try and learn reading skills from the teacher*). In this way, we see how Sha's attitude toward English language literacy is, without any exaggeration, of a different order than that of Edwin, Yan and Wen.

Recall that for Edwin, Yan and Wen, reading aloud represents a classroom activity that they are not comfortable with at all. This undoubtedly affects their ability to take full advantage of the educational environment. As Miller[3] tells us:

In education contexts, speaking audibly and without anxiety in another language is an enormous challenge for all but the most extrovert and intrepid students ... Reticence in speaking, particularly in the early stages, is a natural and very common phenomenon and may manifest itself as silence, minimal responses or extreme soft-spokenness (Tsui 1996). Mainstream interactions may also be inhibited by sociopsychological and in-group factors (Davison and Williams 2001). (Miller, 2004: 295–296)

These three adolescents grapple with the fear of embarrassing themselves in front of their classmates and what this means is that most of their efforts and resources are directed toward managing their anxieties about what to do should the teacher call upon them (Chapter 6). And therefore, their behaviors stand in stark contrast to that of Sha, whose relative lack of anxiety allows him to participate more fully in the class activities. Again, Miller's observations resonate here:

It seemed to me that 'knowing English' and 'being outgoing' were related to identity work at school. And (Miller, 2004: 301):

Yet, with limited English, the temptation to withdraw to the safety of one's language group must be great. (Miller, 2004: 301)

But in some of the more drastic cases, even withdrawing to 'one's language group' may not be enough. As in the case of Yan, only the seclusion of her home provides her with the sense of security she needs to practice reading aloud in English.

Asking the Teacher for Help

(23)
I: OK, now do you ask questions during English lesson?
S: Sometimes if I don't understand or if I want an idea.
. . .
I: Do you think asking questions will help in learning of English?
S: Of course, definitely. If you don't ask anything either it means you don't understand or you are doing something too simply. The thing is too simple, then you don't have to ask questions. You have to ask questions.

The fact that Sha and his friends enjoy learning English lessons also means that there is no fear of derision if he takes the initiative to ask the teacher questions. Notice how adamant he is that one should ask questions.

(24)
S: There have been certain occasions when like during Physics, lah, when the teacher is speaking, sometimes I don't really understand what she is saying, lah.
I: Why?
S: Because I mean the teacher she said herself that the English is not the first language, Chinese is. And she spoke, she was explaining it using a lot of Singlish, lah. I really didn't understand exactly what she was saying.
I: What do you do then? Do you ask?
S: I asked her to repeat, lah, but I asked like 'Can you write it down on the board?' I didn't openly ask her to repeat it properly?
I: Why?
S: Because I didn't want to embarrass her in class or something.

There is some irony to the fact that on the occasions when Sha does not ask questions, it is not because he is worried about being embarrassed. Rather, he is worried about embarrassing others whose English he feels is not quite up to scratch. For example (24), during the Physics class, he tries to not ask

the teacher questions in order to avoid embarrassing her because he thinks
her English is not as good as his.

Against Code-Switching in Off-Site Arenas

Finally, unlike Edwin, Wen and Yan, who code-switch with their peers
during group work, Sha is insistent that the group sticks to English and only
English as far as possible.

(25)

S: Planning ... Planning for composition today is very easy a group work
for me, lah. I just sit there. Sometimes the teacher asks us to plan a
compo for so many subjects. I just tell them which subject I will try
... I will just give them many ideas for any subject. Then I will tell
them your turn, lah. You give me ideas.

I: So you are usually the one contributing?

S: Yah. But I will also try and ask them don't speak mother tongues, lah.
Speak English so I will understand.

I: OK, how do you feel when they do, when they speak mother tongue
there?

S: How I feel? Normally I will just tell them to speak English. I don't
understand, yah. Normally they will speak English. Sometimes they
speak mother tongue then I will ask them 'Wait, wait, wait, what is
the problem? What is the idea? Tell me the idea!' I want to know the
idea. Then they will just speak English from there always, lah.

Public Speaking

Recall that among our five previous informants, it was Ping who
expressed the greatest confidence in English, and who also claimed to be
good at public speaking, although we saw that she was hampered by her
inability to speak impromptu. It is therefore perhaps fitting that we end our
discussion of Sha with some remarks on his experience of public speaking.

(26)

I: In English. Ok, what sort of circumstances, when do you do public
speaking?

S: Sometime when the school opening ceremony, normally I am chosen
when they ask me to be the MC, then I have to public speaking lah.

I: Ok, who ... who is your audience? How big is the audience?

S: Sometimes it's the whole school, sometimes there is a parents around. Sometimes there is a lot of important people. But most of time it's just the school lah, school and teachers.

As (26) indicates, Sha is 'normally chosen' to emcee a school event. Being 'normally chosen' suggests that he is widely recognized by his teachers as being a good public speaker.

(27)
S: Normally I speak from a script lah. So whatever they write I have to speak about. But normally I will just invite the guest of honor on stage for prize giving or something. But there are certain certain circumstances when I have to speak about the topic, like in Sec one they have the plain English speaking contact then I normally speak what I think most people will like to hear ... I personally like to talk about.

Being an emcee means, of course, that Sha cannot always rely on a prepared script. So, while a script is usually available, the vagaries of stage events mean that he needs to have the presence of mind as well as the concomitant linguistic skills to be able to improvise should the situation call for it.

(28)
I: Do you think that ... is there anything you can do to improve to make sure you are an effective speaker, impromptu speaker?
S: Read more books on impromptu speaking. Speak ... speak without ... when I actually do public speaking try not to follow exactly what the script say. Try and memorize only the main points and work around them.
I: Has that proved to be effective?
S: On certain occasions it was like the opening ceremony, I didn't use exactly the entire script that was given to me. Cause I need to go back and forth. I ask her a question and she answers. She asks me a question. So normally I will just put the ... a point in a question then I ask her then for the answer basically I will just leave it up to the impromptu. I never have the written answer down.

Like Ping, then, Sha understandably feels more at ease when he does not actually have to depart from a script. But unlike Ping, who was unable to cope with any need to improvise, Sha is more confident in comparison. He does in fact make a conscious effort to not follow the script exactly, and he also tries to improve his language skills by reading about impromptu speaking.

Miller (2004) provides some similar observations in her description of experiences of two girls, Alicia and Nora, who were both asked to give oral presentations. According to Miller:

> The doing of 'orals' raised several issues for Nora and Alicia. They were, as Nora described, 'critical moments' in a number of senses. They entailed the stress of standing very visibly in front of the class, being observed and listened to in a way that was unfamiliar, by class members who, due to limited interaction within and outside the class, were also unfamiliar. There were judgments made on what was heard, and presumably on what was inaudible, informally by students, and formally by the teacher. Finally, the accepted practice of doing orals incorporated a full written script, and, often, when students used palm cards, the cards basically contained every word of the talk. (Miller, 2004: 306–307)

Here, we see again how all-too-common is it that oral presentations are understood as little more than the oral recitation of a written script. The emphasis then is on memory work and perfect delivery rather than on the ability to interact and respond in a more improvised and naturalistic manner. Seen in this light, Sha's willingness to deliberately grapple with the challenges posed by impromptu deliveries emerges as relatively rare and admirable.

The pedagogical challenge here, then, is to 'transform learning activities, such as oral presentations, into experiences which take into account these students' identities' and would have to include 'rethinking the oral presentation as a contextualized spoken performance, rather than a formal speech which had to be drafted in entirety' (Miller, 2004: 307).

Conclusion

As we have already noted, identity work in the form of style involves the element of bricolage, so that different individuals, while undoubtedly drawing upon features and values associated with large-scale social categories, also to a significant degree assemble these features in ways that reflect more localized pressures and constraints, such as the desire to satisfy norms associated with particular peer groups. This means that different individuals tend to approach literacy practices in different ways, ways that are undeniably traceable to larger sociocultural values, but only indirectly so. For example, we have seen that reading aloud in class clearly constitutes a specific literacy event. However, what is at one level the same event is obviously viewed differently by our individual student informants. In particular, Sha enjoys the opportunity to read aloud while the others (Edwin, Yan and Wen) clearly dread it. Construed more broadly as forms of practice, we might be tempted to directly link their different attitudes toward reading aloud to their occupation of various large-scale categories such as teenager, male/female, Chinese/Malay/Indian and so on. However, this would obscure the mediating effects of their peers, effects that are comparatively more subtle in nature, but certainly no less real.

For Sha and his friends, reading aloud among themselves is also treated as an enjoyable social activity and thus constitutes an acceptable social practice within their group. In contrast, no such out-of-class analog exists for the other three students. Thus, the notion of literacy practice allows us to reflect the fact that for Sha, reading aloud both in class and among friends are activities that allows him to engage in the kind of identity work that both he and his friends value. For example, it is clear that Sha sees himself as someone who speaks English well and who enjoys displaying his language skills. This display of language skills, especially with his friends, allows him and his friends to gain symbolic capital from each other by enjoying a high degree of peer approval or recognition. And this is something that Ping, Fandi, Edwin, Yan and Wen feel compelled to avoid doing *for the very same reason*. That is, with the others, peer approval is dependent on *not* displaying a proficiency in English.

The observations in this and the preceding two chapters give us a good sense of how the concern with identity work, especially, identity work that is motivated by peer evaluation, can affect students' English language literacy practices. In the course of the discussion, we have also noted the various challenges such identity work poses for English language teaching. In the next chapter, we will attempt to suggest a pedagogical response to these challenges.

Notes

(1) We point out that the use of the metadiscursive label 'Standard English' is Sha's own. This self-ascription of what kind of English is spoken in Sha's household may admittedly still show some divergences from what might be considered standard English in other linguistic markets (cf. Blommaert, 2003). But be that as it may, more significant from an ethnographic perspective is that the choice of this label is intended to mark a distinction between what he thinks is the kind of English his own family uses, and what he considers to be the kind of English spoken by most other Singaporeans. As we pointed out above, this indicates Sha's appreciation of a difference in social class.

(2) Again, this indicates Sha's own awareness that he belongs to a rather different social class when compared to many of his friends. This is by no means atypical. Wee (2005), for example, points out that Colin Goh – a strong defender of Singlish, but also a highly educated individual who is very competent in standard English – occasionally

refers to the Singlish that he supports as 'broken English'. And as we have already noted (Chapter 2), the use of Singlish is one of the linguistic means by which Singaporeans attempt to neutralize class differences. Such uses of Singlish, undoubtedly intended as sincere attempts at creating a sense of solidarity across social divides, are reminiscent of what Bourdieu (1991) refers to as a strategy of condescension. As Bourdieu remarks:

Such a strategy is possible whenever the objective disparity between the persons present (that is, between their social properties) is sufficiently known and recognized by everyone (particularly those involved in the interaction, as agents or spectators) so that the symbolic negation of the hierarchy (by using the 'common touch', for instance) enables the speaker to combine the profits linked to the undiminished hierarchy with those derived from the distinctly symbolic negation of the hierarchy – not the least of which is the strengthening of the hierarchy implied by the recognition accorded to the way of using the hierarchical relation. (Bourdieu, 1991: 68)

In other words, someone like Sha can use Singlish as a means of 'negating the hierarchy' only because it is understood that he is not limited to using Singlish, but instead has the capacity to use a more standard form of English. The so-called monolingual speakers of Singlish – that is, those speakers who are construed as not having any significant command of the standard variety but who are 'forced' to use Singlish because that is the only kind of English they possess – would not be able to reap the symbolic profits accruing to a strategy of condescension for the simple reason that their use of Singlish stems not from a matter of choice, but from the lack of any choice. And perhaps more importantly, as Bourdieu points out, when speakers engage in strategies of condescension, the effect is not to undermine or negate the indexical ranking of linguistic varieties. Rather, it merely serves to reinforce or strengthen the prevailing indexical order.

(3) Miller (2004) is describing her observations of how migrant students are attempting to adapt to life in Australia. For these students, the difficulty arises from them being positioned as ESL students in contexts where other students are 'native speakers' of English. Moreover, these migrant students oftentimes find themselves the victims of racial slurs (Miller, 2004: 293). While students like Edwin, Yan and Wen are clearly not migrants, their difficulties with the English language are nonetheless similar to those faced by the students described by Miller (2004).

8 Pedagogy, Literacy and Identity[1]

In this book, we have emphasized how the literacy practices of individuals can be tied to macrosocial structures and the political economy of Singapore. We have seen in Chapter 2, for example, that despite the government's intention to promote the equal status of both English and the officially assigned mother tongue, it is English that acquires a higher value and status. As a consequence of this, multilingualism in Singapore is very dominated by the hegemony of the English language, and young adolescents are left having to grapple with the tensions that arise when their multilingual practices are in conflict with the indexical orders associated with the broader political economy. These conflicts were described in greater detail in Chapters 5 through 7, where we saw how the different expectations and influences of the home and the peer group can significantly impact on English language literacy practices in the classroom. In particular, choices about how and whether to participate in the activities organized within the language classroom were intimately bound up with the adolescents' considerations of the consequences these choices might have for identity work.

In line with these insights, we want to suggest, in this penultimate chapter, that policies for language education – and English language literacy in particular – must be formulated against a reexamination of prevalent assumptions about the nature of literacy. Our discussion of this issue of language education policy and its grounding in assumptions about literacy also leads us to touch on the more general question of what literacy studies can offer to sociolinguistics in general and *vice versa*. We then close by offering some pedagogical strategies that we think can be usefully brought to bear on the question of how language and literacy teaching can be conducted in ways that do not force students to compromise peer-oriented identities that they might heavily value.

Two Approaches to Language Education

It is well known that language plays a gate-keeping role in society, such that knowledge of particular varieties can provide individuals with access to social and economic goods while conversely, lack of such knowledge leads to the denial of such access. In light of this situation, responses to the gate-keeping role of language can be classed into two broad strategies. The first strategy is to argue that the hitherto 'powerless varieties' ought to be used in prestige domains (Phillipson & Skutnabb-Kangas, 1995). The second, essentially a converse of the first, is to argue that the 'power varieties' ought to be made more accessible to larger segments of society (Corson, 2001: 106). Both these approaches, though, face a number of problems.

As regards the first approach, calling for the use of powerless varieties in prestige domains such as education is a key aspect of what is sometimes referred to as the Linguistic Human Rights (LHRs) paradigm (Phillipson & Skutnabb-Kangas, 1995; Skutnabb-Kangas, 2000), which is especially concerned to ensure that speakers of minority languages are not penalized because of language barriers. Phillipson and Skutnabb-Kangas (1995: 483), for example, call for minority groups to be educated through the medium of their various mother tongues. While this may go some way toward providing speakers who lack knowledge of the power varieties with at least some wider form of participation in society, it needs to come to terms with the fact that there are built-in limitations. At some point, it becomes unrealistic, if not impossible, to participate in particular socioeconomic activities without knowledge of the relevant power varieties that have become the lingua franca by which these activities are conducted. Fishman (1989: 233) refers to such power varieties as languages of wider communication (LWCs) and notes that it is the spread of English, more so than any other LWC, which raises a number of problems for the status of various indigenous languages (see also Phillipson, 1992). But there are in fact more serious problems for the LHRs paradigm.

The notion of LHRs presupposes the existence of a 'language community' since it assumes that the promotion of the mother tongue is the best way to ensure the protection of speakers' socioeconomic interests. But if we are interested in the socioeconomic conditions of speakers, it is the 'speech community' that we should be concerned with instead. The distinction between these two notions of how community and language are connected is critical. Whereas the notion of a language community assumes that it is unproblematic to treat the interactions as revolving around an easily demarcatable and definable named linguistic variety, the notion of a speech community is more sensitively geared toward recognizing that interactions

– even among those who are putatively members of the same community – may be quite heterogeneous. As Silverstein points out:

> This [i.e. language community: CS & LW] contrasts with a "speech community", a much more general term. This term indicates that there are perduring, presupposable regularities of discursive interaction in a group or population. When we can recognize an implicit normativity to such indexical semiosis as informs and underlies communicative acts of identity and groupness, we have a speech community. Denotational function – and the degree of successful denotational communication – is not here to the point. Speech communities, even more than language communities, are highly variable in manner and degree of stability and extent over populations, times, institutional formations, places, and other determinants.
>
> ... speech communities are frequently plurilingual, that is, they encompass speakers who belong to more than one language community ... (Silverstein, 1998: 407)

Confusing language and speech communities (see Wee, 2005) leads to the belief that 'native speakers will maintain or preserve their cultures if they continue speaking their language' but this ignores 'the fact that in the first place they would not stop speaking it if they valued its association with their ancestral culture over their necessary adaptation to the current world order – a simple matter of prioritising things in their struggle for survival' (Mufwene, 2002: 23). In short, the gate-keeping role of language requires speakers to make choices about what languages to keep and what languages to give up, depending on what they consider to be important or relevant to them as individuals, to their communities, or to the kinds of futures they envision for their children. This is not to blithely assume that such choices are easily made, but neither should we assume that it is somehow intrinsically 'wrong' or an automatic violation of language rights if speakers do decide to shift away from a language that they have been historically affiliated with.

But perhaps what is of greatest relevance to the arguments being developed in this book is that the LHRs paradigm fails to give proper recognition to the fluid nature of identities, assuming instead that identities can be unproblematically linked to particular languages and ethnic groups and in the process, eliding the heterogeneous nature of such groups (May, 2001: 8). The result is that the LHRs paradigm may serve to aggravate rather than alleviate social discrimination. For example, Stroud (2001: 346–347) argues that by singling out specific 'minority' languages for special treatment, LHRs are 'potentially discriminatory and socially divisive' as claims to limited resources are being argued for along ethnolinguistic lines. Instead, Stroud suggests that it is more useful to appreciate 'the situation where speakers themselves exercise control over their language, deciding *what* languages are, and what they may *mean*' (Stroud, 2001: 353, italics in original). This point is reinforced by Stroud, who emphasizes the need for careful ethnographic and historiographic work to better appreciate 'the specific ways in which power and language are interrelated in historically and culturally distinct speech communities' (Stroud, 2002: 250).

The other approach, as a means of mitigating the gate-keeping role of language, aims instead to make the power varieties more widely accessible. Here, the goal is to ensure that an LWC is 'wide' not merely because it is used across a broad number of domains, but also because it is being made available to people of divergent socioeconomic and sociocultural backgrounds. The problem faced by this approach is a slightly different one. The relevant question here is the extent to which, as a language comes to be used by people of diverse backgrounds, these different users can all be said to have equal say or control over the use of the language. Perhaps the most systematic attempt to deal with this problem, at least as far as educational linguistics is concerned, comes from the 'genre approach' (Cope & Kalantzis, 1993), which stresses the need to provide explicit instruction in the kinds of linguistic structures that are considered necessary for gaining access to dominant cultures and economies. A comprehensive critique of this approach, however, can be found in Luke (1997), who points out that the genre approach unfortunately tends to 'separate ideology from function ... and thereby to represent particular genres as principally geared for doing intellectual work, rather than as *always* sites for the contestation of difference' (Luke, 1997: 318, italics in original). In other words, the genre approach treats genres as *forms of technology*, that is, they are understood to exist independently of particular individuals, and they (so the promise goes) can be acquired by just about anyone who undergoes the requisite training. Thus, Luke argues that '[w]ithout reconsidering its own social and cultural consequences, genre teaching runs the risk of becoming an institutional technology principally engaged in self-reproduction of the status and privilege of a particular field of disciplinary knowledge, rather than part of a broadly based political project for remaking the institutional distribution of literacy and its affiliated forms of capital' (Luke, 1997: 334).[2] In other words, the genre approach fails to seriously consider the situatedness of knowledge, that what appears to be 'the same' kind of knowledge can in fact be differently valued depending on the source of that knowledge. This is particularly the case with knowledge pertaining to language proficiency since the conventions of language use – including genre conventions – are ultimately impossible to specify explicitly or exhaustively, owing mainly to the fact that such conventions are constantly evolving. This means that at any particular moment, considerations of what counts as 'appropriate', 'proficient' or even 'grammatical' are all intersubjectively negotiated between producer and recipient. Here, the issue of power comes to the fore since the outcomes of such negotiations, that is, the ability to *define* a particular linguistic product as 'good' or 'bad' is often a function of the status and roles that various producers/recipients bring to the interaction.

But even if we put these criticisms of the LHRs paradigm and the genre approach aside, it is worth noting that neither of these proposals is capable of addressing the challenges posed by the issue of identity work among adolescents. Such identity work may involve ethnic identities but it also need not. Concerns with identity work may instead be class-based, such that gender and ethnicity are more accurately construed as ancillary identity markers. And even in cases where ethnic identity becomes foregrounded, it is important to note that the issue can sometimes be one of 'new ethnicities' (Back, 1996; Cohen, 1999), where by definition, the identities being indexed are often hybridized and emergent ones. New ethnicities are typically 'sites of cultural crossings, thresholds that young people move across as they carry on with their cultural business' (Bucholtz, 2002) and identities based on such hybrid or liminal considerations therefore cannot be easily reconciled with the essentializing stance toward identity that is adopted by LHRs proponents. In the case of the genre approach, this seems to take for granted that adolescents are already motivated to acquire the dominant linguistic structures. As a consequence, the overriding concern here is how to make these dominant linguistic structures accessible to the otherwise disprivileged adolescents. But as we have already seen in the preceding chapters, these adolescents are actually often put in positions of conflict. For example, in the classroom, adolescents may be torn between the need to observe the rules regulating the on-floor activities that take place under the authority of the teacher, and the desire to cater to the norms characterizing the off-site interactions that are governed by their peers (Canagarajah, 2004a). So, a more fundamental issue needs to be tackled right at the outset, and this concerns the reevaluation of assumptions about literacy, and seeing it as part of a broader matrix of socialization into communicative practices that cannot be easily disengaged from notions of performance and identity.

Assumptions about Literacy

Both the LHRs and genre approaches rather unfortunately 'reify literacy as an end product of instruction (i.e. a generic measurable outcome in terms of knowledge or skills) instead of as a variable set of processes contingent on textual, cognitive and social factors' (Kern, 2000: 3). That is, both approaches assume the existence of a delimited and ontologically stable entity (a named variety of language in the case of the first and a collection of linguistic structures in the case of the second) that, having been identified by, among others, educational authorities, can then be transplanted from an earlier set of contexts to future contexts that the learners might be expected to be involved in. This kind of assumption treats literacy skills as decontexualized products. And as Kern points out:

> Consequently, educators' efforts are oriented towards defining boundary lines of acceptable normative standards and a search for what might constitute a minimum criterion level. How well must learners read and write (in general) to be considered functional? How many novels must one read, how many cultural 'facts' must one absorb, to be deemed (culturally) literate? (Kern, 2000: 3–4)

This view of literacy recalls Street's (1984) description of an autonomous model of literacy in contrast to that of an ideological model (see also Chapter 1). The latter recognizes literacy as a series of sociocultural practices whose legitimacy and value are ultimately always relativized to changing contexts of power. As a consequence, once literacy is understood to be ideological, there follows an urgent need to appreciate 'how those ideological effects actually are used and deployed to shape capital, social relations and forms of identity, access to material and discourse resources' (Luke, 2004: 333). In this regard, Kern usefully provides the following definition of what he describes as a 'sociocognitive view of literacy':

> Literacy is the use of socially-, historically-, and culturally-situated practices of creating and interpreting meaning through texts. *It entails at least a tacit awareness of the relationships between textual conventions and their contexts of use and, ideally, the ability to reflect critically on those relationships.* Because it is purpose-sensitive, literacy is dynamic – not static – and variable across and within discourse communities and cultures. It draws on a wide range of cognitive abilities, on knowledge of written and spoken language, on knowledge of genres, and on cultural knowledge. (Kern, 2000: 16, emphasis added)

This definition importantly draws our attention to the situated and because of this, dynamic nature of literacy practices. More pertinently, given our discussion of the various adolescents in the earlier chapters, it needs to be emphasized that successfully literate individuals are those who have, in Kern's words, 'at least a tacit awareness of the relationships between textual conventions and their contexts of use' as well as 'the ability to reflect critically on those relationships'. Among our six adolescents discussed, Sha, of course, best represents the individual most successfully literate in English. And we have already seen abundant evidence that Sha is distinguished from the other five adolescents by his ability and indeed willingness to critically reflect how conventions of language can be connected to varying contexts. But in addition to this, as we have also seen, Sha is perfectly at ease when engaging in language performances, whether these be highly conscious and deliberate, or whether they be more naturalistic and mundane. Sha's relative ease with language performances and the concomitant reflexive awareness that this ease helps to cultivate is in no small part attributable to his sense of himself as the very kind of person for whom such performances are acceptable activities. In turn, this social acceptability is traceable to the reactions of his family and friends.

But here we come to an important question about language education policy, which still tends to construe the teaching of English as the teaching of a language whose final authority on what should be considered grammatical, standard or even interactionally appropriate still rests with the traditional native speaker, with all the consequences for the identity investments of the students that this entails. However, as has been pointed out by various scholars (Jenkins, 2000; Widdowson, 1994), the English language occupies a rather different status than a foreign language. Unlike, say, learning Italian in order to interact with traditional native speakers of Italian, learners of English are just as likely – if not more so – to be interacting with nontraditional speakers, that is, speakers from what Kachru (1985, 1986, 1991) has been described as the Outer and Expanding Circle of countries. Combining this observation with our own observations about Sha and the other adolescents, it seems clear that a successful policy for cultivating English language literacy needs to be one that is willing to embrace, or at least allow, for the possibility that these learners could come to see themselves as nontraditional native speakers of English – but native speakers nonetheless. This insight means that Singapore's language policy thus needs to appreciate that patterns of multilingualism are increasingly constructed around the dynamics of language choice and change informed by a logic of life-style consumption and mobility (Stroud & Wee, 2007). However, this type of multilingual dynamics runs the risk of giving rise to difficult social inequities, as speakers will not all have equal access to valued linguistic capital. Especially because it is widely recognized that differential levels of literacy in English can be highly consequential for the socioeconomic trajectories of speakers and in turn, if this is not managed carefully, can lead to the entrenchment of systemic social inequality, one of the major challenges for education policy is to broaden the remit of English language education.

In the following chapter, we introduce a notion of *linguistic citizenship* that we feel better addresses ramifications for language policy of the complex and contingent relationship between language and identity and the plurality of public voices and positions of subjectivity that find variable semiotic expression in speakers' choice of language and language variety. Here, we suggest that the concerns we have raised with respect to language education in a wider policy context can be approached through a language pedagogical focus that takes the notion of voice (Bakhtin, 1981; Jakobson, 1980;) as a central point of departure, rather than the idea of 'language' as system and structure. Voice is fundamentally about who says what in which way to whom. It is situationally, socially and institutionally determined, and is indicative of the ideological and institutional position of the speaker. Canagarajah (2004b) sees voice as 'the manifestation of one's agency in discourse through the means of language'. Bakhtin (1981) relates the definition of voice to the notion of heteroglossia, 'the co-existing, contextually and functionally determined varieties of linguistic forms in a language', emphasizing that:

No voice is single – voice is always plural and multiple, and bears the traces of other times and other places: Every word is entangled, shot through with shared thoughts, points of view, alien value judgements and accents, weaves in and out of complex interrelationships, merges with some, recoils from others ... and having taken meaning and shape at a particular historical moment in a socially specific environment, cannot fail to brush up against thousands of living dialogic threads. (Bakhtin, 1982: 276 quoted in Blackledge & Creese, 2009: 570)

Voice is highly commensurate with the idea of linguistic citizenship. Just as importantly, it also provides a heuristic with which to understand the complex dynamics of classrooms, especially how everyday, situated and local interactions are simultaneously enacting features of the larger sociopolitical and historical framing context. Blackledge and Creese note how in the classrooms they studied 'children and adults alike frequently made meaning through representing other voices within their own voices' (Blackledge & Creese, 2009: 124). And Bailey argues for how a Bakhtinian perspective is 'fundamentally about intertextuality, the ways that talk in the here-and-now draw meanings from past instances of talk' (Bailey, 2007: 269).

Voice can articulate with formal aspects of language in various ways. An important notion is *genre* or *register* (Agha, 2003, 2007), on the one hand, and the recent, extended, idea of *repertoire* (Blommaert & Backus, 2011), on the other. Genre/register is the 'distinctive forms of language, speech and non-linguistic semiosis associated by users with differentiating typifications of person, situation, relationship, behaviour used as a normal part of social inter-action' (Agha, 2007: 186). An important feature of register is that there is a reflexive, metapragmatic awareness among producers and receivers of linguis-tic form and its indexical and social meanings. Register (style or genre) orga-nizes multilingual (and multimodal) resources into complexes of functions and forms that encode communicative events recognizable by community members as conventional performances of a particular type of communicative act (Briggs & Bauman, 1992; Blommaert, 2008). It sets up a particular set of expectations among interlocutors as to the topic/form, attitudinal stance, and interactional roles appropriate to a given speech event, and thus serves to orientate interlocutors to the production, reception and evaluation of dis-courses. Registers articulate the social, ideological, historical, political and economic aspects of context beyond any single instance of reception and pro-duction (Bakhtin, 1986; French, 2000: 160), allowing for the performance of different subject positions, or voices. The way that registers are executed may be subject to evaluation by others in respect of ideologies of competence/ expertise, allegiance or authenticity (Park & Wee, 2009). Competence refers to 'linguistic fluency or proficiency according to specific sets of linguistic cri-teria'; authenticity refers to 'the perception that a speaker bears particular racial, ethnic, or other background attributes and allegiance relates to how choice of language may be seen as implying an attitude of loyalty toward the social group associated with the language' (Park & Wee, 2009: 196).

The notion of *repertoire* was originally coined in (modernist) sociolinguis-tics (Hymes, 1972) to refer to 'the totality of distinct language varieties, dialects and styles employed in a community'. It has recently undergone a renaissance (Blommaert, 2010; Blommaert & Backus, 2011) in the context of studies of language in contexts of superdiversity, where it is taken to refer to the 'biographically organized complexes of resources ... that follow the rythms of human lives' (Blommaert & Backus, 2011: 9). Repertoires can be understood as involving knowledge of genres and styles, how they are mani-fested formally and the attendant subjectivities associated with them (Blommaert & Backus, 2011: 9), and serve as 'records of mobility: of move-ments of people, language resources, social arenas, technologies of learning and learning environments' (Blommaert & Backus, 2011: 22). A repertoire, or multilingual portfolio, actually comprises a 'patchwork of competence and skills' (Blommaert & Backus, 2011: 2), as different types of exposure to, and modes of learning, different languages result in different distributions of forms and functions across languages.[3]

These notions suggest an overarching approach to language pedagogy built around an understanding of how the adolescents construct their voice and subjectivity across a range of genres, registers and languages, that is, how meanings are made and transported across languages (and other forms of multimodal semiosis) in multilingual repertoires. Makoni and Pennycook (2007: 36) have also argued for a language policy in education which focuses on *translingual* language practices, as has more recently Garçia, who points to the need for pedagogical practices 'firmly rooted in the multilingual and multimodal language and literacy practices of children in schools in the 21st century' (Garçia, 2009: 8). Likewise, Blackledge and Creese advocate 'teaching bilingual children by means of a bilingual pedagogy', and argue for a 'a release from monolingual instructional approaches' (Blackledge & Creese, 2010: 201). In this context, *translanguaging* and resemiotization are two notions that could provide a way forward. *Translanguaging*, a term taken up by Garçia (originally from Cen Williams) refers to 'the act performed by bilinguals of accessing different linguistic features or various modes of what are described as autonomous languages' (Garçia, 2009: 141) that 'goes beyond what has been termed code-switching' and includes hybrid language use, that is, a 'systematic strategic, affiliative and sense-making process' (Gutiérrez *et al.*, 2001: 128). *Resemiotization* is about how meaning shifts from context to context, from practice to practice, or from one stage of a practice to the next (Iedema, 2003: 41). These notions share with other like concepts such as, for example, *crossing* (Rampton, 2006), *transcontextualization* (Cowan, 2005, 2008) and *transculture repositionings* (Richardson-Bruna, 2007), an appreciation of the significance of the (language/code) boundary for a creative and constructive negotiation of meaning, and an understanding of the critical multivocality of young people in the semiotic repositioning of themselves through movement between a known language and the target language. As they exploit this movement, pupils simultaneously forge new subjectivities in aligning, or rejecting, cultural and institutional voices and those of their peer group and their self-image. As Blackledge and Creese (2009) phrase it, this type of approach is tantamount to putting emphasis on the *user* rather than the code or language (Rampton, 2006), 'moving away from an emphasis on language and their different codes towards an account which describes the individual engaged in meaning making and identity work' (Blackledge & Creese, 2009: 555).

The classroom is reconstituted, in other words, as an arena for the negotiation of difference and commonality, rather than the assumption or imposition of commonality of speech norms (in language speech norms or identity), which means that English would be taught as one semiotic means in a plurilingual, heteroglossic context with attention to other languages, varieties, and voices. In other words, from a narrow concern with prescribing grammatical rules or even generic structures of communication, the English language teacher must instead address the complex web of intercultural, linguistic and political issues with which the language has become associated. As Gee points out:

> The English teacher can cooperate in her own marginalization by seeing herself as 'a language teacher' with no connection to ... social and political issues. Or she can accept the paradox of literacy as a form of interethnic communication which often involves conflicts of values and identities, and accept her role as one who socializes students into a world view that, given its power here and abroad, must be viewed critically, comparatively, and with a constant sense of the possibilities of change. Like it or not, the English teacher stands at the very heart of the most crucial educational, cultural and political issues of our time. (Gee, 1990: 67–68, in Kern, 2000: 316)

One possible way in which this can be achieved is by having English language teachers encourage learners to approach both the texts they encounter and their own uses of language with questions such as: What voice are the texts assuming? What positions? What resemiotizations or rewritings has the text gone through? For what purposes? As Kramsch emphasizes:

> These questions have no right or wrong answers, only plausible responses based on the historical and social context ... [And] Bringing back an historical dimension into the concept of communicative competence, and a dialogic dimension into the concept of textual competence could better prepare learners of English for the challenges of the global age. It would make learners conscious of a speaker's subject position, his/her history, status and interests ... [and] instill in learners a salutary circumspection vis-à-vis language. (Kramsch, 2007: 67–68)

This kind of approach means adopting a performance perspective, since learners are encouraged to examine how others use language and the assumptions undergirding these uses, as well as their own, and offer these evaluations of use for public critique and scrutiny (Wee, 2008). At the very least, it requires increasing the language awareness of teachers and, in particular, how such awareness can be fruitfully brought to bear on issues in language education (James & Garrett, 1991). But one immediate challenge with language awareness is the question what it actually means to be aware of language. At one level, many teachers still need to be better trained in linguistics (Brumfit, 1991). At another level, however, there is the question of what actually goes into such training. According to Mitchell and Hooper, there is still:

... a strong tendency to equate KAL [knowledge about language: CS and LW] with morpho-syntactic knowledge of a traditional kind, centered on the written language system ...

[missing] were some key topics in contemporary 'expert' models of language ... notably, the structure of discourse beyond the level of the individual sentence, the spoken language in all its aspects, and first/second language acquisition and development. (Mitchell & Hooper, 1991: 49)

So, it would seem that what counts as language awareness is still highly conservative in orientation, and perhaps more significantly, even if discourse and spoken language were to be included, this still leaves untouched the more 'radical' issues of language use as performance, the importance of attending to style and identity, and the willingness to explore how all these can and should be taken into consideration in the development of appropriate pedagogical strategies. From what we have said so far, teachers essentially need to become aware of, and to be able to feed into their classroom practices, a conceptualization of language learning as the attainment, appropriation, rejection, reformulation, parody, or echoing of multiple voices emanating from multiple historical, social, political and economic locations. Teachers need to be able to create the conditions that can support learners in performing and negotiating subjectivities and voices, and how these performances can be deployed as aids in learning the language. This, of course, must be preceded by the teachers gaining a better understanding of the worlds and subjectivities of their charges (Blackledge & Creese, 2009: 143). Teachers need to be aware that the socially fragmented world of pupils finds expression in multiple subjectivities and competing voices, and how a Bakhtinian perspective on classroom interaction can sensitize them to the multiple positions from which learners come, and into which they are inserted in mobile multilingual space. Shifting the pedagogical focus to the speaker and his/her voice rather than staying with formal aspects of language at whatever scale (morpho-syntax, discourse) would assist the teacher in engaging with Singaporean teenagers' concerns with identity that they bring to the classroom, and with the ways in which their constructions and representations of self in the classroom finds expression in rejection, incorporation and appropriation of formal aspects of the target language. Thus, teachers need to appreciate that working with formal aspects of language are very much about working through expressions of identity (as seen in the notion of register/genre).

An essential item of knowledge that teachers need to be in possession of is that metalinguistic reflexivity and its outcomes in terms of formal or stylistic expression is subject to 'keying' and the outcome of a keyed reflection is in turn subject to local interactional and ideological constraints. Ervin Goffman has discussed the notion of 'keying' in terms of moments of disengagement from 'the routine flow of unexceptional business', where 'activity is understood as somehow special, not to be taken straight or treated naively' (Goffman, 1974: chap. 3).

Thus, in all essentials, language awareness means awareness of language as heteroglossic, rather than monoglossic. It means taking a stance on the importance of the production and recognition of multiple voices as a way for pupils and teachers to engage with conflicts and competitions of identities. And it means understanding how conditions can be created for the productive exploration of language forms through keyed moments of metalinguistic reflexivity.

We have been emphasizing all along that any attempt to implement this performance perspective in the classroom has to be pedagogically sensitive to the obstacles that learners may face as they engage in enactments of language use. We have already observed that, among adolescents at least, the extent to which language performance is considered acceptable among peers can result in markedly disparate attitudes and degrees of success in the classroom. So, even though we have managed to identify the various elements that facilitate English language literacy, observing from our data how these elements are present or missing – all to varying degrees – across different individuals, and how their relative absences create obstacles to such literacy, this leaves us with the following pedagogical challenge: How can the language teacher actively attempt to create a pedagogical environment that maximizes the chances of individual students acquiring English language literacy? That is, how can the language teacher encourage a sense of ease with language performances while minimizing the possibility of individual students alienating their peers or drawing derision from the same?

In the next section, we explore one possible way of responding to this challenge.

Anxiety and Identity in the Language Classroom

Discussions of language learning have been concerned with sources of student anxiety, recognizing, quite rightly, that such anxiety can have a detrimental effect on language learning. Unfortunately, with few exceptions, it is generally assumed that student anxiety in the language classroom is *competence-based*. By this we mean that it is assumed that students become anxious because they are insecure about their language abilities, and because of this, are concerned about how their use of the target language will be evaluated by the teacher or by the target community of native speakers. Treating anxiety as competence-based is particularly common in theories of Second Language Acquisition. For example, Spolsky (1989: 115) suggests that 'there is a specific kind of anxiety that in the case of many learners interferes with second language learning', and Krashen's affective filter hypothesis (Krashen, 1981, 1982) treats a lack of self-confidence and anxiety as pertinent factors that contribute to poor language learning.

While we do not wish to downplay the reality and effect of competence-based anxiety, we think it is important to remember that in addition to competence-based anxiety, there is also *identity-based anxiety*, where an individual may be more concerned with maintaining his or her relationship with particular groups than with his or her language abilities. Such relationships are identity-based because 'identity references desire – the desire for recognition, the desire for affiliation and the desire for security and safety' (Norton, 2000: 8). A good example of identity-based anxiety, though not in a language education context, comes from Bourdieu (Thompson, 1991: 17–18), who notes various articulatory differences between the speech styles of working-class and upper/middle-class individuals in France, and points out that such differences index both social as well as sexual identities. Consequently, working-class males who wish to adopt the more prestigious styles of speech run the risk of appearing effeminate, a risk that is obviously not applicable to their female counterparts. Identity-based anxiety is thus motivated by a desire to maintain particular group relationships, such as acceptance by one's peers or a desire to avoid ridicule from them. It manifests itself in worries that particular uses of language – including language used in the classroom – may or may not jeopardize those relationships. In the previous section, we have suggested that a productive way of conceiving identity-based anxiety is in terms of the play of Bakhtinian voices, and we shall explore the implications this might carry for remediation in the classroom below. First, though, we provide some examples of identity-based anxiety.

Some Examples of Identity-based Anxiety

In the discussions of literacy practices among Singaporean teenagers that we presented in the preceding chapters, we have noted a strong orientation toward how they are perceived by their peers, and while this peer orientation understandably influences their choice of leisure activities, it also affects how they conduct themselves in the English language classroom. Classroom activities can be categorized as being either teacher-initiated or student-initiated. An example of a teacher-initiated activity would be the teacher's nomination of a particular student to read a text out loud, which is a common enough activity. As we have noted, because texts are read out loud, the teacher typically uses this activity to gauge students' ability to recognize and pronounce particular words. An example of a student-initiated activity might be a student's decision to begin an exchange with the teacher, perhaps with the goal of clarifying a part of the lesson that he or she does not understand (see Chapters 6 and 7 for details).

Recall that one of the Singaporean teenagers in our study, Edwin, describes his reaction to the teacher-initiated activity of reading out loud in terms of competence-based anxiety. Edwin indicates that he is 'not used to speaking out loud', and he feels 'shy and embarrassed' that he might make a mistake while reading. Because Edwin is concerned about making mistakes, this is clearly a case of competence-based anxiety. And to deal with this, it would help if the teacher were to find ways of assuring Edwin that mistakes are part of the learning process, for example, or for the teacher to allow Edwin more time for rehearsal, if this is what Edwin wants (see below for a discussion of such strategies for dealing with competence-based anxiety).

In contrast to Edwin's competence-based anxiety, his reluctance to initiate an exchange with his teacher can be understood in terms of identity-based anxiety. As we already observed, even when Edwin has problems understanding what is being said, he does not want to 'stand up and ask the teacher' because he might be accused by his classmates of being an 'attention-seeker'. In such a case, it does not matter how friendly, understanding or approachable the teacher might be; it is not the teacher, but Edwin's peers that provide the source of the anxiety. And as we suggest below, dealing with this identity-based anxiety calls for a different approach to language teaching.

Edwin's concern with the opinion of his peers and how it affects his participation in the classroom are mirrored in Shamim's (1996) study of an English language class in Pakistan. Shamim observes that students who sit at the back of class are under great pressure from their peers not to appear too hardworking:

It seems that only a few students who sit in the back have the necessary willpower and determination to move into the action zone [the front: CS & LW] in the face of all the odds, *including pressure from their peers*. But once they are successful in gaining membership to the front zone, they automatically gain access to other privileges, such as increased attention from the teacher. Although a few students manage to move from the back to the front of the classroom, it was found in this study that the location of the students generally remains stable during the course of an academic year. (Shamim, 1996: 140, italics added)

Thus, Shamim's study suggests two things. One, it is possible for the desire for peer acceptance to detrimentally affect language learning. Two, because such peer groupings or cliques are relatively stable, most students find it difficult to break away and so identity-based anxiety can continue to affect a student not just occasionally, but it can in fact become a significantly pervasive aspect of their experience of classroom culture.

Yet another interesting example of identity-based anxiety comes from Allwright and Bailey (1991), who note that there are cases where even very competent learners deliberately make mistakes. They do so because they do not wish to stand out from, and be resented by, their peers. In such cases, worries over how the teacher might evaluate their language abilities (which is competence-based) are overridden by worries over how their peers might perceive them (which is identity-based) (for more recent research on identity-based anxiety, see, for example, Goldstein, 2003).

Implications for Language Teaching

Looking at anxiety from an identity-based, rather than competence-based, perspective sheds a different light on student behavior in the classroom. As we have seen, with competence-based anxiety, it is the teacher whose evaluations (about students' language competence) matter, which means that the teacher can more easily take steps to assuage students' worries over how they are being evaluated. But if the teacher is no longer the source of the anxiety, as with identity-based anxiety, it becomes much more difficult to find ways of reassuring the students, raising different considerations when it comes to the issue of developing appropriate pedagogical strategies.

For example, Hilleson (1996: 271) proposes dealing with student anxiety by having a skills study workshop where teachers can help the students to 'recognize their own anxieties as irrational and unproductive'. He also considers the use of role play and drama, suggesting that 'performing the works of others, *thoroughly rehearsed* in terms of both verbal and non-verbal language' will allow students to experience less 'communication anxiety' (Hilleson, 1996: 272, italics added).

It is clear that the strategies proposed by Hilleson are more useful if one is dealing with competence-based anxiety, since they assume that the teacher and the classroom activities conducted by the teacher are the main sources of anxiety. As Hilleson puts it, these strategies are intended to help teachers find ways to 'protect students from demotivating experiences' (Hilleson, 1996: 272). Thus, if the teacher is the source of anxiety, then it helps having the teacher assure students that their anxieties are irrational. And it might also help if students are given the opportunity by the teacher to 'thoroughly rehearse' their language use.

However, identity-based anxiety is different. Since it is the opinion of the student's peers that matters, assurances from the teacher that the student's anxiety is irrational hold no water. And opportunities for rehearsal do not help since, as we saw above, even highly competent students will deliberately underperform if they think this will spare them ridicule.

Identity-based anxiety means that we need to ask how language teaching can be conducted in ways that do not threaten students' relationships with their peers. If students feel that being a good language learner might actually compromise their acceptance among their peers, then they may act in order to preserve that acceptance, even if this means jeopardizing their ability to learn the language. One suggestion is to approach this problem from the pedagogical vantage point of Bakhtinian voice that we introduced above. In fact, from the perspective of how pupils negotiate multiple voices, identity anxiety can be seen as the constructive, dialogic engagement of pupils' multilayered subjectivities with the authoritative voice of the teacher, on the one hand, and the monitoring and parodying voice of peers, on the other. Constructively engaging with different voices, including that of silence, is a way for pupils to 'counteract[ing] the alienating effects of the teacher's authoritative discourse' (Luk, 2008: 127, cited in Blackledge & Creese, 2009: 134), and taking up 'mock-ESL positions' (Blackledge & Creese, 2010), in an attempt to 'populate traditional discourse with their own local social languages and voices for their own purposes' (Lin & Luk, 2005: 89). Such purposes may include parodying the voice of the teacher and seeking alignment with the voices of the peer group – even though this may on occasion merely serve to reaffirm the authority of the educational establishment. Blackledge and Creese (2010) provide the case of how students in a complementary school Gujarati class insist in completing a language task in English despite the teacher's prompting that the task should be completed in Gujarati. They note how this practice could be seen as a way for the pupil to save face by 'disguising' their lack of proficiency in Gujarati, thus using their bilingualism as a style resource (Androutsopoulos, 2007) for identity performance to peers. Creese et al. (2006) detail how students in heritage classroom take on a 'freshie' voice that situates them as less proficient and more new than they are in reality, and Talmy (2004: 164) refers to 'linguicism at work' in the social practice of some pupils to publically tease and humble their classmates of lower L2 English proficiency (cited in Blackledge & Creese, 2009: 131), thereby stylizing the 'ethnic other' as less proficient, and thus endorsing their own proficiency. In other words, what we have been calling identity anxiety is negotiated against the complex collisions and creative deployment of ideological worlds, emplacement of subjectivities, and language learning where students introduce 'surreptitious layers of talk of their own initiation' to carve out their own subject position (Luk, 2008: 127, quoted in Blackledge & Creese, 2010: 134).

Stylization

A possible strategy for addressing identity-based anxiety comes from Rampton's (2002, 2006, 2011) discussion of *stylization*, which refers to a reflexive communicative action in which speakers produce specially marked and often exaggerated representations of languages, dialects accents, registers or styles that lie outside their habitual repertoire (with the caveat at least as this is *expected* within the situation at hand, our italics) (Agha, 2007: 187). Rampton notes how '[w]hen someone switches into a stylized voice or exaggerated accent, there is a partial and momentary disengagement from the routine flow of unexceptional business' (Rampton, 2006: 225). Stylization is relevant here because it refers to cases where adolescents deliberately adopt styles of language that need not 'directly' be associated with their identities, and because it a process where the speaker deliberately engages in modeling utterances and voices in focused practices of metalinguistic reflexivity. A key characteristic of stylization is that language use is typically seen to be playful or nonserious. For example, Rampton (2002) discusses a case where monolingual boys of Anglo and African Caribbean descent were invited by their Punjabi friends to either say things in Punjabi or respond to Punjabi questions. Crucially, as Rampton points out, '(t)hese invitations to use another language normally contained elements which lay just beyond the learner's grasp, and the fact that an important element of what was being said to the second-language learner was incomprehensible was crucial, generating a great deal of the entertainment' (Rampton, 2002: 520). Lin and Luk (2005: 86) demonstrate 'how students are able to resist the routines of regular classroom practice by populating prescribed utterances with playful, ironic accents' (Blackledge & Creese, 2009: 125). Thus, during stylization, learners are partaking of language practices associated with identities that they have no investment in, and because of this, learners also make no claims to competence; in fact, lack of competence may even be viewed positively since it is incomprehension that provides much of the entertainment. It is precisely because of this that adolescents can stylize without anxiety, whether it is competence-based or identity-based anxiety. We have also noted by way of reference to Goffman's notion of 'keying' that how, when and where styling occurs in utterances, and with what effects depends on a range of locally specific interactional and ideological factors, as 'metalinguistic reflexivity never takes place in an interactional vacuum' and 'whether and to what extent a person will develop new features [of style] will depend on the keying of the occasion in which they are made aware of them: the key will steer or constrain their responses' (Rampton, 2011: 36). Closely observing the type of stylization gives us an idea of the kinds of conditions under which students might be willing to adopt language styles that bear no relationship to identities that they are already invested in.

Some Pedagogical Possibilities

Van Lier (2008: 54; Blackledge & Creese, 2009: 202) has suggested that the teacher engage the learner in pedagogic actions with the goal of developing 'a wide panoramic view of self' in order that new identity positions associated with language learning may emerge. In the Singapore situation, students typically converse among themselves using a complex mixture of mother tongue and Singlish (a colloquial variety of English). This kind of language use, we have found, carries over into the English language classroom even. Thus, a challenge for the English language teacher is to get the students to adopt more a standard variety of English. But students who adopt such ways of speaking can be seen as 'putting on airs' since these ways of speaking are not typically associated with how the students identify themselves. In fact, one other student in our study, Yan, specifically voices such a concern. She is afraid that if she insists on speaking (standard) English too often, she will be perceived as being snobbish.

Thus, we need to find ways in which teachers will find it easier to encourage students to engage in language use while minimizing levels of competence-based and identity-based anxiety (cf. Kramsch, 2009 for a range of interesting possibilities here). One approach could be to create an imaginary context, framed by the teacher as being 'playful' or 'nonserious', that will allow language use to be presented as nonthreatening, so that students do not see their use of language as implicating either their language capabilities or their invested identities. For example, the teacher may suggest a number of activities, specifically framed as playful uses of language, where students are encouraged to imagine themselves in different personae associated with the target language. One possibility is for students to take turns as 'teacher', and for the teacher, at these times, to adopt the role of 'student'.

Some students may use the opportunity to mock these other uses of language and their associated identities, and such mockery needs to be accepted by the teacher as part of the spirit of stylization. The notion of translanguaging is a useful heuristic with which to understand the possibilities inherent in this type of situation. Translanguaging as a pedagogical practice in Singaporean classrooms: 'the hearing, signing or reading of lessons in one language, and the development of the work (the oral discussion, the writing of passages, the development of projects and experiments) in another language' (Garcia, 2009: 302) is 'an arrangement that normalizes bilingualism without functional separation' (Baker, 2001). In a South African basic literacy course for adults, Kerfoot (ftc) found that the various recoding moves whereby content was recontextualized in different registers, languages and as well as various multisemiotic means of encoding (e.g. mindmaps and bullets) served 'to reshape existing distinctions between formal and informal speech along with the power relations bound up with them, as well as erased hierarchy and constructed participants as equals capable of collectively addressing social issues' (Kerfoot, ftc: 25). This allowed voices previously silenced to be heard in ways not possible through 'normative' literacy practices. This was partly because such recoding and resemiotizing practices created 'new social arrangements and knowledge structures, altering the channels along which ideas flowed' (Kerfoot, ftc: 25).

The option of engaging the students in their identity work directly is also an option. In this case, the teacher needs to somehow initiate a discussion with the students about his or her linguistically mediated identity work. For example, Ong (2003) discusses an example where an English teacher provides feedback to his students' on their writing of an assigned topic 'The Beach' (Teacher: *Don't write like this. ... Are you referring to the people building the sandcastles who look fantastic or the sandcastle itself?*). As the feedback process goes on, the teacher starts switching more into Singlish, as indicated by the use of the particle *lah* (Teacher: *Along the beach lah, beachside.*). The switch to Singlish is accompanied by a greater exchange of humorous remarks between the teacher and students (Student: *Cher, my imagination not very good leh.*). This is no coincidence since the teacher's switch to Singlish signals that the formal or serious nature of the lesson is being temporarily abandoned, and this encourages the students to respond accordingly. The disengagement thus accomplished creates the space for focusing on form in a less threatening and authoritative manner.

Exactly how these types of pedagogical arrangement can be realized in different educational contexts is a matter of further research. For example, we acknowledge that the use of role play in language teaching has had mixed success (Al-Arishi, 1994). But its value lies in the fact that by virtue of occupying a role, participants still have jobs to do and problems to solve, so that they are driven to communicate because of 'the duties inherent in their functions' rather than because of a 'teacher-directed need' (Jones, 1982: 9). Furthermore, feedback from other participants can be instantaneous if the language used is considered inappropriate since it may affect the effective performance of a role (Jones, 1982: 7–8). This is why we consider role play a potentially effective means for overcoming identity-based anxiety.

However, our goal here is to highlight the importance of developing a wide range of pedagogical strategies that consciously address identity-based anxiety, and we are aware that culture-specific norms will have to be taken into account. We need to be conscious of the point made earlier with respect to how local interactional and ideological conditions determine how meta-linguistic and metapragmatic reflexivity is manifest. In some cultures, 'playful' talk may be culturally inappropriate given local understandings of the teacher–student relationship; also, there may be gender-based constraints such that same-sex joking could be considered more acceptable than cross-sex jocularity. Clearly, though, more work needs to be done in developing language teaching strategies that take into account students' identity-based anxiety. But for this to happen, teachers need to be actively involved in proposing possible strategies, and this requires that the scope of Language Awareness in English language teacher education (James & Garret, 1991; Wright & Bolitho, 1993) be broadened, so that it includes not just grammar and discourse, but also a greater understanding of current sociolinguistic theorizing.

Concluding Remarks

We noted at the beginning of this book that a major concern for sociolinguistic investigation is the social distribution and valuation of linguistic resources. This concern has gradually led sociolinguistics (and the related field of linguistic anthropology) to develop various concepts that can help us better understand how some language practices come to be viewed as resources over others, and how, concomitant with this, there may be consequences for social access to material and symbolic goods.

What we have attempted to do is to employ these concepts (style, performance, indexical values, etc.) in specific relation to the study of literacy, focusing on the acquisition of English language literacy in Singapore as a case study. Literacy provides a particular important area for sociolinguistics' concern with the distribution of resources, since the characterization and social ratification of particular ways of using language as 'literate' constitutes an especially influential means by which individuals and communities – and indeed, successive generations of the same – may garner and ultimately accrue various forms of capital, sometimes to the point where relationships of social inequality may become entrenched or even misrecognized as natural or inevitable.

By carefully attending to the language practices and identity concerns of the adolescents in our study, and by situating these in relation to the multiple markets of the home, school and peer interaction, we hope to have shown how a sociolinguistics of literacy can not only take advantage of current and ongoing sociolinguistic scholarship, but also how the choice of literacy can provide sociolinguistics with a prism through which questions about the allocation of social and linguistic resources can received a particularly critical and applied perspective.

Notes

(1) The discussion in this chapter draws on Stroud and Wee (2006).
(2) See Hasan (1999) for a defense of the genre approach, especially in response to Luke (1997).
(3) The notion of repertoire is similar to the idea of sociolinguistic consumption (Stroud & Wee, 2007, and Chapter 9).

9 The Dynamics of Language Distribution in Late-Modern Multilingual Singapore

In today's global world, extant language policies are increasingly inadequate for managing and regulating the complex sociolinguistic dynamics of highly transforming communities characterized by pervasive transnational mobility and an extensive domestic reconstruction of social, political and economic life. This is the case for Singapore, whose late-modern structure requires an approach to the management of multilingualism that departs radically from that of the founding years of the nation. As we saw in Chapter 2, Singapore's language policy remains grounded in a politics of national (re)construction and mobilization, and a concern with ethnolinguistic harmony. It was designed as a strategy for managing a multiethnic society, via a mother-tongue policy that encouraged Singaporeans to be bilingual in English and an official mother tongue (i.e. a language assigned by the state as representative of a community's ethnic identity). This policy, which is still in effect today, is based on a historically and culturally context-specific theory of governance that defined national construction and ethnic/racial harmony in terms of a specific conception of language and its relationship to individual and group identities.

But as the foregoing chapters have demonstrated, if English language education is to at all address the challenges faced by younger Singaporeans, there must be a willingness to revisit fundamental assumptions concerning how English is to be positioned in relation to identity work. While the preceding chapter explored possible pedagogical strategies, we are also aware that language education policy is only one part of a broader set of national policies that are aimed at preparing Singaporeans for economic competition in a highly globalized world, fostering national cohesiveness even as many Singaporeans work and live abroad, and attracting 'foreign talent' to replace those Singaporeans who have decided to give up their citizenship. In this concluding chapter, we want to suggest that a different approach to policy-making is therefore required in late-modern, multilingual societies such as Singapore. The impetus behind this rethinking of policy is not only based on the issue of language education (although this is undoubtedly a significant part of it), but as will be made clear, there are other reasons why a revisiting of Singapore's language policy is also needed.

In the following, we argue that refiguring language policy in late-modern Singapore comes with the cost of rethinking some very fundamental assumptions on the nature of citizenship and language, how the one relates to the other, and the structural and institutional changes that are required in order to accommodate forms of late-modern citizenship, with a new political philosophy of language. In order to grasp the import of contemporary multilingual dynamics, we turn to theorizations of citizenship in late modernity, as any political philosophy of language is in all essentials an articulation of a wider discourse of citizenship and governance (cf. Stroud, 2009), and elaborate in this context the idea of *linguistic citizenship*. This is a notion that it is designed to not only draw attention to the essential role language plays in emerging new forms of citizenship, but also to how citizenship as a set of dynamic political practices is formative of new forms of language. It is a construct that combines the principles of cosmopolitan and deliberative democracy within an emerging reflexive citizenship, and that attends particularly to the role of language and multilingualism as a political resource in complex, transnational, scaled societies. Our task in this chapter is thus twofold: first, to understand the changing nature and practice of citizenship in late modernity and to explore what late modernity means more generally for government and governance, thereby critically examining extant practices of institutions and their ideological underpinnings, and second, to discuss what this means for language, and for language policy in particular.

Consuming Singapore

Bauman, writing about advanced Western democracies more generally, notes how

Ours is a 'consumer society' in a similarly profound and fundamental sense in which the society of our predecessors ... used to deserve the name of a 'producer society' ... The way present-day society shapes up its members is dictated first and foremost by the need to play the role of the consumer, and the norm our society holds up to its members is that of the ability and willingness to play it. ... The difference is one of emphasis, but that shift does make an enormous difference to virtually every aspect of society, culture and individual life. The differences are so deep and ubiquitous that they fully justify speaking of our society as a society of a separate and distinct kind – a consumer society. (Bauman, 1998: 24)[1]

This statement in fact admirably depicts the contemporary Singaporean condition (cf. Chua, 2003). One salient aspect of consumption in late-modern societies is its importance for individuals' identity constructions, and since a consumer society is defined largely by the wide variety of goods that can serve as markers of identity, the notion of *choice* (Bauman, 1998: 30; Giddens, 1991: 197) becomes of utmost importance. The consumer can be held responsible for the choices s/he makes in the kinds of objects or activities s/he consumes *regardless* of whether or not such choices are freely exercised (Warde, 1994: 881). With responsibility and choice comes the need to be *reflexive*. For Beck (1992: 131) and Giddens (1991: 81), reflexivity is an especially important feature since the outcomes of sociocultural (as well as scientific–technological) practices involve risks, and therefore need to be constantly monitored and fed back into the conduct of the practices themselves. Thus, actors who are more reflexively oriented can be said to have an advantage over actors who are less so. The emphasis on choice also makes it a rational strategy for the consumer to avoid being overly committed to a particular commodity or identity since this might preclude future choices. As Bauman puts it:

> Identities, just like consumer goods, are to be appropriated and possessed, but only in order to be consumed, and so to disappear again. As in the case of marketed consumer goods, consumption of an identity should not – must not – extinguish the desire for other new and improved identities, nor preclude the ability to absorb them. (Bauman, 1998: 28)

Language is also increasingly an object of consumption, where the choice of what language to learn and/or to pass on to children is less determined by traditional ethnic linguistic heritage, and more by the calculated decision on what purchase knowing a particular language may bring to a range of symbolic and material markets. English, as noted earlier, has been promoted by the state as a modern language with significant economic value, and because of this, it has become strongly associated with educational achievements and material wealth, making it a desirable and important language in the minds of Singaporeans. Furthermore, the languages people choose to 'consume' on a day-to-day basis are impacting upon (traditional) macro-level sociolinguistic ordering of languages, to the extent that the state's energetic and encompassing promotion of its ethnolinguistic principle of language ordering has all been but abandoned on practice (see Chapter 2). The increased use of English in the homes has even resulted in a number of cases where Singaporeans are describing themselves as literate in *only* English, which obviously contradicts the state's desire to promote bilingual proficiency in *both* English and the official mother tongue. Table 9.1 (adapted from Leow, 2000: 75) shows that a significant number of Singaporeans in their mid-40s or younger are claiming to be monolingual in English, indicating that English language monolingualism might be an emerging trend rather than one that is passing.

One interpretation of these developments is that Singaporeans tend to 'put the instrumental value of a language above the sentimental or symbolic value' (Li *et al.*, 1997: 380; see Chapter 2). It is true that Singlish is also of great symbolic value for many Singaporeans as a marker of their national identity. But the observation by Li Wei *et al.* still holds because supporters of Singlish have suggested, contrary to the state's position on this matter, that the presence of Singlish does not jeopardize or compromise Singaporeans' ability to acquire 'standard/good' English (Wee, 2005). They see no reason why the two varieties of English cannot coexist, and therefore reject the state's argument that continued use of Singlish will only lead to 'ghettoization' (cf. Freeland & Patrick, 2004: 17).

Even the Chinese 'dialects', which in Singapore commonly refer to Chinese languages other than Mandarin, are seen as valuable linguistic resources in today's consumerist context of late modernity. In spite of their use still being discouraged by the Speak Mandarin Campaign, Singaporeans have not eliminated them from their linguistic repertoire. Rather, they have created a space to resignify these languages as 'instrumental' or 'practical'. In other words, the dialects are seen as neither crucial to the speakers' ethnic identity nor to the preservation of tradition, and their continued use provides a nice illustration of how the prime effect of the Speak Mandarin Campaign has been to *delink* dialects from local identities.

In all these cases, socioeconomic and pragmatic considerations appear to strongly determine choice of language or how languages are conceived, arguably more so than issues of identity or ethnicity. Even where identity is highlighted, as in the case of Singlish and its supporters, it is on the basis that this can be maintained without threatening economic growth. This development is also apparent in the emergence of widespread (unofficial) bilingualism that cuts across ethnic boundaries, resulting in speakers acquiring languages

TABLE 9.1 RESIDENT POPULATION AGED 15 YRS AND ABOVE: LITERATE IN ONLY ENGLISH

Total = 353,801

15–24 yrs	25–34 yrs	35–44 yrs	45–54 yrs	55–64 yrs	above 65
12.6%	18.1%	28.9%	26%	9.1%	5.3%

(other than English) that bear no official association with their designated (ethnolinguistic) identities. In one sense, this is an outcome of state-funded housing and school policies, which, aimed at preventing the creation of ethnic enclaves, provide structural and institutional encouragement for spontaneous language acquisition across ethnic groups. Edwin, a young Chinese student, illustrates this well when he indicates that, in addition to English and Mandarin, he also speaks some Malay. For convenience, we reproduce below some relevant extracts from Chapters 5 and 6:

(1)
Edwin: My friends, most of them are Malays.
Interviewer: All from other classes?
Edwin: Yes, sometimes I can converse with them in a bit of Malay

However, the converse desire to acquire Mandarin among Malay families also results in patterns of unofficial bilingualism. This is illustrated by Fandi, a Malay teenager, whose multilingual home environment is underscored by the fact that, in addition to using English and Malay, he and his family enjoy watching Chinese [Mandarin] television programs.

(2)
Fandi: Cause they are . . . I mean compared to Malay and some
                     English sitcoms, lah, I find it Chinese . . . Chinese sitcoms or
                     [VCDs], lah, quite better cause there are better actor,
                     actresses, actors all sometimes like that. Then the scripts
                     they do then the jokes they make, the comedy all, I think
                     Chinese are better, lah. . . . . Actually the whole family
                     watch, lah. Then the volume is up then I will under-
                     stand some of the Chinese words. Then I will bring them to
                     school, talk to the Chinese friends in Chinese, like that, lah.

Another example of how Chinese dialects are used as productive linguistic resources in social interactions *across linguistic and ethnic groupings* is that many male Singaporeans have found knowledge of Hokkien to be extremely valuable during National Service, where young men of varied socioeconomic backgrounds are forced to work and interact together. National Service therefore provides for many young Singaporean males (mainly Chinese, and to a lesser extent, Malays and Indians) a set of experiences in which the Chinese dialects, in particular Hokkien, are resignified as important lingua franca for getting along with fellow soldiers as well as for simply getting things done (Chapter 2). The desire to avoid drawing attention to class distinctions even between coethnics is a further indication that status may be attaining a more fundamental role in Singapore society than ethnicity. The foregoing examples suggest that Singaporeans are making primarily instrumental choices in matters of language. The dynamics of Singaporean multilingualism is no longer simply organized along the lines of ethnically determined local identities, nor regulated in terms of linguistic ownership and authenticity. Languages have become hierarchically ordered in economic systems of value even where official policy explicitly tried to rule this out. Speakers now learn and acquire languages for a variety of reasons that have more to do with their perceived use-value than inherent ownership or the performance of ethnic identities.

These developments are also reflected in respect of state-sanctioned language practices. In response to the rise of English, the growing demand for Mandarin among a broad spectrum of ethnic groups and the rise of new, heterogeneous populations, the state is having to rethink the kinds of linguistic practices it expects of Singaporeans, by offering freedom of linguistic choice. As we have noted, the high degree of importance and prestige attached to English by many Singaporeans has led it to displace the official mother tongues from the home environment, which means that more Singaporean students are entering the school system with their official mother tongue effectively a foreign language. Instead, for many Singaporeans, it is English (including Singlish) that is the language of the home (and as we will see later, this carries significant implications for the state's policy that English is unacceptable as an official mother tongue).

Thus, as we noted in Chapter 2, the state has had to acknowledge that a significant number of Chinese Singaporeans actually have great difficulty coping with Mandarin. The trend toward English as the home language appears to have grown even further lately. Thus, consider the following recent newspaper report ('More SAP pupils from English-speaking homes'):

It is not just the usual suspects, such as mission schools, that face difficulties in teaching the Chinese language because their students come mostly from English-speaking homes. Several Special Assistance Plan (SAP) schools and schools affiliated to Chinese associations – the bedrock of Chinese learning here – said, they, too, face similar challenges these days.

At Nanyang Primary School, for instance, about 80 per cent of Primary 1 pupils this year come from predominantly English-speaking homes.

Said school principal Lee Hui Feng: 'We crossed the 70 per cent mark about two to four years ago. I has been 72, 73 per cent and, this year, it has gone up.'

...

In six years – comparing its current Primary 6 and Primary 1 cohorts – the percentage of pupils from English-speaking home in Nan Chiau [a primary school affiliated to a Singapore Hokkien clan association: CS and LW] has gone up from around 40 per cent to 60 per cent.

...

As a result, these schools are seeing more pupils struggling with Chinese.

The head of department for Chinese language at Kong Hwa [a SAP school: CS and LW], Mr Kuah Yi Piao, said: 'There are pupils who respond in English when asked questions in Mandarin, or end up using English during discussions in Chinese class.' (*The Straits Times* March 13, 2010)

Essentially, underlying the dynamics of language choices and the small shifts and transformations in mother-tongue policy that we may be witnessing are the more general and more encompassing practices of *reflexive* citizenship. This is a notion of reflexivity with a slightly different emphasis to how it is used by Bauman and Giddens. Ellison has coined the notion of *reflexive citizenship* to refer to

the general process, driven by social, political and economic change by which social actors, confronted with the erosion or transformation of established patterns of belonging, readjust existing notions of rights and membership to new conceptions of identity, solidarity and the institutional foci of redress. (Ellison, 1997: 711)

This conception of citizenship attempts to address the fact that people are linked in many different ways within and across institutions of different levels of scale and formality, and that their interests and subject positions vary greatly and may not coincide with groupings such as ethnicity, race, gender, language or sexuality, or even large homogeneous categories such as social class assumed by a modernist politics. This challenges an approach to language that has traditionally been built around the idea of 'linguistic distinctness', a perspective on language that 'takes the world to be a neat patchwork of separate monolingual, geographical areas almost exclusively populated by monolingual speakers' (De Schutter, 2007: 3), or what Heller (2007) calls the 'structural-functional view', where languages are perceived as bounded and delimitable systems that occupy equally bounded and delimitable spaces and functions. In the late-modern public sphere, much of what goes on involves encounters between speakers of different languages in multiple and various urban spaces, both real and virtual, a form of contemporary multilingualism that Aronin and Singleton call a new 'linguistic dispensation' (Aronin & Singleton, 2008: 1) in which 'sets of languages[,] rather than single languages, now perform the essential functions of communication' (Aronin & Singleton, 2008: 2).

Rescaling Singapore

Not only is life in late modernity a world of consumption, it is also a world of objects in motion. 'These objects include ideas and ideologies, people and goods, images and messages, technologies and techniques. This is a world of flows' (Appadurai, 2001: 5). And as Giddens observes, a key characteristic of such constant flows is 'the intensification of worldwide social relations which link localities in such a way that local happenings are shaped by events occurring many miles away and vice versa' (Giddens, 1990: 64). The inevitable result of such flows is rescaling, since entities defined at one level of abstraction no longer necessarily interact with entities defined at corresponding levels (as would be in a Westphalian framework that envisages international interactions as primarily state-to-state). Instead, an entity such as the state may have to deal (simultaneously) with concerns that manifest themselves at the suprastate, substate as well as cross-state levels. Jacquemet observes that, as a result

> Sophisticated technologies for rapid human mobility and electronic global communication ... are advancing a process of constructing localities in relation to global sociopolitical forces ... Three of the most significant outcomes of this process are: (1) the sustained development of diasporic social formations, in which people bear multiple linguistic allegiances and cultural belongings; (2) the emergence of media idioms (such as the use of global English in news broadcasting, advertising, or electronic mailing lists); and (3) the formation of global power elites and locally based semiotic operators that use knowledge of international languages as commodities and tools to secure, in the former case, a dominant position in the world, and for the latter, to engage in a process of social and geographical (mostly south-north) mobility. (Jacquemet, 2005: 261)

Clearly, in such a world, social trajectories are increasingly unpredictable in the sense that individuals can neither expect to be doing the same job nor live in the same society for much of their lives. New skills will need to be acquired, often in new environments, with concomitant implications for the kinds of registers or 'social languages' that are deemed relevant (Gee, 2001).

In Singapore, the state's acknowledgement of this can be seen in how it has emphasized to the general population the importance of constant job retraining, where older workers need to be willing to shift into a 'second career' as new jobs in new growth sectors arise (*The New Paper* May 2, 2007).

One implication of rescaling is that individuals now find themselves participating in a variety of sites in competition for resources distributed along multiple levels of scale, such as the nation, the supranation, the local and the regional. Increasingly, in many nation-states, private organizations, non-governmental organization, and multinational corporations are providing the economic, symbolic, and material opportunities (e.g. medical care, security, transport, sewage disposals) that were traditionally either the provenance of the state or delegated to local governments. In other words, the resources and agencies available to citizens to a large extent depend more and more upon what organizations, channels, and institutions outside of, or along with, the state proper they are able to access. The Singaporean state has also recognized that many Singaporeans are now traveling and working abroad, and even emigrating. In 1997, Goh Chok Tong (then Prime Minister) therefore spoke of 'Singapore communities in other cities' (3).[2] Since Singaporeans are no longer defined in terms of being located on the island, Goh appealed to a sense of national loyalty and familial ties they will (hopefully) feel *regardless* of where they may be.

(3)
> In a very mobile world, more Singaporeans will go abroad to work. ... There are ... sizeable Singapore communities in other cities – Sydney, Perth, London, Paris, Tokyo, Beijing, Bangkok, Manila. ... It is a facet of globalization and regionalization that we need to reflect on and address ... Abiding bonds to family and friends and deep loyalties to Singapore are crucial in this new situation. We must never forget that Singaporeans owe one another an obligation, and the more able ones, in whom Singapore has invested the most, have a special obligation to society. We must all join hands to keep Singapore together.

Citizenship has generally been closely identified with historically gendered and racialized practices exercised within a uniform and shared public space within the boundaries of a territorially defined nation-state. However, as a response to such global flows, the Singaporean state has decided to reposition itself as 'a cosmopolitan, global city' in order to attract talented foreigners as potential new citizens, thus replacing those Singaporeans who may decide to emigrate permanently.

(4)

Our ... strategy to meet future competition is to gather talent and make Singapore a cosmopolitan city ... Attracting global talent is essential for creating the best for Singaporeans. ... Singapore must become a cosmopolitan, global city, an open society where people from many lands can feel at home.

These developments in Singapore find parallels elsewhere as recent years' horizontal and vertical processes of globalization, although refigured through the particularities of the local urban context and local institutions, have ushered in new political formations in contexts of massive demographic change and technological innovation. The importance for individual agency of multiple transnational alliances at different levels of scale and formality is contributing to the delinking of citizenship narratives from conventional imaginings of the nation-state as a space of inclusion and exclusion of particular ethnicities, genders or linguistic groupings. However, despite the clear cosmopolitan character of contemporary citizenship, democratic participation at the local level remains an essential prerequisite of democratic structures at the transnational levels, with Held (2006) claiming that 'the recovery of an intensive participatory and deliberative democracy at local levels as a complement to the deliberative assemblies of the wide-global order [portends] a political order of democratic associations, cities and nations as well as regions and global networks' (Held, 2006: 309). Calhoun also emphasizes the (continued) importance of the local in the reimagining of social solidarity, stating:

Local communities are often precisely the settings ... in which social relationships establish bridges across race, religion, or other lines of categorical difference. The importance of the local resides in 'public discourse' and the production and reproduction of 'shared culture', which changes peoples' identities and understandings as 'commonalities' with others are established, not found. (Calhoun, 2001: 25–27)

Citizenship narratives thus have to reimagine local public space as central to both a sense of inclusive 'belonging' as well as a nexus for the establishment of cosmopolitan engagement. In the Singaporean context, we have an implicit admission by the state that Singapore's national identity may need to be reconstructed into one less dependent on an Asian 'us' versus Western 'them' dichotomy.

(5)

Therefore we must incorporate into our society talent from all over the world, not just Chinese, Malay or Indians, but talented people whatever their race or country of origin – East Asians, Southeast Asians, South Asians, Arabs from the Gulf and Middle East, North Americans, Europeans, Australasians, even Latin Americans and Southern Africans ... Some will integrate into our society and settle here. For them we hope this spirit will eventually evolve into one of loyalty and rootedness to Singapore. ... We must therefore welcome the infusion of knowledge which foreign talent will bring.

However, at the same time that the state recognizes choice and autonomy, and formulates policy around mobility, flux and change in many areas, it also wishes to keep a sense of a bounded Singaporean Asian community, apparent in Goh's assertion that this very same strategy of becoming a cosmopolitan city is also part of how Singapore can 'maintain our Asian heritage'.

(6)

Our strategies – to maintain sound macroeconomic policies, to welcome talent, to maintain our Asian heritage, to be cosmopolitan city, and to involve everyone in building our best home – will only succeed if we become one people, one Singapore.

Even as Goh argues that Singapore society must be more 'open', he insists on maintaining the society's 'Asian heritage'. In this way, arriving at a judicious balance between a thoroughgoing cosmopolitanism – one informed by more pragmatically oriented responses to the challenges of late modernity – and the retention of a robustly Asian national identity remains an ongoing challenge for Singapore. Below, we will suggest how that alternative ideological discourses of a reimagined nation-state can be built around the social, economic and political imperatives of commitment to shared values and the instrumentality and political expediency of diversity.

Rescaling, as noted earlier, occurs when relations between demographic or political units are realigned, often in complex and unpredictable ways. This in turn affects activities and interactions because it necessarily involves 'the recontextualization within [an] entity of social practices, forms of discourse, forms of institution and organization, forms of governance and styles and genres which are operative elsewhere' (Fairclough, 2006: 167). Rescaling will clearly impact upon the organization of multilingualism in Singaporean society. To take one example, the success of the foreign talent policy will eventually impact upon Singapore's language policy, especially the mother-tongue policy, because the foreign talent policy aims to persuade such talent to take up Singaporean citizenship, and the success of this policy could well change the nation's demographics (Wee & Bokhorst-Heng, 2005). Japanese, Korean, French or American foreign talent who become citizens obviously cannot be expected to embrace Mandarin, Malay or Tamil as their official mother tongues. This poses an almost insurmountable conundrum for contemporary Singaporean language policy, the solution to which requires a radical departure from many of its founding assumptions.

The other side of the coin is that language practices among Singaporeans themselves are increasingly likely to be *transidiomatic*, as Singaporeans located across the globe communicate among themselves as well as with individuals of other nationalities. This is because '(d)iasporic and local groups alike recombine their identities by maintaining simultaneous presence in a multiplicity of sites' so that groups are 'using different languages and communicative codes simultaneously present in a range of communicative channels, both local and distant' (Jacquemet, 2005: 264–265). In other words, language practices will typically involve mixed codes and multiple communicative frames rather than occur within the (monolingual) boundaries of delimited languages (Jacquemet, 2005: 274). Because these transidiomatic practices take place in diasporic transnational contexts, they are much harder for the state to 'police' despite the fact that their very hybrid nature puts them at odds with the mother-tongue policy favored by the state.

The mother-tongue policy has also had to be more flexible because the children of Singaporean expatriates returning to Singapore would probably not have been studying their official mother tongue while studying abroad. This has led the Ministry of Education to acknowledge that these children might need to be exempted from the mother-tongue requirement (*The Straits Times*, March 20, 1998), significantly putting the lie to early nation-building ambitions of full bilingualism in an Asian language and English.

From the preceding discussion, we see that Singaporean late modernity has involved a shift in the meaning of notions such as ethnicity, nationhood and identity in constructions of citizenship, with a resulting tension between local, nation-centered and ethnically shaped citizen identities, on the one hand, and transnational diasporic identities of consumer citizenship, on the other. This tension is also reflected in both the workings of Singaporean language policy and its understandings of language. Language is fundamentally a politically construed ontology (Heller, 2008b), as what may comprise a language and the significance accorded to it and its speakers is determined by a states' institutional, symbolic and linguistic resources, and promoted through a variety of concrete political, administrative and linguistic (discursive) processes. Issues of language are negotiated within delimited and set fields of tension and contradiction, where only certain types of arguments count. Clearly, the political ontology of language in late-modern Singapore has until now remained fundamentally 'modernist', constructed around the formation and maintenance of the South-East Asian nation-state. Thus, the central institutions and discourses of language are those of a traditional national public sphere and unified markets such as education and the work place, and the tensions and contradictions in public debate on language revolve around the axis of ethnolinguistic management. However, the original intention of Singaporean language policy as a tool in ethnolinguistic management is unable to accommodate a class dynamics that crosscuts and undermines ethnicity, and that transforms the field of policy into an arena for the negotiation and contestation of consumption. What current language dynamics instead show is an orientation toward reflexivity and choice, and a growing recognition of language as (a type of) commodity and even life-style product. These practices highlight the tensions inherent in reconciling such choices with equitable (linguistic) citizenship and linguistic justice. Reflexive citizenship on increasingly disaggregated public spheres carries with it concerns of social and redistributive justice (Ellison, 1997), to the extent that 'some groups will be more adept than others in adjusting to more fluid social and political forms' (Ellison, 1997: 714), with 'reflexivity winners and users' (Ellison, 1997: 714) as a result. One challenge for late-modern societies is to balance concerns of social equity and more traditional concerns of nation building with the less widely recognized challenges posed by the language–consumption–mobility nexus. And linguistic justice involves ensuring mechanisms for access and acquisition of a wide range of languages that were earlier not possible.

At the same time, there is a need to reconcile global developments and influences with local conditions (and national ambitions), that is, issues are raised that require attention to a sociolinguistics of scale. Developments in late-modern and globalized societies have thus laid the political, economic and social foundations, not only for the emergence of variegated forms of citizenship, but also for a new politics of language, where Singaporean narratives of linguistic identity in late modernity need to embrace multilingualism and cosmopolitanism as core values of nation building.

Revisiting Language Policy in Late-Modern Consumerist Singapore

In the pursuit of linguistic justice in a transnational consumerist world, one guiding principle behind a new Singaporean language policy could be to attempt to increase choices in consumption open to different classes. Its core design features should therefore be built around consumption, choice/autonomy and reflexivity. The idea of *linguistic citizenship* captures these alternative formulations or questions on language, and their attendant implications for a late-modern approach to a politics of language. Linguistic citizenship refers to the linguistic implications of reflexivity in a cosmopolitan world, and to the ramifications that forms of deliberative democracy and social and linguistic justice carry for language. This approach to language politics recognizes that 'multilinguality' is 'constitutive of being human' (Agnihotri, 2007: 80); that communities today increasingly need to be recognized as comprising complex translocal, multilayered, polycentric, and stratified semiotic spaces; and that a late-modern politics of language thus needs to address tensions between *identity* and *identification*, recognize a *plurality of public voices and positions* and *new public spheres* outside of the state proper, as well as deal with the blurring of the borders between *public* and *private*. A fundamental point of departure for linguistic citizenship is that linguistic diversity and difference are one prime means (rather than an insurmountable problem) for the material realization of democracy, to the extent that speakers negotiate their access to resources and agency across manifold sites, building both local and transnational solidarities through interpersonal negotiation in multiscaled and multilingual spaces. However, as we have noted above, the importance of diversity in and across languages for a reflexive citizenship remains largely unrecognized in much contemporary discourse on language and policy, thereby excluding many forms of linguistic (and metalinguistic) practice essential for agency and social justice. The collocation *linguistic citizenship* has thus been deliberately coined in order to highlight the power of the trope of citizenship historically to draw attention to inequities suffered by those whose voices have been systematically excluded and structurally marginalized, such as women, children and migrants, and is intended to bear a family resemblance to how the notion of citizenship is used in phrases such as 'intimate citizenship' (Plummer, 2001), and 'sexual citizenship' (Stychin, 2001). Thus, in using linguistic citizenship as a sensitizing concept, our intention is also to draw attention to acts of (linguistic) reflexivity and agency that reveal tensions between modernist, nation-state language policies, on the one hand, and late-modern dynamics of multilingualism, on the other. We interpret such tensions and contradictions at the *interstice* of modernity and late modernity as politically salient key events that require radical political change and structural transformation. Throughout this chapter, we have attempted to sketch what these tensions might comprise of in the Singaporean context, and we are now ready to formulate some questions around Singaporean late-modern sociolinguistic dynamics and explore what their significance for policy might be. First, what does it mean to approach language as an object of consumption, and what mechanisms are available to ensure that there is an optimal alignment between consumption and social and linguistic justice? How can we reconcile an instrumental, consumption-oriented and (re)distributive notion of language with a role for language in recognition and identity work? These questions address the conundrum of how Singaporean language policy can be better aligned with transnational developments in society in general, and the deeper issues these raise of a political nature. A fourth question concerns what implications the answers to the preceding questions may carry for structural changes and transformations of policy discourses. Finally, what are the implications of a plural and autonomous linguistic choice for narratives of national (linguistic) unity, and the role of language policy in late-modern Singapore? We suggest that the answers we seek to these questions within a framing of linguist citizenship stake out a radically different approach to questions of language and policy than to what is currently in place. In order to account for speakers' linguistic practices and patterns of language acquisition, as well as the target forms acquired in multilingual contexts, we introduce the notion of *sociolinguistic consumption*. This refers to the portfolio of linguistic forms, both at the sublanguage level and at the 'supralanguage' level as chains of multilingual, cross-linguistic resources, and to the multiple ways in which speakers invest in this portfolio. On the question of how to optimally align social justice with sociolinguistic consumption, we suggest an approach in terms of radical *deliberative* procedures around questions of language, and make the point that deliberation in a plural and complex world requires a focus on how meanings are contextualized and recontextualized or *resemitotized* across multiple modes of semiotic practice. This implies a departure from a conventional emphasis on the importance of mother tongues and ethnic languages for political participation and deliberation. However, this does not mean that we merely need to revise a politics of linguistic recognition in order to accommodate multiple languages or linguistic varieties. On the contrary, we argue that linguistic equity can only be accomplished by deconstructing the very fundament upon which disputes of equity are raised in the first place, namely the notion of a mother tongue and claims of identity based on this. We base this claim on the argument that material redistribution in a conventional politics of diversity affirmation necessarily implies the very erasure of the notion of linguistic identity on which the idea of linguistic recognition rests. We go on to discuss the implications of such a move for nation-state discourses, and propose some possibilities for how new nation-state discourses may emerge, and other forms of linguistic normativity be systematically developed around the idea of cosmopolitanism. Finally, we discuss the implications of our analyses for policy and how the engagement of multiple actors with a variety of different state discourses may be facilitated.

Sociolinguistic Consumption

What, then, does it mean to claim that language is an object of consumption? How does language as an object of consumption differ from other forms of consumption? How should access to and regulation of linguistic consumption be regulated – if at all – and by whom? What is the role of individual choice?

We present the notion of *sociolinguistic consumption* as a way of approaching the question of language in late modernity. An advantage of the notion is that it situates language choice as consumption firmly within a framework of social class, access and privilege – central aspects of the current study. It also allows us to forge links between what Bucholtz (2009) has called a 'sociolinguistics of identity' and the trappings and aesthetics of language as forms of life-style commodity among many others. More specifically, the notion of *sociolinguistic consumption* captures a reconceptualization of language in terms of how it functions in different social domains that reflect the social and historical trajectories of speakers and their material constraints. For example, in understanding sociolinguistic consumption, it is important to distinguish language as the direct object of consumption from language that one is socialized into indirectly, as a consequence of consuming something else, such as participation in various activities. An example of the former might be the desire to learn English because the language itself is seen to bestow strong socioeconomic advantages on its speakers (cf. Phillipson, 1992: 271ff). An example of the latter might be the acquisition of French in the course of wine-tasting activities. In the former, the intended targets are the autonomous denotational systems themselves (Silverstein, 1998) while in the latter, particular registers are acquired in the context of specific activity types (Levinson, 1992). This distinction is useful because it suggests that even languages that are perceived to be relatively valueless *qua* denotational codes may acquire renewed relevance when associated with activities that are considered important or worth engaging in.

Combining the aforementioned distinction with that of choice, we arrive at the following four-way typology of sociolinguistic consumption in Figure 9.1.

Though the dimensions are clearly continua, for ease of exposition, we will discuss four types of examples, where each might be placed in the regions we have numbered from 1 to 4.

Consumption of language:

		More direct	Less direct
	More constrained	1	3
Choice of language:			
	Less constrained	2	4

Figure 9.1 Typology of sociolinguistic consumption

Singapore's explicit language policy in all essentials addresses only language in region 1. In Singapore, the state expects its citizens to be proficient in both English and an officially assigned mother tongue. Region 1 therefore describes the state's mother-tongue policy, which requires Singaporeans to learn English and the mother tongue. Region 2 describes a situation where the individual voluntarily decides to learn a language, which in Singapore, would typically be in addition to English and the official mother tongue. Region 3 refers to cases where a register is learnt in the context of activities that the individual is obligated to participate in. These might include working and, for Singaporean male individuals, spending at least two years in the army as part of National Service. Region 4 refers to cases where a language is learnt in the context of activities that the individual freely participates in, for fun or entertainment. Typical examples include playing soccer, computer games or viewing certain programs. Consumption of these activities may then lead the actors to acquire the associated registers.

In other words, late modernity thus means that a variety of actors and modes of acquisition determine what comprises multilingual resources and their meanings, with an emerging polycentricity and heterogeneity in the multilingual landscapes as a consequence. One feature of multilingualism that emerges out of this complex set of tensions around language is that rather than merely a collection of *languages*, multilingualism needs to be reconceptualized more broadly as a complex of *specific* semiotic resources, some of which belong to a conventionally defined 'language', while others belong to another 'language' or even sublanguages (Blommaert, 2008), or other representational resources. These repertoires of resources are organized across individuals, institutions and at local or translocal levels of scale in ways that reflect the fluidity and flux of translocal speech communities; prescribed standard forms of a language may coexist with hybrid and nonstandard elements from other languages, but also with elements from other media and modalities. On close inspection, most speakers' multilingual portfolios present as complexly piecemeal, semiotic traces of their life histories of personal, social and geographical movement (Blommaert, 2008: 115; Grosjean, 2008; Vigouroux, 2009).

An approach to language attuned to the implications of multitude of identities, subject positions, and positions of interest needs to reframe semiotic practices of citizenship away from a totalizing sense of language and toward such notions as fracturedness, hybridity, partiality and perspective. Canagarajah (2007: 98) notes how 'situatedness, materiality, diversity, hybridity, and fluidity [is] at the heart of language and identity'.

A notion that promises to provide for (new) positions of subjectivity and ways of talking about and managing social transformation in late modernity is *genre* or *register*. Genres organize multilingual resources into 'complexes of communicative-formal features that make a particular communicative event recognizable as an instance as a type' (Blommaert, 2008; cf. Briggs & Bauman, 1992), recognizable by community members as conventional performances of subjectivities and activities. Importantly, new genres comprise the textual practices for 'cultural innovation and change' and offer new epistemological or cultural forms for the formation and expression of particular types of identity (Blommaert, 2008: 47).

It should be clear from our discussion above that the state's language policy cannot be considered in isolation from its other policies and initiatives, since language figures in all domains of social life. In other words, language policy and planning is not just limited to what can be found in explicit language policies or public proclamations of the state regarding what it sees as a desirable sociolinguistic situation (i.e. quadrant 1). Language policies can be implicit and they occur in a variety of social domains, since ideologies about language are prevalent regardless of whether these lead to overt formulations or not (cf. Blommaert, 2010; Ramanathan, 2005; Ricento, 2006; Shohamy, 2006, 2007; Spolsky, 2004; Wright, 2004). Thus, we also need to pay attention to how the state's policies outside of language policy proper already show the impact of sociolinguistic consumption, in response to the challenges of late modernity. Furthermore, given the range of actors engaged in 'grassroots' language policy, it is imperative to investigate ways of bringing their perspectives and choices to bear on official state policy.

Reflexive Citizenship and Deliberation

One body of thinking that has addressed the question of how to create expanded participatory spaces for the expression of diversity, attending to the issue of fluid and multiple political identities, broad alliances, and a flexible notion of public and private, is *deliberative democracy*. The founding idea of deliberative democracy is that all citizens who may be directly subject to a particular decision, as well as their representatives, ought to be able to deliberate on problems in a rational and reflective way, with mutual respect for the values and interests of others, taking into account all perspectives in the search for framings and formulations of common concern on decisions that may hold more generally across various categories of citizens (Deveaux, 2005). Deliberation is especially useful with respect to minority groups undergoing social transformation, where 'a deliberative democratic approach to multicultural politics' inserts individuals centrally into 'processes of cultural communication, contestation and resignification ... within civil society' (Benhabib, 2002: 7). Deliberative democracy also highlights the distinction between notions of interest versus rights versus needs as organizing tropes of citizenship activism, in which '[i]nterests are constructed in different sites and based in the subject positions of speakers' (Maher, 2002) and are able to accommodate different contradictory ideas of speakers. Procedures of deliberation then attempt to address the fact that communities are not homogeneous, and that public space is not uniform.

However, much criticism has been leveled against deliberative democracy in some of its various interpretations. One such criticism has been that deliberative democracy may fall foul of a potential lack of democratic legitimacy in so far as only a few representatives and stakeholders will ever actively take part in any deliberations – something that is far from the 'unconstrained deliberation of all about matters of common concern' (Benhabib, 2002: 7). Dryzek (2000) proposes a notion of discursive democracy in order to deal with this problem, emphasizing 'the contestation of *discourses* in the public sphere' ... [where discourse is] 'a shared way of comprehending the world embedded in language' (Dryzek, 2000: 10) – a bundle of assumptions, stances and takes on an issue that many or few may identify with and see as a proxy for their own participation.

Related to this is another point of critique directed against the notion, one that holds interesting ramifications for language, namely, that deliberative democratic practices are potentially antipluralist and exhibit an elitist bias. The claim here is that deliberative democracy assumes an ethnocentrically narrow, class and culture-determined concept of rational communication as a ground rule upon which all stakeholders must agree and around which they will want to reach consensus – some (abstract) notion of common good. The 'deficit' in this regard is not just a question of certain groups being excluded because of lack of material resources or insufficient educational backgrounds, so simply increasing the social distribution of competencies relevant to deliberation more widely will not work (Sanders, 1997). Rather, it is something more fundamental, a question of epistemological authority;

a narrow focus on rationality, it is argued, may exclude the feelings and complaints of disenfranchised groups and may constrain alternative rhetorical means through which a group may habitually choose to express its voice (cf. Stroud, 2009). This point thus also problematizes the idea of a rational, uniform and shared public sphere that dominates and determines the form that political expression can take, what is considered legitimate language, and the import of epistemological authority.

Similar arguments have been put forward by feminist and poststructuralist thinkers on citizenship who have underscored the necessity of taking cognizance of 'a more refined understanding of difference' at the same time as they level critique at the nature of the public sphere which is traditionally construed in terms of universal values that tend to homogenize diversity rather than accommodate difference. Young claims that

> in a heterogeneous public, differences are publicly recognized and acknowledged as irreducible, by which I mean that persons from one perspective or history can never completely understand and adopt the point of view of those with other group-based perspectives and histories. (Young, 1989: 258)

and suggests that answers are the outcome of a plurality of perspectives that cannot be reduced to a unity (Young, 1987: 69). Sassoon also remarks on how citizenship in late-modern contexts needs to be refigured as 'a process in which differences and highly differentiated needs are addressed in their specificity and peculiarity, in which it is recognized that the universal can be as misleading as the specific' (Sassoon, 1991: 102).

In later versions of deliberative democracy, an important recurrent theme has thus been the deconstruction or deemphasis of a sovereign and privileged Habermasian public sphere in favor of multiple, hierarchically layered, and contested public spheres. The idea of multiple spheres with more fluid boundaries is also in line with the rejection of a single unitary subject or identity (Stychin, 2001, 294) and toward recognition of diversity and difference, which are prerequisites for a more encompassing sense of citizenship. Fraser (1998) speaks of subaltern counterpublics in the sense of 'the emergence of arenas in response to an exclusionary civil society' ... [which] 'provide important spaces both for withdrawal from official civil society and also for engagement with it to rectify exclusions' (Stychin, 2001: 288). Such a multiplicity of spheres allows 'reconciliation ... between normalization and transgression' (Stychin, 2001: 288) – that is, the recognition of other orders of normativeness – and thus provides one way of attending to the issue of diversity raised by those critics of deliberative democracy who would see consensus and agreement as hegemonic and centrifugal powers, whereas contest and negotiation allow for more dissent in individual voice to be heard.

With respect to linguistic citizenship, acknowledging and making space for different languages, but also for different genres and registers, styles and narrative formats, is essential in order that different voices may be heard on issues of local and scaled concern. For example, Deveaux (2005) speaks of bargaining rather than consensus, which better captures the idea of negotiation of interests whereas Sanders (1997) suggests that narrative and testimony specifically express an alternative type of 'rationality' that is more accessible to many and that can thus comprise a more inclusive public discourse. However, this means that language is both the *target* of deliberation and the *means* and medium through which this is pursued, which suggests that the problem of diversity and difference in forms of participation needs to be approached through acknowledging the legitimacy in *deliberation* of the very forms and tropes that are *contested*. Furthermore, given the linked and manifold public spheres on which deliberation needs to take place, attention needs to be paid not just to the portfolios of language and varieties that individuals bring to the 'negotiating table', but equally to the range of genres, registers and multisemiotic means that speakers need to *traverse* in their collective forms of meaning-making. This is because meanings need to travel and flow across multilingual chains, so central to linguistic citizenship in late modernity is the idea of a sociolinguistics of multilingual *mobility*. Here, issues of how multiple encodings of a discourse are transfigured across contexts and languages are in focus – that is, a focus on, what Iedema (2001, 2003) has termed resemiotization, the 'inevitably transformative dynamics of socially situated meaning-making processes' (Iedema, 2001: 30).

Language Groups as Bivalent Collectivities

Recognition of linguistic diversity, an essential feature of a deliberative and reflective citizenship, raises the question of how to reconcile linguistic recognition and identity work with an instrumental and consumption-oriented view of language. This question can be answered partially by way of reference to Fraser's notion of *bivalent collectivities*, which are groups that are differentiated

> ... by virtue of *both* the political-economic structure *and* the cultural-valuational structure of society. When disadvantaged, they may suffer injustices that are traceable to both political economy and culture simultaneously. Bivalent collectivities, in sum, may suffer both socio-economic maldistribution and cultural misrecognition in forms where neither of these injustices is an indirect effect of the other, but where both are primary and co-original. (Fraser, 1998: 27, italics in original)

Advantaged bivalent collectivities enjoy both a valorization of cultural resources and access to socioeconomic goods. However, as we noted above, for disadvantaged collectivities, those whose voices may not be heard in deliberation, the core of the problem lies in the mutually reinforcing problem of linguistic nonrecognition coupled to the lack of access to resources and distribution. The notion of bivalent collectivities suggests that attempts at redistributive justice that merely affirm inherited cultural affiliations will always end up privileging some collectivities over others – despite the best of intentions. A better direction to pursue would be to aim for a deconstruction of how individuals' membership in group categories are construed, so as to open up the possibility of multiple socioeconomic and cultural pathways that are minimally constrained by the provenance of one's group membership (Stroud, 2001).

Linguistic citizenship highlights the importance of recognizing the complex, constructed and contingent relationship between language and identity, and the need to open up this relationship for public mediation. Linguistic citizenship acknowledges that speakers in multilingual contexts are often faced with dynamic and changing relationships between particular languages – ethnicity minority languages and LWCs, between inherited and aimed for identities, and between sociopolitical affiliations at the local, regional and more global levels. Given these complexities, it is critical that speakers not be locked into essentializing positions that prescribed from the outset the kinds of linguistic obligations that they are expected to embrace. This means that any proposed policy, including language education policies, should emphasize the commonality that exists between individuals and groups rather than entrench their differences:

Attention to what unites actors with respect to language, however, does not preclude sensitivity to issues that divide speakers of different minority languages and how they are positioned in relation to each other. Language activists do not have to agree on a unified and coherent vantage point. Just as the meanings of the sociopolitical role of gender and implications have developed over the years, so too can we envisage that debates on the importance and reach of language as a sociopolitical category will develop in like manner. Debates on linguistic citizenship will offer contending representations of speakers and their rights, hosted by conflicting political interests, as has been the case with gendered citizenship. The important point is that this approach to minority language issues also draws on the power of *linguistic* identity to mobilize minority language speakers, but in ways that transcend essentialist ascriptions of identity to language by viewing the language-identity link as contingent and constructed in discourse. (Stroud, 2001: 348, italics in original)

This clearly does not mean that ethnic, linguistic or national identities cease to be important, since decisions regarding sociolinguistic consumption often implicate dimensions of identity, or identification, work. For example, Fandi's reference (see (2)) to picking up some Chinese words and using them with his Chinese friends in school is an indication of how his instrumental-pragmatic language choices interact in important ways with ethnic identity considerations. As a Singaporean studying in the English-medium educational system, Fandi is all too aware that competence in English carries great symbolic value as a marker of prestige. And being Malay, Fandi knows that there is a social expectation that he speak Malay since it is supposed to mark his ethnic identity. But because Chinese has no bearing at all on either his identity as a Singaporean or as a Malay, Fandi can afford to 'dabble' in Chinese without worrying about being marked as an 'unsophisticated' Singaporean or as a Malay who has lost touch with his ethnic roots. In this sense, the use of Mandarin also allows Fandi to liminally slip between established and regulated categories and identities.

What a redistributive approach to language does mean, though, from the perspective of linguistic citizenship is for the language policy to facilitate individual choices that are as unfettered as possible by sociocultural obligations. Essentially this means radically rethinking the idea that equity means the recognition of multiple, legitimate linguistic identities as a basis for redistribution, Ellison's (1997) problematization of the idea of a universal and unified public sphere, similar in purpose in many respects to Fraser's multiplication of subaltern publics, offers a way forward. In his conception, a public sphere is an increasingly disintegrated and complex arena, where citizens will

> inhabit a series of putatively fixed empirical positions themselves subject to variation depending on prevailing political and social conditions' [and where] particular identities will emerge and disappear as a result of a complex interplay of conditions. (Ellison, 1997: 710)

His conception of citizenship in the 21st century is of a variegated practice of 'defensive engagement' by groups or individuals who seek a diverse range of solidarities in times of social change 'in a variety of possible settings, divorced from traditional institutional locations or modes of belonging' (Ellison, 1997: 710). This implies a politics of broad affiliation in which speakers may capitalize on fluid political identities in order to construct broad alliances with other constituencies, not necessarily based in any particular commonality of ethnicity, language, gender or race (cf. Phelan, 1995; Stychin, 2001) – a politics of affinity (Phelan, 1995) where new collective social experiences create multiple, contested, and constantly changing social identities (Mouffe, 1992). Singapore's language policy, then, needs to be more explicit in recognizing and catering to the kind of unofficial socio-linguistic consumption that Fandi's acquisition of Mandarin exemplifies. However, in the specific Singaporean case, a redistribution of resources also means questioning and deconstructing the very basis of linguistic capital, namely linguistic ownership grounded in the linking of ethnic identities to mother tongues. There is also a need to adopt a more realistic and tolerant view of the sociolinguistic dynamics of English, since nativization is likely if not inevitable once a society starts using the language with enthusiasm. In the case of English, it is ironic that the state seems unwilling or unable to appreciate that the emergence of a nativized variety can be considered an encouraging sign, since it is possible to suggest that a *sine qua non* of effective use of English is the willingness of speakers to consider themselves native speakers of their own dialectal variant, which has been hailed as a viable marker of a national identity. With this in mind, appropriations of English by speakers for various social activities – including its manifestation in the form of Singlish – can and probably should be seen as encouraging signs that English is taking root to the point where speakers are becoming comfortable with the language. In other words, what is at stake with regard to the ques-tion of equitable (re)distribution is a radical transformation of the basis of (linguistic) recognition, namely the deconstruction of any link between *identity* and a specific language; both with respect to mother tongues and the role of English, claims to identity need to be rethought as statements of *identification*. We pursue the ramifications of deconstructing the notion of mother tongue for national identities in the next section.

National Identities and the Deconstruction of Mother Tongues

We have noted an increasingly autonomous and fluid construction of a language–identity link, and a reconfiguration of identities in terms of con-sumerist, life-style choices. Furthermore, what was already a heterogeneous Singaporean population to begin with looks set, in the context of late moder-nity, to become even more increasingly varied in its sociolinguistic profile, as new technologies and industries emerge, as citizens who have lived overseas return to the country, and as foreign talent from different parts of the world take up Singaporean citizenship. We have discussed the importance of delib-eration as a way of accommodating a differentiated and reflexive citizenship, and detailed some of the challenges that this poses for linguistic recognition and redistribution. Throughout, we have emphasized the importance of a rescaled notion of 'language' to encompass both forms of *sublanguage*, as well as chains of multilingual and multisemiotic varieties.

In this context, the notion of mother tongue loses much of its appeal for Singaporean language politics. The state's mandatory assignation of a specific mother tongue, or even a limited set of mother tongues, onto this kind of ethnolinguistic diversity is simply unrealistic. Expanding the set of mother tongues available for adoption means that the number of mother tongues will need to be increased to the point where the privileging of Asian mother tongues over Western ones – including English – will be impossible to sustain. The state will also need to abandon its stance that English is unacceptable as a mother tongue and, instead, recognize that its insistence on opposing this 'Western' language to the 'Asian' mother tongues is no longer tenable (see below), since some of those foreigners taking up Singaporean citizenship will already have English as a mother tongue and they join the growing number of young Singaporeans for whom English (including Singlish) is also a mother tongue. As Wee and Bokhorst-Heng observe:

> This might mean that, in so far as the state is still intent on encouraging Singaporeans to keep in touch with their mother tongues, this will have to be done 'softly', via persuasion but accepting that the final choice lies with the individual. Furthermore, once the mother tongue issue is ceded more toward the personal domain, then it becomes clear that what language a particular Singaporean may consider his or her mother tongue is also something that can no longer be mandated by the state; this, too, will be a matter of personal choice … Thus, it seems to us that the most reasonable option for the state is for it to shift away from the current mother tongue policy with its Asian-centricity towards a more 'open' bilingual policy. By this we mean that, in addition to English, students … can learn whichever language they want for any number of reasons: either because they consider this other language interesting, they see it as a part of their heritage, or simply because they think it is economically useful. The state may then still want to encourage Singaporean citizens to learn their various mother tongues, but this would no longer be part of an official policy which would be mandatory in the schools. Instead, Singaporeans would be able to exercise their own choice in deciding what language they consider to be their mother tongue. (Wee & Bokhorst-Heng, 2005: 176–177)

Approaches to the politics of language and policy formulation have only recently attempted to come to terms with flux and contact of multilingual networks. We have seen that multilingualism in late modernity manifests as differentiated repertoires of competences in different 'languages' and as *truncated* complexes of resources (Cook, 1992; Dyers, 2008). This means that notions such as mother tongue, first language and second language, with their assumed differences of access and proficiency, no longer adequately capture the way new emerging multilingual semiotic economies are organized. Policy then needs to work with a more differentiated and composite notion of multilingualism that can capture the varied forms of semiosis that make up speakers' or groups' *multilingual portfolios*. This notion resonates with a reflexive linguistic citizenship and is one way of articulating the idea of the four quadrants of sociolinguistic consumption. The notion of multilingual portfolio also carries a critique of modernist views of language, that construct sociolinguistic ordering, regularization, and hierarchization of language ecologies that may not be readily acceptable (or accessible) to indigenous communities (Stroud, 2001; Stroud & Heugh, 2004). However, the idea of a multilingual portfolio, or repertoire of linguistic skills and practices is, not a construct easily accommodated in current policy thinking, which relies predominantly on a conventional understanding of 'language'. So far, official attempts to accommodate the ongoing trends in Singaporean society that we noted earlier in this chapter have meant reinforcing the mother-tongue logic (e.g. denial of Eurasians' claim to mother-tongue status of English) or in allowing small digressions to this logic (permitting Malay speakers to learn Mandarin – which carries the additional problem of revising the status of Mandarin to become an instrumental, economic language rather than a mere heritage language of ethnic identification). Deconstructing the notion of mother tongue – from one that is tied to specific ethnic identities to one that is more reflective of an individual's lived experiences – would allow the language policy to better accommodate the growing diversity of the population. It would require dispensing with narratives that insist on positioning English as a purely instrumental language that should, purely by state fiat, have no place in the Singaporean identity. All of this suggests that new nation-state narratives constructed around an idea of linguistic cosmopolitanism need to be formulated. The spatially situated mother tongue that for so long has been indexical of nation-states and their borders can poorly serve such a function in late-modern Singapore. Rather than a focus on an Asian language and English, these new discourses should highlight the reality of its linguistic and ethnic mix and hybridity. As Singapore has traditionally carried a national narrative of pragmatism, endurance, the spirit of survival in a harsh and unrelenting world, and cosmopolitanism, many potential narratives would seem to offer themselves in reimagining a new collective engagement in a multilingual nation. Such narratives are already beginning to find expression within contemporary Singaporean discourses on language in other fields, such as linguistic entrepreneurship in an expanding global knowledge economy, and representations of the modern Singaporean citizen as globally mobile and infinitely flexible.

The question of course is how such new discourses may emerge in social debate. The recent Swedish national debates on language and immigration provide an illustration of how such shifts toward alternative discourses of nationalism based in common values might be constructed in practice. In that country, public debates have over the years highlighted lighter shades of feminism as core values of Swedish society. This has helped to shift the meaning of being Swedish toward a more complex, intersectional discourse of national identity and belonging. In recent media debates on immigrant youth, young men in particular have been portrayed as chauvinist and gender conservative, and language complaints that immigrant varieties of Swedish contain a rich vocabulary of gender denigration have figured prominently in the debates as evidence for this (cf. Milani, 2010). Interestingly, although this reimagination of what it means to be a Swede still feeds off traditional national sentiment against immigrants, by opening up various subject positions around gender issues, language and immigrant status, it nevertheless provides for the possibility for immigrants to step outside their stigmatized and constructed (imagined and imposed) association with male chauvinism to take up a new masculinity based in respect for women, thereby adopting core values of the new nationalism. At the same time, by suggesting that they reconstruct themselves through a more appropriate Swedish, the debate also serves to reaffirm the importance of the language for national identity, but this time admitting of a more inclusive speakership that also encompasses the 'immigrant'. Thus, while retaining a nation-state representation of language, the debates that make explicit reference to immigrants (as traditionally 'outside' the nation-state and a problem for many European countries to deal with inclusively) refigure their identities as national in terms of core values. Such renarration in public and ideological debates is a reflexive process of late modernity common to many transforming states, and is a process in which (re)constructions of language often figure prominently (cf. Blommaert, 1999).

Language Policy in Late-Modern Singapore

What then does an approach in terms of linguistic citizenship imply for the general design of Singaporean language policy? In late modernity, '[m]any of the key cornerstones of public policy analysis have become problematic as processes of globalization have disrupted the traditional analytical and conceptual frameworks through which policy-making and implementation have been understood' (Kennett, 2008: 3). Newman reminds us how 'the image of a hierarchical relationship between state and citizenry ... is displaced by the idea of multiple parallel spaces in which power is encountered and negotiated' (Newman, 2005: 4). One reason for this, of course, is that globalization has been accompanied by a proliferation and 'increasing visibility of NGOs, the rhetoric of decentralization, local partici-pation, self-help and partnership' (Kennett, 2008: 7–8). Rhodes (1997) notes how policy-making is now often carried out through networks and personal contacts than through hierarchical relationships between individuals, groups and the state (Kennett, 2008: 6; Blommaert, 2010). However, this does not mean that the state is no longer a force to reckon with in policy contexts, only that the discursive fields across which principles of policy need to travel have multiplied and become more diverse, giving rise to what Ellison (1997) has characterized as a disintegrated and complex public sphere. Thus, rather than the importance of government policy and procedure having been usurped, national governments now have a wider range of relationships and institutions across which to develop policy. Weiss (1998) has termed this 'state adaptivity' (as opposed to state retreat) or 'state augmentation' (Weiss, 2005) where globalization is actually strengthening the role of national institutions (Kennett, 2008: 11).

Thus, in a context of linguistic citizenship, actors at different levels of scale – the transnational, regional and subnational level, civil society and the corporate sphere – attempt to exercise control over language, deciding what languages are and what they may mean, and how language issues can be discursively tied to a wider range of social issues (Stroud, 2001). Language policy needs to move toward giving greater space to autonomy, such that individuals and levels of organization are allowed to decide for themselves many linguistic matters that are currently the purview of the state. The role of the state would then be to ensure that choices are made in a critically reflexive environment, one characterized by a sophisticated appreciation of language dynamics and their possible consequences. On the one hand, this places demands on government structures to prioritize questions of social justice and equity, suggesting that 'the role of government is to enable inter-actions, encourage many and varied arrangements for coping with policy, and ensure equitable distribution of services between actors through self and co-regulation' (Kennett, 2008: 5), a stance on politics that Kooiman (2003) has termed 'sociopolitical governance or interactive governance'. On the other hand, it requires of nonstate interests to find flexible ways of engaging with state structures, which manifest as various forms of Foucauldian dis-courses of governmentality (cf. Stroud, 2009). This remains a challenge not only for language policy but policymaking in late modernity generally.

Conclusion

We have noted that the implications of the tendencies, trends and proposals for a revised language policy cannot be easily managed in the existing state machinery and available political discourse on language. Both Singaporean institutions and discourses of language and citizenship remain inappropriately attuned to the sort of change and development that we have sketched in earlier sections of this chapter. At first glance it might appear as though allowing more nonethnic Chinese to learn Mandarin in government schools, or revising the mother-tongue policy to accommodate the influx of foreign talent is just a matter of tweaking a few policy paragraphs and making resources available to the relevant institutions. However, in the wider social policy context, the state's ethnolinguistically oriented language policy stands out as something of an anomaly, especially since language policies in general cannot be isolated from broader social concerns. A discussion of the language policy proper also shows how sociolinguistic reality significantly diverges from what the state intends to achieve. Such divergences, we suggested, illustrate the overriding weight of socioeconomic considerations and the critical state of ethnolinguistically based language policy models. We have noted that a sociolinguistic ordering around notions of ethnicity and nation does not fit easily with the multilingual dynamics of late-modern societies. Societal development in late modernity, we have argued, is generating linguistic hierarchies of value that are massively reconfiguring issues of language and ethnicity into questions of language and class.[3] Singapore's language policy thus needs to appreciate that patterns of multilingualism are increasingly constructed around the dynamics of language choice and change informed by a logic of life-style consumption and mobility, that is, sociolinguistic consumption. We also argued that one important principle suggested by the notion of sociolinguistic consumption is that language policy needs to move toward giving greater space to autonomy, such that individuals are allowed to decide for themselves many linguistic matters that are currently the purview of the state. The role of the state would then be to ensure that choices are made in a critically reflexive environment, one characterized by a sophisticated appreciation of language dynamics and their possible consequences. In this connection, it is encouraging to note that Singapore's Ministry of Education is currently exploring the introduction of a preuniversity program, envisaged to cover basic topics in sociolinguistics, grammar and psycholinguistics. This initiative can be expected to raise the general level of metalinguistic awareness among younger Singaporeans. The impetus at present, however, is less due to a desire to enhance autonomy and critical reflexivity in language choices than to the desire to improve students' learning of the English language. Be that as it may, this is certainly an important if tentative step in the right direction, since the state's top-down approach in deciding for its citizens what should properly constitute a politics of language, based on its own conceptual division between (ethnic) identity and instrumentalism, between a private, noneconomic sphere of action and a public economically suffused sphere, is no longer a tenable project.

In other words, adapting existing institutions and ways of conceptualizing language that leaves underlying structures of authority and decision-making on language intact will not suffice. A more radical approach in terms of linguistic citizenship needs to be developed, and in many respects, Singapore is already responding to the conditions of life in late modernity by embarking on a variety of initiatives in the direction.

Notes

(1) To accept this is not to deny that societies may differ in the kinds of consumption available and acceptable to members (Savage *et al.*, 1992).
(2) All quotations from Goh in this section are from his 1997 National Day Rally Speech.
(3) Since access to, and distribution of, goods and practices are highly correlated with socioeconomic standing, we treat consumption as an indicator of class. It is of course possible to approach class as an objective macrostructural category with attention given to the social trajectories of relatively large populations. However, it is also possible to conceive of class in more interactional terms (cf. Bradley, 1996: 45), and instead treat it as 'a social category which refers to the lived relationships surrounding social arrangements of production, exchange, distribution and consumption ...' (Bradley, 1996: 19–20). Where such relationships implicate inequalities or even differences, it is plausible to speak of an incipient sense of class consciousness and, in this way, considerations of class can mediate other characteristics such as ethnicity, gender, age and sex to the extent that these are also part of the complex set of social categories indexed by differential access to social goods (cf. Rampton, 2006: 232; see also Abercrombie & Warde *et al.*, 2000: 145ff).

References

Abercrombie, N. Warde, A., with Deem, R., Penna, S., Soothill, K., Urry, J., Sayer, A. and Walby, S. (2000) *Contemporary British Society*. Cambridge: Polity Press.

Adams, M. (2003) The reflexive self and culture: A critique. *British Journal of Sociology* 54, 221–238.

Adams, M. (2006) Hybridizing habitus and reflexivity: Towards an understanding of contemporary identity? *Sociology* 40, 511–528.

Adkins, L. (2003) Reflexivity: Freedom or habit of gender? *Theory, Culture and Society* 20, 21–42.

Agha, A. (2003) The social life of cultural value. *Language and Communication* 23, 237–273.

Agha, A. (2007) *Language and Social Relations*. Cambridge: Cambridge University Press.

Agnihotri, R.K. (2007) Towards a pedagogical paradigm rooted in multilinguality. *International Multilingual Research Journal* 1, 79–88.

Al-Arishi, A.Y. (1994) Role-play, real-play, and surreal-play in the ESOL classroom. *ELT Journal* 48, 337–346.

Allwright, D. and Bailey, K. (1991) *Focus on the Language Classroom: An Introduction to Classroom Research for Language Teachers*. Cambridge: Cambridge University Press.

Alsagoff, L. (2007) Singlish: Negotiating culture, capital and identity. In V. Vaish, S. Gopinathan and Y-B. Liu (eds) *Language, Capital, Culture: Critical Studies of Language and Education in Singapore* (pp. 25–46). Rotterdam, The Netherlands: Sense Publishers.

Althusser, L. (1971) *Lenin and Philosophy and Other Essays*. London: Verso.

Amin, A. and Thrift, N. (eds) (2004) *The Blackwell Cultural Economy Reader*. Oxford: Blackwell.

Androutsopoulos, J. (2007) Bilingualism in the mass media and on the internet. In M. Heller (ed.) *Bilingualism: A Social Approach* (pp. 207–232). London: Palgrave Macmillan.

Appadurai, A. (2001) Grassroots globalization and the research imagination. In A. Appadurai (ed.) *Globalization* (pp. 1–21). Durham, NC: Duke University Press.

Aronin, L. and Singleton, D. (2008) Multilingualism as a new linguistic world order. *International Journal of Multilingualism* 5, 1–16.

Auer, P. (1995) The pragmatics of code-switching: A sequential approach. In L. Milroy and P. Muysken (eds) *One Speaker, Two Languages: Cross-Disciplinary Perspectives on Code-Switching* (pp. 115–135). Cambridge: Cambridge University Press.

Auer, P. (1998) Introduction: Bilingual conversation revisited. In P. Auer (ed.) *Code-Switching in Conversation: Language, Interaction and Identity* (pp. 1–24). London: Routledge.

Back, L. (1996) *New Ethnicities and Urban Culture: Racisms and Multiculture in Young Lives*. London: University College London Press.

Bailey, B. (2007) Heteroglossia and boundaries. In M. Heller (ed.) *Bilingualism: A Social Approach* (pp. 257–274). New York: Palgrave Macmillan.

Baker, C. (2001) *Foundations of Bilingual Education and Bilingualism* (3rd edn). Clevedon: Multilingual Matters.

Bakhtin, M. (1981) *The Dialogic Imagination*. Austin, TX: University of Texas Press.

Bakhtin, M. (1986) *Speech Genres and Other Late Essays*. Austin, TX: University of Texas Press.

Bamgbose, A. (1992) Standard Nigerian English: Issues of identification. In B.B. Kachru (ed.) *The Other Tongue: English Across Cultures* (2nd edn) (pp. 125–147). Urbana, IL: University of Illinois Press.

Barton, D. and Hamilton, M. (1998) *Local Literacies: Reading and Writing in One Community*. London: Routledge.

Baudrillard, J. (1988) *Selected Writings*. Cambridge: Polity Press.

Bauman, R. (1977) *Verbal Art as Performance*. Prospect Heights, IL: Waveland Press.

Bauman, R. (1989) Performance. In E. Barnouw (ed.) *International Encyclopedia of Communication* 3 (pp. 262–266). New York: Oxford University Press.

Bauman, R. and Briggs, C. (1990) Poetics and performance as critical perspectives on language and social life. *Annual Review of Anthropology* 19, 59–88.

Briggs, C. and Bauman, R. (1992) Genre, intertextuality and social power. *Journal of Linguistic Anthropology* 2, 131–172.

Bauman, Z. (1998) *Work, Consumerism and the New Poor*. Buckingham: Open University Press.

Baynham, M. (2000) Narrative as evidence in literacy research. *Linguistics and Education* 11, 99–117.

Beck, U. (1992) *Risk Society*. London: Sage.

Beck, U. (1994) The reinvention of politics: Towards a theory of reflexive modernization. In U. Beck, A. Giddens and S. Lash (eds) *Reflexive Modernization: Politics, Tradition and Aesthetics in the Modern Social Order* (pp. 1–55). Cambridge: Polity Press.

Bell, A. (1984) Language style as audience design. *Language in Society* 13, 145–204.

Bell, A. (1997) Language style as audience design. In N. Coupland and A. Jaworski (eds) *Sociolinguistics: A Reader and Coursebook* (pp. 240–249). London: Macmillan.

Bell, A. (2001) Back in style: Reworking audience design. In P. Eckert and J.R. Rickford (eds) *Style and Sociolinguistic Variation* (pp. 136–169). Cambridge: Cambridge University Press.

Benhabib, S. (2002) *The Claims of Culture: Equality and Diversity in the Global Era*. Princeton, NJ: Princeton University Press.

Benjamin, G. (1976) The cultural logic of Singapore's multiracialism. In R. Hassan (ed.) *Singapore: Society in Transition* (pp. 115–133). Kuala Lumpur: Oxford University Press.

Benwell, B. and Stokoe, E. (2006) *Discourse and Identity*. Edinburgh: Edinburgh University Press.

Bhatia, T.K. and Ritchie, W.C. (2004) Bilingualism in the global media and advertising. In T.K. Bhatia and W.C. Ritchie (eds) *Handbook of Bilingualism* (pp. 513–546). Oxford: Blackwell.

Bills, D.B. (2004) *The Sociology of Education and Work*. Oxford: Blackwell.

Blackledge, A. and Creese, A. (2008) Contesting 'language' as 'heritage': Negotiation of identities in late modernity. *Applied Linguistics* 29, 533–554.

Blackledge, A. and Creese, A. (2009) Meaning-making as a dialogic process: Official and carnival lives in the language classroom. *Journal of Language, Identity and Education* 8, 236–283.

Blackledge, A. and Creese, A. (2010) *Multilingualism: A Critical Perspective*. London: Continuum Press

Blommaert, J. (1999) The debate is open. In J. Blommaert (ed.) *Language Ideological Debates* (pp. 1–38). Berlin: Mouton de Gruyter.

Blommaert, J. (2003) Commentary: A sociolinguistics of globalization. *Journal of Sociolinguistics* 7, 607–623.

Blommaert, J. (2005) *Discourse*. Cambridge: Cambridge University Press.

Blommaert, J. (2008) *Grassroots Literacy: Writing, Identity and Voice in Central Africa*. London: Routledge

Blommaert, J. (2010) *The Sociolinguistics of Globalization*. Cambridge: Cambridge University Press.

Blommaert, J. and Backus, A. (2011) Repertoires revisited: Knowing language in super-diversity. *Working Papers in Urban Language and Literacies* 67. London: King's College.

Bokhorst-Heng, W. (1998) Language and imagining the nation in Singapore. PhD dissertation, University of Toronto.

Bokhorst-Heng, W. (1999) Singapore's Speak Mandarin Campaign: Language ideological debates in the imagining of the nation. In J. Blommaert (ed.) *Language Ideological Debates* (pp. 235–265). Berlin: Mouton de Gruyter.

Bokhorst-Heng, W. (2005) Debating Singlish. *Multilingua* 24, 185–209.

Bohman, J. (1999) Practical reason and cultural constraint: Agency in Bourdieu's theory of practice. In R. Shusterman (ed.) *Bourdieu: A Critical Reader* (pp. 129–152). Oxford: Blackwell.

Bourdieu, P. (1977) *Outline of a Theory of Practice*. Cambridge: Cambridge University Press.

Bourdieu, P. (1984) *Distinction: A Social Critique of the Judgment of Taste*. Cambridge, MA: Harvard University Press.

Bourdieu, P. (1986) The forms of capital. In J.G. Richardson (ed.) *Handbook of Theory and Research in the Sociology of Education* (pp. 241–258). New York: Greenwood Press.

Bourdieu, P. (1990) *The Logic of Practice* (R. Nice, trans.). Cambridge: Polity Press.

Bourdieu, P. (1991) *Language and Symbolic Power*. Cambridge, MA: Harvard University Press.

Bourdieu, P. and Passeron, J-C. (1977) *Reproduction in Education, Society and Culture*. London: Sage.

Bourdieu, P. and Passeron, J-C. (1979) *The Inheritors: French Students and Their Relation to Culture*. Chicago: University of Chicago Press.

Bradley, H. (1996) *Fractured Identities: Changing Patterns of Inequality*. Cambridge: Polity Press.

Brandt, D. and Clinton, K. (2002) Limits of the local: Expanding perspectives on literacy as a social practice. *Journal of Literacy Research* 34, 337–356.

Brooks, A. and Wee, L. (2008) Reflexivity and the transformation of gender identity: Reviewing the potential for change in a cosmopolitan city. *Sociology* 42, 503–521.

Brumfit, C. (1991) Language awareness in teacher education. In C. James and P. Garrett (eds) *Language Awareness in the Classroom* (pp. 24–39). London: Longman.

Brysk, A. (2002) Introduction: Transnational threats and opportunities. In A. Brysk (ed.) *Globalization and Human Rights* (pp. 1–16). Berkeley, CA: University of California Press.

Bucholtz, M. (2002) Youth and cultural practice. *Annual Review of Anthropology* 31, 525–552.

Bucholtz, M. (2009) From stance to style: Gender, interaction, and indexicality in Mexican immigrant youth slang. In A. Jaffe (ed.) *Stance: Sociolinguistic Perspectives*. Oxford: Oxford University Press.

Bucholtz, M. and Hall, K. (2004) Language and identity. In A. Duranti (ed.) *The Blackwell Companion to Linguistic Anthropology* (pp. 369–394). Oxford: Blackwell.

Calhoun, C. (1993) Habitus, field and capital: The question of historical specificity. In C. Calhoun, E. LiPuma and M. Postone (eds) *Bourdieu: Critical Perspectives* (pp. 61–88). Chicago: University of Chicago Press.

Calhoun, C. (2001) The necessity and limits of cosmopolitanism: Local democracy in a global context. Paper presented at the meeting of UNESCO on Identity and Difference in the Global Era, Rio de Janeiro, Brazil.

Calhoun, C. (2003) Pierre Bourdieu. In G. Ritzer (ed.) *The Blackwell Companion to Major Contemporary Social Theorists* (pp. 274–309). Oxford: Blackwell.

Cameron, D. (1995) *Verbal Hygiene*. New York: Routledge.

Cameron, D. (2000) Styling the worker: Gender and the commodification of language in the globalized service economy. *Journal of Sociolinguistics* 4, 323–347.

Canagarajah, S. (1999) *Resisting Linguistic Imperialism in English Teaching*. Oxford: Oxford University Press.

Canagarajah, S. (2004a) Subversive identities, pedagogical safe houses, and critical learning. In B. Norton and K. Toohey (eds) *Critical Pedagogies and Language Learning* (pp. 116–137). Cambridge: Cambridge University Press.

Canagarajah, S. (2004b) Multilingual writers and the struggle for voice in academic discourse. In A. Pavelenko and A. Blackledge (eds) *Negotiation of Identities in Multilingual Contexts* (pp. 266–289). Clevedon: Multilingual Matters.

Canagarajah, S. (2007) Lingua franca English, multilingual communities, and language acquisition. *The Modern Language Journal* 91, 923–939.

Canale, M. and Swain, M. (1980) Theoretical bases of communicative approaches to second language teaching and testing. *Applied Linguistics* 1, 1–47.

Carrington, V. and Luke, A. (1997) Literacy and Bourdieu's sociological theory: A reframing. *Language and Education* 11, 96–112.

Cheshire, J. (1982) Dialect features and linguistic conflict in schools. *Educational Review* 14 53–67.

Chng, H.H. (2003) 'You see me no up': Is Singlish a problem? *Language Problems and Language Planning* 27, 45–62.

Chua, B.H. (1983) Re-opening ideological discussion in Singapore: A new theoretical direction. *Southeast Asian Journal of Social Science* 11, 31–45.

Chua, B.H. (2003) *Life is Not Complete without Shopping: Consumption Culture in Singapore*. Singapore: Singapore University Press.

Clammer, J. (1985) *Singapore: Ideology, Society, Culture*. Singapore: Chopman.

Clarke, D. (1989) Communicative theory and its influence on materials production: State-of-the-art article. *Language Teaching* 22, 73–86.

Cohen, P. (ed.) (1999) *New Ethnicities, Old Racisms*. London: Zed Books.

Cohen, R. (1997) *Global Diasporas: An Introduction*. London: University College London Press.

Collins, J. (1993) Determination and contradiction: An appreciation and critique of the work of Pierre Bourdieu on language and education. In C. Calhoun, E. LiPuma and M. Postone (eds) *Bourdieu: Critical Perspectives* (pp. 116–138). Chicago: University of Chicago Press.

Collins, J. (1995) Literacy and literacies. *Annual Review of Anthropology* 24, 75–93.

Cook, V. (1992) Evidence for multi-competence. *Language Learning* 42, 557–591.

Cook, V. (2001) Using first language in the classroom. *Canadian Modern Language Review* 57, 402–423.

Cope, B. and Kalantzis, M. (eds) (1993) *The Powers of Literacy: A Genre Approach to Teaching Writing*. London: Falmer Press.

Corson, D. (2001) *Language Diversity and Education*. Mahwah, NJ: Lawrence Erlbaum.

Coupland, N. (2001) Language, situation, and the relational self: Theorizing dialect-style in sociolinguistics. In P. Eckert and J.R. Rickford (eds) *Style and Sociolinguistic Variation* (pp. 185–210). Cambridge: Cambridge University Press.

Coupland, N. (2004) Sytlised deception. In A. Jaworski, N. Coupland and D. Galasinski (eds) *Metalanguage: Social and Ideological Perspectives* (pp. 249–273). Berlin: Mouton de Gruyter.

Coupland, N. (2007) *Style: Language Variation and Identity*. Cambridge: Cambridge University Press.

Cowan, P. (2005) Putting it out there: Revealing Latino visual discourse in the Hispanic Academic Program for middle school students. In B. Street (ed.) *Literacies Across Educational Contexts: Mediating Learning and Teaching* (pp. 145–169). Philadelphia, PA: Caslon Publishers.

Cowan, P. (2008) The transcontextualization of Chicano visual discourse. *57th Annual Yearbook of the National Reading Conference*. Chicago: National Reading Conference.

Craib, I. (1994) *The Importance of Disappointment*. London: Routledge.

Creese, A., Bhatt, A., Bhojani, N. and Martin, P. (2006) Multicultural heritage and learner identities in complementary schools. *Language and Education* 20, 23–44.

Crowley, T. (1999) Curiouser and curiouser: Falling standards in the Standard English debate. In T. Bex and R. Watts (eds) *Standard English: The Widening Debate* (pp. 271–282) London: Routledge.

Crystal, D. (1997) *English as a Global Language*. Cambridge: Cambridge University Press.

Da Silva, E., McLaughlin, M. and Richards, M. (2007) The globalized new economy: The commodification of bilingualism and the emergence of the language worker. In M. Heller (ed.) *Bilingualism: A Social Approach* (pp. 183–206). Macmillan Publishers.

Davies, A. (1999) Standard English: Discordant voices. *World Englishes* 18, 171–186.

Davison, C. and Williams, A. (2001) Integrating language and content: Unresolved issues. In B. Mohan, C. Leung and C. Davison (eds) *English as a Second Language in the Mainstream: Teaching, Learning and Identity* (pp. 51–70). London: Longman.

De Schutter, H. (2007) Language policy and political philosophy: On the emerging linguistic justice debate. *Language Problems and Language Planning* 31, 1–23.

Deveaux, M. (2005) A deliberative approach to conflicts of culture. In A. Eissenberg and J. Spinner-Halev (eds) *Minorities within Minorities: Equality, Rights and Diversity* (pp. 340–362). Cambridge: Cambridge University Press.

Dryzek, J. (2000) Discursive democracy vs. liberal constitutionalism. In M. Saward (ed.) *Democratic Innovation* (pp. 78–89). London: Routledge.

Du Gay, P. (1996) *Consumption and Identity at Work*. London: Sage.

Duranti, A. (1992) Intentions, self, and responsibility: An essay in Samoan ethnopragmatics. In J.H. Hill and J.T. Irvine (eds) *Responsibility and Evidence in Oral Discourse* (pp. 24–47). Cambridge: Cambridge University Press.

Duranti, A. and Goodwin, C. (eds) (1992) *Rethinking Context: Language as an Interactive Phenomenon*. Cambridge: Cambridge University Press.

Dyers, C. (2008) Truncated multilingualism or language shift? An examination of language use in intimate domains in a new non-racial working class township in South Africa. *Journal of Multilingual and Multicultural Development* 29, 110–126.

Eckert, P. (2000) *Linguistic Variation as Social Practice*. Oxford: Blackwell.

Eckert, P. (2001) Style and social meaning. In P. Eckert and J.R. Rickford (eds) *Style and Sociolinguistic Variation* (pp. 119–126). Cambridge: Cambridge University Press.

Eckert, P. (2005) Variation, convention and social meaning. Paper presented at the Annual Meeting of the Linguistic Society of America, January 7, 2005. Oakland, CA.

Eckert, P. and Rickford, J. (eds) (2001) *Style and Sociolinguistic Variation*. Cambridge: Cambridge University Press.

Ellison, N. (1997) Towards a new social politics: Citizenship and reflexivity in late modernity. *Sociology* 31, 697–717.

Erickson, F. (2001) Co-membership and wiggle room: Some implications of the study of talk for the development of social theory. In N. Coupland, S. Sarangi and C. Candlin (eds) *Sociolinguistics and Social Theory* (pp. 152–181). London: Longman.

Fairclough, N. (2006) *Language and Globalization*. London: Routledge.

Ferguson, G. (2006) *Language Planning and Education*. Edinburgh: Edinburgh University Press.

Fishman, J. (1989) *Language and Ethnicity in Minority Sociolinguistic Perspective*. Clevedon: Multilingual Matters.

Frankfurt, H. (1988) *The Importance of What We Care about*. Cambridge: Cambridge University Press.

Fraser, N. (1998) From redistribution to recognition? Dilemmas of justice in a 'post-socialist' age. In C. Willett (ed.) *Theorizing Multiculturalism* (pp. 19–49). Oxford: Blackwell.

Freeland, J. and Patrick, D. (2004) Language rights and language survival: Sociolinguistic and sociocultural perspectives. In J. Freeland and D. Patrick (eds) *Language Rights and Language Survival: Sociolinguistic and Sociocultural Perspectives* (pp. 1–33). Manchester: St. Jerome Publishing.

French, B. (2000) The symbolic capital of social identities: The genre of bargaining in an urban Guatemalan market. *Journal of Linguistic Anthropology* 10, 55–89.

Foucault, M. (1982) The order of discourse. In M. Shapiro (ed.) *Language and Politics* (pp. 108–138). London: Blackwell.

Fowler, B. (1997) *Pierre Bourdieu and Cultural Theory: Critical Investigations*. London: Sage.

Gal, S. and Irvine, J.T. (1995) The boundaries of languages and disciplines: How ideologies construct difference. *Social Research* 62, 967–1001.

Garçia, O. (2009) *Bilingual Education in the 21st Century: A Global Perspective*. Oxford: Wiley.

Gee, J.P. (1990) *Social Linguistics and Literacies*. London: Falmer Press

Gee, J.P. (2000) New people in new worlds: Networks, the new capitalism and schools. In B. Cope and M. Kalantzis (eds) *Multiliteracies: Literacy Learning and the Design of Social Futures* (pp. 43–68). London: Routledge.

Gee, J.P. (2001) Educational linguistics. In M. Aronoff and J. Rees-Miller (eds) *The Handbook of Linguistics* (pp. 647–663). Oxford: Blackwell.

Giddens, A. (1982) *The Constitution of Society*. Berkeley, CA: University of California Press.

Giddens, A. (1990) *The Consequences of Modernity*. Cambridge: Polity Press.

Giddens, A. (1991) *Modernity and Self-Identity: Self and Society in the Late Modern Age*. Cambridge: Polity Press.

Giddens, A. (1992) *The Transformation of Intimacy*. Cambridge: Polity Press.

Giddens, A. (1994) Replies and critiques. In U. Beck, A. Giddens and S. Lash (eds) *Reflexive Modernization* (pp. 174–215). Cambridge: Polity Press.

Goffman, E. (1974) *Frame Analysis*. New York: Harper & Row.

Goffman, E. (1981) *Forms of Talk*. Philadelphia, PA: University of Pennsylvania Press.

Goldberg, A.E. (1995) *Constructions: A Construction Grammar Approach to Argument Structure*. Chicago: University of Chicago Press.

Goldstein, T. (2003) Contemporary bilingual life at a Canadian high school: Choices, risks, tensions and dilemmas. *Sociology of Education* 76, 247–264.

Goodwin, M.H. (2006) *The Hidden Life of Girls: Games of Stance, Status and Exclusion*. Oxford: Blackwell.

Goodwin, C. and Goodwin, M.H. (2004) Participation. In A. Duranti (ed.) *A Companion to Linguistic Anthropology* (pp. 222–244). Oxford: Blackwell.

Gopinathan, S., Pakir, A., Ho, W.K. and Saravanan, V. (eds) (1998) *Language, Society and Education in Singapore: Issues and Trends*. Singapore: Times Academic Press.

Grosjean, F. (2008) *Studying Bilinguals*. Oxford: Oxford University Press.

Gumperz, J. (1982) *Discourse Strategies*. Cambridge: Cambridge University Press.

Gupta, A.F. (1994) *The Step-Tongue: Children's English in Singapore*. Clevedon: Multilingual Matters.

Gupta, A.F. (1998) The situation of English in Singapore. In J.A. Foley, T. Kandiah, Z.M. Bao, A.F. Gupta, L. Alsagoff, C.L. Ho, L. Wee, I.S. Talib and W. Bokhorst-Heng (eds) *English in New Cultural Contexts: Reflections from Singapore* (pp. 106–126). Singapore: Oxford University Press.

Gupta, A.F. and Siew, P.Y. (1995) Language shift in a Singapore family. *Journal of Multilingual and Multicultural Development* 16, 301–314.

Gutiérrez, K., Baquedano-Lopez, P. and Alvarez, H.H. (2001) Literacy as hybridity: Moving beyond bilingualism in urban classrooms. In M. Reyes and J.J. Halcón (eds) *The Best for Our Children: Critical Perspectives on Literacy for Latino Students* (pp. 122–141). New York: Teachers College Press.

Hall, D. (1995) Materials production: Theory and practice. In A. Hidalgo, D. Hall and G. Jacobs (eds) *Getting Started: Materials Writers on Materials Writing* (pp. 8–24). Singapore: SEAMEO Regional Language Centre.

Han, F. K., Fernandez, W. and Tan, S. (1998) *Lee Kuan Yew: The Man and His Ideas*. Singapore: Times Academic Press.

Hasan, R. (1999) The disempowerment game: Bourdieu and language in literacy. *Linguistics and Education* 10, 25–87.

Hawkins, M.R. (2005) Becoming a student: Identity work and academic literacies in early schooling. *TESOL Quarterly* 39, 59–82.

Heath, S.B. (1983) *Ways with Words*. Cambridge: Cambridge University Press.

Heath, S.B. (1994) What no bedtime story means: Narrative skills at home and school. In J. Maybin (ed.) *Language and Literacy in Social Practice: A Reader* (pp. 73–95). Clevedon: Multilingual Matters.

Hebdige, D. (1979) *Subculture: The Meaning of Style*. London: Methuen.

Heelas, P. (1996) Detraditionalization and its rivals. In P. Heelas, S. Lash and P. Morris (eds) *Detraditionalization* (pp. 1–20). Oxford: Blackwell.

Held, D. (2006) *Models of Democracy* (3rd edn). Cambridge: Polity Press.

Heller, M. (1995) Code-switching and the politics of language. In L. Milroy and P. Muysken (eds) *One Speaker, Two Languages: Cross-Disciplinary Perspectives on Code-Switching* (pp. 158–174). Cambridge: Cambridge University Press.

Heller, M. (1999a) Alternative ideologies of *la francophonie*. *Journal of Sociolinguistics* 3, 336–359.

Heller, M. (1999b) *Linguistic Minorities and Modernity: A Sociolinguistic Ethnography*. London: Longman.

Heller, M. (2001) Undoing the macro/micro dichotomy. In N. Coupland, S. Sarangi and C. Candlin (eds) *Sociolinguistics and Social Theory* (pp. 212–234). London: Longman.

Heller, M. (ed.) (2007) *Bilingualism: A Social Approach*. New York: Palgrave Macmillan.

Heller, M. (2008a) Language and the nation-state: Challenges to sociolinguistic theory and practice. *Journal of Sociolinguistics* 12, 504–524.

Heller, M. (2008b) Bourdieu and 'literacy education'. In J. Albright and A. Luke (eds) *Pierre Bourdieu and Literacy Education* (pp. 50–67). New York: Continuum.

Heller, M. and Martin-Jones, M. (2001) *Voices of Authority: Education and Linguistic Difference*. London: Ablex Publishing.

Hill, J. H. and Irvine, J.T. (eds) (1992) *Responsibility and Evidence in Oral Discourse*. Cambridge: Cambridge University Press.

Hilleson, M. (1996) 'I want to talk with them, but I don't want them to hear': An introspective study of second language anxiety in an English-medium school. In K.M. Bailey and D. Nunan (eds) *Voices from the Language Classroom* (pp. 248–278). Cambridge: Cambridge University Press.

Hing, K. (2004) Chinese dialects in Singapore: Reversing language shift. Honours thesis, National University of Singapore.

Hochschild, A.R. (1983) *The Managed Heart: Commercialization of Human Feeling*. Berkeley, CA: University of California Press.

Hull, G. and Schultz, K. (2002) Connecting schools with out-of-school worlds. In G. Hull and K. Schultz (eds) *School's Out! Bridging Out-of-School Literacies with Classroom Practice* (pp. 32–57). New York: Teachers College Press.

Hymes, D. (1972) Models of the interaction of language and social life. In J. Gumperz and D. Hymes (eds) *Directions in Sociolinguistics: The Ethnography of Communication*. Oxford: Blackwell.

Iedema, R. (2001) Resemiotization. *Semiotica* 137, 23–39.

Iedema, R. (2003) Multimodality, resemiotization: Extending the analysis of discourse and multi-semiotic practice. *Visual Communication* 2, 29–57.

Irvine, J.T. (1985) Status and style in language. *Annual Review of Anthropology* 14, 557–581.

Irvine, J.T. and Gal, S. (2000) Language ideology and linguistic differentiation. In P. Kroskrity (ed.) *Regimes of Language* (pp. 35–83). Santa Fe, N M: School of American Research.

Jacquemet, M. (2005) Transidiomatic practices: Language and power in the age of globalization. *Language & Communication* 25, 257–277.

Jaffe, A. (1999) *Ideologies in Action: Language Politics on Corsica*. Berlin: Mouton de Gruyter.

Jakobson, R. (ed.) (1980) *The Framework of Language*. Ann Arbor, MI: University of Michigan Press.

James, C. and Garrett, P. (eds) (1991) *Language Awareness in the Classroom*. London: Longman.

Jenkins, J. (2000) *The Phonology of English as an International Language*. Oxford: Oxford University Press.

Jenkins, R. (1992) *Pierre Bourdieu*. London: Routledge.

Johnstone, B. (1990) *Stories, Community and Place: Narratives from Middle America*. Bloomington, IN: Indiana University Press.

Johnstone, B. (2000) *Qualitative Methods in Sociolinguistics*. New York: Oxford University Press.

Johnstone, B. (2001) *Discourse Analysis*. Oxford: Blackwell.
Johnstone, B. (2004) Place, globalization, and linguistic variation. In C. Fought (ed.) *Sociolinguistic Variation: Critical Reflections* (pp. 65–83). New York: Oxford University Press.
Jones, K. (1982) *Simulations in Language Teaching*. Cambridge: Cambridge University Press.
Kachru, B.B. (1985) Standards, codification, and sociolinguistic realism: The English language in the outer circle. In R. Quirk and H.G. Widdowson (eds) *English in the World: Teaching and Learning the Language and Literature* (pp. 11–30). Cambridge: Cambridge University Press.
Kachru, B.B. (1986) *The Alchemy of English*. Oxford: Pergamon Press.
Kachru, B.B. (1991) Liberation linguistics and the Quirk concern. *English Today* 25, 3–13.
Kachru, B.B. (2005) *Asian Englishes: Beyond the Canon*. Hong Kong: Hong Kong University Press.
Keat, R. and Abercrombie, N. (eds) (1991) *Enterprise Culture*. London: Routledge.
Kennedy, P. (2001) Introduction: Globalization and the crisis of identities? In P. Kennedy and C. Danks (eds) *Globalization and National Identities: Crisis or Opportunity?* (pp. 1–28). New York: Palgrave Macmillan.
Kennett, P. (ed.) (2008) *Governance, Globalization and Public Policy*. Cheltenham: Edward Elgar.
Kerfoot, C. (forthcoming). Making and shaping participatory spaces: Resemiotization and citizenship agency. In L. Lim, C. Stroud and L. Wee (eds) *The Multilingual Citizen: Towards a Politics of Language for Agency and Change*. Manchester: St. Jerome Press.
Kern, R. (2000) *Literacy and Language Teaching*. Oxford: Oxford University Press.
Kooiman, J. (2003) *Governing as Governance*. London: Sage.
Kramsch, C. (2007) The uses of communicative competence in a global world. In J. Liu (ed.) *English Language Teaching in China* (pp. 55–74). London: Continuum.
Kramsch, C. (2009) *The Multilingual Subject*. Oxford: Oxford University Press.
Kramsch, C. and Whiteside, A. (2008) Language ecology in multilingual settings: Towards a theory of symbolic competence. *Applied Linguistics* 29, 645–671.
Krashen, S. (1981) *Second Language Acquisition and Second Language Learning*. Oxford: Pergamon.
Krashen, S. (1982) *Principles and Practice in Second Language Acquisition*. Oxford: Pergamon.
Kwan, M.Y. (2003) *The Speak Good English Movement: A Debate of the Englishes*. MA thesis, National University of Singapore.
Kwan-Terry, A. and Luke, K.K. (1997) Tradition, trial and error: Standard and vernacular literacy in China, Hong Kong, Singapore and Malaysia. In A. Tabouret-Keller, R.B. Le Page, P. Gardner-Chloros and G. Varro (eds) *Vernacular Literacy: A Re-evaluation* (pp. 271–315). Oxford: Clarendon Press.
Labov, W. (1966) *The Social Stratification of English in New York City*. Washington, DC: Center for Applied Linguistics.
Labov, W. (1972) *Language in the Inner City*. Philadelphia, PA: University of Pennsylvania Press.
Labov, W. and Waletzky, J. (1967) Narrative analysis: Oral versions of personal experience. In J. Helms (ed.) *Essays on the Verbal and Visual Arts* (pp. 12–44). Seattle, Washington, DC: University of Washington Press.
Langacker, R.W. (1987) *Foundations of Cognitive Grammar, Vol. 1: Theoretical Prerequisites*. Stanford: Stanford University Press.
Lareau, A. (2003) *Unequal Childhoods: Class, Race, and Family Life*. Berkeley, CA: University of California Press.

Lash, S. (1993) Pierre Bourdieu: Cultural economy and social change. In C. Calhoun, E. LiPuma and M. Postone (eds) *Bourdieu: Critical Perspectives* (pp. 193–211). Chicago: University of Chicago Press.

Lash, S. (1994) Reflexivity and its doubles: Structure, aesthetics, community. In U. Beck, A. Giddens and S. Lash (eds) *Reflexive Modernization* (pp. 110–173). Cambridge: Polity Press.

Lash, S. and Urry, J. (1994) *Economies of Sign and Space.* London: Sage.

Lau, K.E. (1993) *Singapore Census of Population 1990. Statistical Release 3.* Singapore: SNP Publishers.

Lave, J. and Wenger, E. (1991) *Situated Learning: Legitimate Peripheral Participation.* New York: Cambridge University Press.

Lawler, S. (2003) Narrative in social research. In T. May (ed.) *Qualitative Research in Action* (pp. 242–258). Thousand Oaks, CA: Sage.

Lee, C.D. (1993) *Signifying as a Scaffold for Literary Interpretation: The Pedagogical Implications of an African American Discourse Genre.* Urbana, IL: National Council of Teachers of English.

Leidner, R. (1993) *Fast Food, Fast Talk: Service Work and the Routinization of Everyday Life.* Berkeley, CA: University of California Press.

Leow, B.G. (2000) *Census of Population 2000: Education, Language and Religion. Statistical Release 2.* Singapore: Department of Statistics.

Levinson, S. (1992) Activity types and language. In P. Drew and J. Heritage (eds) *Talk at Work: Interaction in Institutional Settings* (pp. 66–100). Cambridge: Cambridge University Press. Originally published in *Linguistics* 17, 356–399.

Lewis, C. (2001) *Literacy Practices as Social Acts: Power, Status and Cultural Norms in the Classroom.* Mahwah, NJ: Lawrence Erlbaum.

Li, W., Saravanan, V. and Ng, J. (1997) Language shift in the Teochew community in Singapore: A family domain analysis. *Journal of Multilingual and Multicultural Development* 18, 364–384.

Lin, A.M.Y. and Luk, J.C.M. (2005) Local creativity in the face of global domination: Insights of Bakhtin for teaching English for dialogic communication. In J.K. Hall, G. Vitanova and L. Marchenkova (eds) *Dialogue with Bakhtin on Second and Foreign Language Learning: New Perspectives* (pp. 77–88). Mahwah, NJ: Lawrence Erlbaum.

Linde, C. (2001) Narrative in institutions. In D. Schiffrin, D. Tannen and H. Hamilton (eds) *The Handbook of Discourse Analysis* (pp. 518–535). Oxford: Blackwell.

Littlewood, W. (1981) *Communicative Language Teaching.* Cambridge: Cambridge University Press.

Lu, L. (2005) *Are We Missing the Point? A Bourdieuian Perspective of Language Planning and Policy in Singapore.* Honours thesis, National University of Singapore.

Luk, J.C.M. (2008) Classroom discourse and the construction of the learner and teacher identities. In M. Martin-Jones, A-M. de Meija and N.H. Hornberger (eds) *Encyclopedia of Language and Education 3: Discourse and Education* (pp. 121–134). New York: Springer.

Luke, A. (1997) Genres of power: Literacy education and the production of capital. In R. Hasan and G. Williams (eds) *Literacy in Society* (pp. 308–338). London: Longman.

Luke, A. (2004) On the material consequences of literacy. *Language and Education* 18, 331–335.

Maher, K. (2002) Who has the right to rights? Citizenship's exclusions in an age of migration. In A. Brysk (ed.) *Globalization and Human Rights* (pp. 19–43). Berkeley, CA: University of California Press.

Makoni, S. and Pennycook, A. (2007) Disinventing and reconstituting languages. In S. Makoni and A. Pennycook (eds) *Disinventing and Reconstituting Languages* (pp. 1–41). Clevedon: Multilingual Matters.

Mani, A. and Gopinathan, S. (1983) Changes in Tamil language acquisition and usage in Singapore: A case of subtractive bilingualism. *Southeast Asian Journal of Social Science* 11, 104–117.

Marginson, S. (1992) After globalization: Emerging politics of education. *Journal of Education Policy* 14, 19–31.

Martin-Jones, M. (1995) Code-switching in the classroom: Two decades of research. In L. Milroy and P. Muysken (eds) *One Speaker, Two Languages: Cross-Disciplinary Perspectives on Code-Switching* (pp. 90–111). Cambridge: Cambridge University Press.

Maschler, Y. (1994) Metalanguaging and discourse markers in bilingual conversation. *Language in Society* 23, 325–366.

May, S. (2001) *Language and Minority Rights*. London: Longman.

Mauzy, D.K. and Milne, R.S. (2002) *Singapore Politics under the People's Action Party*. London: Routledge.

McNay, L. (1999) Gender, habitus and the field: Pierre Bourdieu and the limits of reflexivity. *Theory, Culture & Society* 16, 95–117.

McNay, L. (2000) *Gender and Agency: Reconfiguring the Subject in Feminist and Social Theory*. Cambridge: Polity Press.

McNay, L. (2008) *Against Recognition*. Cambridge: Polity Press.

Mesthrie, R. and Bhatt, R.M. (2008) *World Englishes*. Cambridge: Cambridge University Press.

Michaels, S. (1981) 'Sharing time': Children's narrative styles and differential access to literacy. *Language in Society* 10, 423–442.

Milani, T. (2010) What's in a name? Language ideology and social differentiation in a Swedish print-mediated debate. *Journal of Sociolinguistics*, 14, 116–142.

Miller, J. (2004) Identity and language use: The politics of speaking ESL in schools. In A. Pavlenko and A. Blackledge (eds) *Negotiation of Identities in Multilingual Contexts* (pp. 290–315). Clevedon: Multilingual Matters.

Milroy, J. (2001) Language ideologies and the consequences of standardization. *Journal of Sociolinguistics* 5, 530–555.

Milroy, J. and Milroy, L. (1999) *Authority in Language* (3rd edn). London: Routledge.

Mitchell, R. and Hooper, J. (1991) Teachers' views of language knowledge. In C. James and P. Garrett (eds) *Language Awareness in the Classroom* (pp. 40–61). London: Longman.

Moje, E.B. (2000) 'To be part of the story': The literacy practices of gangsta adolescents. *Teachers College Record* 102, 651–690.

Mouffe, C. (1992) Feminism, citizenship and radical democratic politics. In J. Butler and J. Scott (eds) *Feminists Theorize the Political* (pp. 369–384). New York: Routledge.

Mufwene, S.S. (2002) Colonisation, globalization, and the future of languages in the twenty-first century. *MOST International Journal on Multicultural Societies* 4, 1–48. http://www.unesco.org/most. Last accessed on 15.05.04.

Newman, J. (ed.) (2005) *Remaking Governance: People, Politics and the Public Sphere*. Bristol: Policy Press.

Norton, B. (1995) Social identity, investment and language learning. *TESOL Quarterly* 29, 9–31.

Norton, B. (2000) *Identity and Language Learning: Gender, Ethnicity and Educational Change*. Harlow: Pearson.

Ong, A. (2006) *Neoliberalism as Exception: Mutations in Citizenship and Sovereignty.* Durham: Duke University Press.

Ong, D. (2003) Unsuccessful student writing: An ethnographic study. MA thesis, National University of Singapore.

Pakir, A. (1992) English-knowing bilingualism in Singapore. In K.C. Ban, A. Pakir and C.K. Tong (eds) *Imagining Singapore* (pp. 234–262) Singapore: Times Academic Press.

Pakir, A. (2000) Singapore. In W.K. Ho and R.Y.L. Wong (eds) *Language Policies and Language Education: The Impact in East Asian Countries in the Next Decade* (pp. 259–284). Singapore: Times Academic Press.

Park, J. and Wee, L. (2009) The three circles redux: A market-theoretic perspective on World Englishes. *Applied Linguistics* 30, 389–406.

Pavlenko, A. (2001) Bilingualism, gender and ideology. *International Journal of Bilingualism* 5, 117–151.

Pavlenko, A. and Blackledge, A. (2004) *Negotiation of Identities in Multilingual Contexts.* Clevedon: Multilingual Matters.

Pennycook, A. (1994) *The Cultural Politics of English as an International Language.* London: Longman.

Pennycook, A. (2001) *Critical Applied Linguistics.* Mahwah, NJ: Lawrence Erlbaum.

Pennycook, A. (2003) Global Englishes, Rip Slyme and performativity. *Journal of Sociolinguistics* 7, 513–533.

Phelan, S. (1995) The space of justice: Lesbians and democratic politics. In L. Nicholson and S. Seidman (eds) *Social Postmodernism* (pp. 332–356). Cambridge: Cambridge University Press.

Phillipson, R. (1992) *Linguistic Imperialism.* Oxford: Oxford University Press.

Phillipson, R. and Skutnabb-Kangas, T. (1995) Linguistic rights and wrongs. *Applied Linguistics* 16, 483–504.

Pillai, A.D. (2003) Language use amongst Singaporean Malayalee families. MA thesis, National University of Singapore.

Plummer, K. (2001) The square of intimate citizenship: Some preliminary proposals. *Citizenship Studies* 5, 237–251.

PuruShotam, N. (1998) *Negotiating Language, Constructing Race.* Berlin: Mouton de Gruyter.

Ramanathan, V. (2005) Rethinking language planning and policy from the ground up: Refashioning institutional realities and human lives. *Current Issues in Language Planning* 6, 89–101.

Rampton, B. (1991) Interracial Punjabi in a British adolescent peer group. *Language in Society* 20, 391–422.

Rampton, B. (1995) *Crossing: Language and Ethnicity among Adolescents.* London: Longman.

Rampton, B. (1998) Language crossing and the redefinition of reality. In P. Auer (ed.) *Code-Switching in Conversation* (pp. 290–320). London: Routledge.

Rampton, B. (ed.) (1999) Styling the other. Special issue. *Journal of Sociolinguistics* 3, 421–590.

Rampton, B. (2002) Ritual and foreign language practices at school. *Language in Society* 31, 491–525.

Rampton, B. (2006) *Language in Late Modernity: Interaction in an Urban School.* Cambridge: Cambridge University Press.

Rampton, B. (2011) Style in a second language. *Working Papers in Urban Languages and Literacies* 65. London: King's College.

Rappa, A. and Wee, L. (2006) *Language Policy and Modernity in Southeast Asia.* New York: Springer.

Rhodes, R. (1997) *Understanding Governance*. Basingstoke: Macmillan.

Ricento, T. (ed.) (2006) *An Introduction to Language Policy, Theory and Practice*. Oxford: Blackwell.

Richardson-Bruna, K. (2007) Traveling tags: The informal literacies of Mexican newcomers in and out of the classroom. *Linguistics and Education* 18, 232–257.

Rickford, J.R. (2001) Style and stylizing from the perspective of a non-autonomous sociolinguistics. In P. Eckert and J.R. Rickford (eds) *Style and Sociolinguistic Variation* (pp. 220–231). Cambridge: Cambridge University Press.

Rogers, A. (2001) Afterword. In B. Street (ed.) *Literacy and Development* (pp. 205–222). Cambridge: Cambridge University Press.

Romaine, S. (2001) Multilingualism. In M. Aronoff and J. Rees-Miller (eds) *The Handbook of Linguistics* (pp. 512–532). Oxford: Blackwell.

Rosaldo, M.Z. (1982) The things we do with words: Ilongot speech acts and speech act theory in philosophy. *Language in Society* 11, 203–237.

Rose, N. (1989) *Governing the Soul*. London: Routledge.

Rossner, R. (1988) Materials for communicative language teaching and learning. In C. Brumfit (ed.) *Annual Review of Applied Linguistics* (Vol. 8, pp. 140–163). Cambridge: Cambridge University Press.

Rothenbuhler, E. (1998) *Ritual Communication*. London: Sage.

Rubdy, R. (2001) Creative destruction: Singapore's Speak Good English Movement. *World Englishes* 20, 341–355.

Sanders, L.M. (1997) Against deliberation. *Political Theory* 25, 347–376.

Saravanan, V. (1994) Language and social identity amongst Tamil–English bilinguals in Singapore. In R. Khoo, U. Kreher and R. Wong (eds) *Languages in Contact in a Multilingual Society* (pp. 79–93). Clevedon: Multilingual Matters.

Saravanan, V. (1998) Language maintenance and language shift in the Tamil–English community. In S. Gopinathan, A. Pakir, W.K. Ho and V. Saravanan (eds) *Language, Society and Education in Singapore* (pp. 175–204). Singapore: Times Academic Press.

Sassen, S. (2006) *Territory, Authority, Rights: From Medieval to Global Assemblages*. Princeton, NJ: Princeton University Press.

Sassoon, A.S. (1991) Equality and difference: The emergence of a new concept of citizenship. In D. McLellan and S. Sayers (eds) *Socialism and Democracy*. London: Macmillan.

Savage, M., Barlow, J., Dickens, P. and Fielding, T. (1992) *Property, Bureaucracy and Culture: Middle-Class Formation in Contemporary Britain*. London: Routledge.

Scollon, R. and Scollon, S. (1979) The literate two-year old: The fictionalization of self. *Working Papers in Sociolinguistics*. Austin, TX: Southwest Regional Laboratory.

Searle, J. (1969) *Speech Acts*. Cambridge: Cambridge University Press.

Shamim, F. (1996) In or out of the action zone: Location as a feature of interaction in large ESL classes in Pakistan. In K.M. Bailey and D. Nunan (eds) *Voices from the Language Classroom* (pp. 123–144). Cambridge: Cambridge University Press.

Shohamy, E. (2006) *Language Policy: Hidden Agendas and New Approaches*. London: Routledge.

Shohamy, E. (2007) Reinterpreting globalization in multilingual contexts. *International Multilingual Research Journal* 1, 127–133.

Siddique, S. (1990) The phenomenology of ethnicity: A Singapore case study. *Sojourn* 5, 35–62.

Siegel, J. (1999) Stigmatized and standardized varieties in the classroom: Interference or separation. *TESOL Quarterly* 33, 701–728.

Silverstein, M. (1977) Cultural prerequisites to grammatical analysis. In M. Saville-Troike (ed.) *Linguistics and Anthropology (GURT* 1977) (pp. 139–151). Washington, DC: Georgetown University Press.

Silverstein, M. (1979) Language structure and linguistic ideology. In P. Clyne, W. Hanks and C. Hofbaue (eds) *The Elements: A Parasession on Linguistic Units and Levels* (pp. 193–247). Chicago: Chicago Linguistic Society.

Silverstein, M. (1998) Contemporary transformations of local linguistic communities. *Annual Review of Anthropology* 27, 401–426.

Silverstein, M. (2003) Indexical order and the dialectics of sociolinguistic life. *Language and Communication* 23, 193–229.

Silverstein, M. (2004) 'Cultural' concepts and the language–culture nexus. *Current Anthropology* 45, 621–652.

Sinclair, J. (1988) *New Directions in English Dictionaries*. Unpublished manuscript.

Sinclair, J. and Coulthard, M. (1975) *Towards an Analysis of Discourse: The English Used by Teachers and Pupils*. London: Oxford University Press.

Skeggs, B. (1997) *Formations of Class and Gender: Becoming Respectable*. London: Sage.

Skeggs, B. (2002) Techniques for telling the reflexive self. In T. May (ed.) *Qualitative Research in Action* (pp. 349–374). London: Sage.

Skeggs, B. (2004) Context and background: Pierre Bourdieu's analysis of class, gender and sexuality. In L. Adkins and B. Skeggs (eds) *Feminism after Bourdieu* (pp. 19–33). Oxford: Blackwell.

Skehan, P. (1998) *A Cognitive Approach to Language Learning*. Oxford: Oxford University Press.

Skilton-Sylvester, E. (2002) Literate at home but not at school: A Cambodian girl's journey from playwright to struggling writer. In G. Hull and K. Schultz (eds) *School's Out! Bridging Out-of-School Literacies with Classroom Practice* (pp. 61–90). New York: Teachers College Press.

Skutnabb-Kangas, T. (2000) *Linguistic Genocide in Education – Or Worldwide Diversity and Human Rights?* Mahwah, NJ: Lawrence Erlbaum.

Somers, M.R. and Gibson, G.D. (1994) Reclaiming the epistemological 'Other': narrative and the social constitution of identity. In C. Calhoun (ed.) *Social Theory and the Politics of Identity* (pp. 37–99). Cambridge, MA: Blackwell.

Sperber, D. (1975) *Rethinking Symbolism*. Cambridge: Cambridge University Press.

Spolsky, B. (1989) *Conditions for Second Language Learning*. Oxford: Oxford University Press.

Spolsky, B. (2004) *Language Policy*. Cambridge: Cambridge University Press.

Street, B. (1984) *Literacy in Theory and Practice*. Cambridge: Cambridge University Press.

Street, B. (ed.) (1993) *Cross-Cultural Approaches to Literacy*. Cambridge: Cambridge University Press.

Street, B. (2000) Literacy events and literacy practices: Theory and practice in the 'New Literacy Studies'. In K. Jones and M. Martin-Jones (eds) *Multilingual Literacies: Comparative Perspectives on Research and Practice* (pp. 17–30). Amsterdam: John Benjamins

Street, B. (2001) Introduction. In B. Street (ed.) *Literacy and Development* (pp. 1–17). Cambridge: Cambridge University Press.

Street, B. (2003) Foreword. In J. Collins and R. Blot (eds) *Literacy and Literacies: Texts, Power and Identity* (pp. xi–xv). Cambridge: Cambridge University Press.

Street, B. (2004) Futures of the ethnography of literacy? *Language and Education* 18, 326–330.

Stroud, C. (1998) Perspectives on cultural variability of discourse and some implications for code-switching. In P. Auer (ed.) *Code-Switching in Conversation: Language, Interaction and Identity* (pp. 321–348). London: Routledge.

Stroud, C. (2001) African mother-tongue programmes and the politics of language: Linguistic citizenship versus linguistic human rights. *Journal of Multilingual and Multicultural Development* 22, 339–355.

Stroud, C. (2002) Framing Bourdieu socioculturally: Alternative forms of linguistic legitimacy in postcolonial Mozambique. *Multilingua* 21, 247–273.

Stroud, C. (2009) A postliberal critique of language rights: Toward a politics of language for a linguistics of contact. In J. Petrovic (ed.) *International Perspectives on Bilingual Education* (pp. 191–218). New York: Information Age Publishing.

Stroud, C. and Heugh, K. (2004) Linguistic human rights and linguistic citizenship. In D. Patrick and J. Freeland (eds) *Language Rights and Language Survival: A Sociolinguistic Exploration* (pp. 191–218). Manchester: St Jerome.

Stroud, C. and Wee, L. (2006) Anxiety and identity in the language classroom. *RELC Journal* 37 (3), 299–307.

Stroud, C. and Wee, L. (2007) Consuming identities: Language planning and policy in Singaporean late modernity. *Language Policy* 6, 253–279.

Stychin, C. (2001) Sexual citizenship in the European Union. *Citizenship Studies* 5, 285–301.

Sullivan, A. (2001) Cultural capital and educational attainment. *Sociology* 35 893–912.

Süssmuth, R. (2007) On the need for teaching intercultural skills: Challenges for education in a globalizing world. In M.M. Suárez-Orozco (ed.) *Learning in the Global Era* (pp. 195–212). Berkeley, CA: University of California Press.

Sweetman, P. (2003) Twenty-first century dis-ease? Habitual reflexivity or the reflexive habitus. *Sociological Review* 51, 528–549.

Talmy, S. (2004) Forever FOB: The cultural production of ESL in a high school. *Pragmatics* 14, 149–172.

Thompson, J. (1991) Introduction. *Pierre Bourdieu, Language and Symbolic Power* (pp. 1–42). Cambridge, MA: Harvard University Press.

Tollefson, J. (1991) *Planning Language, Planning Inequality.* London: Longman.

Trudgill, P. (1975) *Accent, Dialect and the School.* London: Edward Arnold.

Tsui, A. (1996) Reticence and anxiety in second language learning. In K. Bailey and D. Nunan (eds) *Voices from the Language Classroom* (pp. 145–167). Cambridge: Cambridge University Press.

Turner, V. (1987) *The Anthropology of Performance.* New York: PAJ.

Van Lier, L. (2008) The ecology of language learning and sociocultural theory. In A. Creese, P. Martin and N.H. Hornberger (eds) *Encyclopedia of Language and Education* 9 (pp. 53–65). New York: Springer.

Varenne, H. and McDermott, R. (1998) *Successful Failure.* Colorado, CO: Westview Press.

Vigouroux, C. (2009) A relational understanding of language practice: Interacting time spaces in a single ethnographic site. In J. Collins, S. Slembrouck and M. Baynham (eds) *Globalization and Language in Contact: Scale, Migration, and Communicative Practices* (pp. 62–84). London: Continuum Press.

Vygotsky, L. (1987) *The Collected Works of L. S. Vygotsky, Vol 1: Problems of General Psychology.* R.W. Rieber and A.S. Carton (eds) New York: Plenum.

Wallace, C. (2002) Local literacies and global literacy. In D. Block and D. Cameron (eds) *Globalization and Language Teaching* (pp. 101–114). London: Routledge.

Wallerstein, I. (2000) *The Essential Wallerstein.* New York: The New Press.

Warde, A. (1994) Consumption, identity-formation and uncertainty. *Sociology* 28, 877–898.

Webb, J. (2004) Organizations, self identities and the new economy. *Sociology* 38, 719–738.

Wee, L. (2002a) *Lor* in colloquial Singapore English. *Journal of Pragmatics* 34, 711–725.

Wee, L. (2002b) When English is not a mother tongue: Linguistic ownership and the Eurasian community in Singapore. *Journal of Multilingual and Multicultural Development* 23, 282–295.

Wee, L. (2003) Linguistic instrumentalism in Singapore. *Journal of Multilingual and Multicultural Development* 24/3, 211–224.

Wee, L. (2005) Intra-language discrimination and linguistic human rights: The case of Singlish. *Applied Linguistics* 26, 48–69.

Wee, L. (2006) The semiotics of language ideologies in Singapore. *Journal of Sociolinguistics* 10, 344–361.

Wee, L. (2007) Linguistic human rights and mobility. *Journal of Multilingual and Multicultural Development* 28 (4), 325–338.

Wee, L. (2008) The technologization of discourse and authenticity in English language teaching. *International Journal of Applied Linguistics* 18, 256–273.

Wee, L. (2010) 'Burdens' and 'handicaps' in Singapore's language policy: On the limits of language management. *Language Policy* 9, 97–114.

Wee, L. (2011) Metadiscursive convergence in the Singlish debate. *Language & Communication* 31, 75–85.

Wee, L. and Bokhorst-Heng, W. (2005) Language policy and nationalist ideology: Statal narratives in Singapore. *Multilingua* 24, 159–183.

Wee, L. and Brooks, A. (2010) Personal branding and the commodification of reflexivity. *Cultural Sociology* 4, 45–62.

Weiss, L. (1998) *The Myth of the Powerless State*. Cambridge: Cambridge University Press.

Weiss, L. (2005) The state-augmenting effects of globalization. *New Political Economy* 10, 345–353.

Wenger, E. (1998) *Communities of Practice*. Cambridge, MA: Cambridge University Press.

Widdowson, H.G. (1978) *Teaching Language as Communication*. Oxford: Oxford University Press.

Widdowson, H.G. (1979) *Explorations in Applied Linguistics*. Oxford: Oxford University Press.

Widdowson, H.G. (1994) The ownership of English. *TESOL Quarterly* 28, 377–388.

Widdowson, H.G. (2003) *Defining Issues in English Language Teaching*. Oxford: Oxford University Press.

Wright, S. (2004) *Language Policy and Language Planning: From Nationalism to Globalization*. Basingstoke: Palgrave Macmillan

Wright, T. and Bolitho, R. (1993) Language awareness: A missing link in language teacher education? *ELT Journal* 47, 292–304.

Young, I.M. (1987) Impartiality and the civic republic: Some implications of feminist critiques of moral and political theory. In S. Benhabib and D. Cornell (eds) *Feminism as Critique*. Oxford: Polity Press.

Young, I.M. (1989) Policy and group difference: A critique of the ideal of universal citizenship. *Ethics* 99, 250–274.

Subject Index

Ambivalence, 5, 23, 37, 39–42, 47, 50, 58, 62, 63, 92, 97, 121
Anxiety, 115, 161, 183
  competence-based and identity-based, 17, 180
Authenticity, 15, 17–18, 38, 176, 195
Autonomy, 4, 24, 54, 59, 68, 109, 145, 200, 203, 217–218
Avoidance strategy, 114, 120, 133

Bilingual policy, 34, 90–91, 97, 117, 214

Citizenship, 3, 190, 196, 198–199, 201, 202, 208, 209, 201, 213, 214
  Linguistic, 175, 191, 202, 203, 207, 210–212, 215–217
Code-switching, 18, 19, 36, 121, 139, 142, 163, 177
Commodification, 38
Communicative competence, 64, 178
Crossing, 18–19, 100, 101, 177
Consumption, 24, 38, 40, 174, 192, 197, 202, 203
  Sociolinguistic, 7, 39, 204, 205

Deliberative democracy, 191, 199, 203, 208, 209
Dialects, 12, 176, 185
  Chinese, 9, 10, 13, 14, 29, 33–36, 40, 41, 47, 85, 90, 97, 193, 194

Economic growth, 3, 193
Elite, elitism, 45, 48, 80, 81, 137, 197

Embarrassment, 133, 136
Emotional labour, 16
English language teaching, 19, 166
Entertainment, 101, 115, 185, 206
Ethnic primordialism, 32
Ethnography, 20, 21
Examinations, 12, 15, 34, 49, 80

Foreign talent, 3, 190, 200, 201, 213, 218

Gatekeeping, of language, 1, 6, 11, 169
Globalization, 2, 24, 38, 198–99, 216–17
Grammar, 8, 10, 86, 188, 218

Heritage, 30, 41, 49, 130, 153, 184, 192, 200, 214, 215
Hybridity, 15, 18, 19, 207, 215

Improvisation, 160
Indexical values, 2, 35, 188
Instrumentalism, see pragmatism

Language ideologies, 22
Learning load, 34
Leisure, 79, 83, 88, 114, 117, 120, 127, 181
Lingua franca, 1, 28–32, 44, 49, 99, 169, 194
Linguistic Human Rights, 169

Literacy, autonomous and ideological
  models, 19, 20, 173

Media, 14, 37, 63, 80, 197, 216
Media Development Authority, 14
Medium of instruction, 28, 48, 63
Migration, 3, 24, 38, 216
Ministry of Education, 48, 80, 91,
  201, 218
Monolingualism, 11, 15, 47, 49, 193
Mother tongue, 1, 2, 9, 28–32, 33, 34–49,
  63, 80, 85, 90, 92, 99, 116, 147, 152,
  186, 190, 195, 201, 213
Motivation, 1, 52, 136, 144
Multiracialism, 21, 29, 32, 46

Narratives, 63, 73, 74, 199, 202, 204, 215
Nationalism, 152, 216
National Service, 44–46, 85–86,
  194, 206

Orders of indexicality, 33, 90

Parents, 2, 33, 41, 49, 69, 83, 88, 90, 95,
  109, 129, 150, 152, 155
Peers, 2, 23, 36, 67, 172, 180
Performance, 4, 16, 39, 47, 64, 69, 76, 100,
  132, 141, 156, 158, 161, 174, 178, 188,
  195, 207,
Personalist ideology, 15–17

Pragmatism, 46, 215
Public speaking, 107, 112, 163

Reading, aloud, 68, 77, 131, 132,
  160, 166,
  For leisure, 114
Reflexivity, 4, 52, 92, 156, 180, 185, 192,
  202, 218

Schools, 5, 11, 15, 28, 49, 70, 75, 79, 106,
  152, 177, 195
Singlish, 9, 10, 13, 14, 29, 36, 46, 83, 86,
  148, 186, 193, 213
Snobbery, 1, 140
Social class, 27, 35, 67, 145, 196, 205
Speak Good English Movement, 9, 13,
  29, 36
Speak Mandarin Campaign, 9, 10, 14, 29,
  31, 33, 42, 47, 85, 90, 193
Standard English, 3, 9, 10–14, 35, 37, 79,
  142, 147, 154, 186
Stigmatized varieties, 8, 137, 216

Technology, of language, 3, 19, 171

Verbal hygiene, 9
Vocabulary, 86, 92, 107, 110, 114, 117,
  126, 137, 148, 216

Workplace, 22, 35

For Product Safety Concerns and Information please contact our EU Authorised Representative:

Easy Access System Europe

Mustamäe tee 50

10621 Tallinn

Estonia

gpsr.requests@easproject.com

www.ingramcontent.com/pod-product-compliance
Ingram Content Group UK Ltd.
Pitfield, Milton Keynes, MK11 3LW, UK
UKHW021843280426
5452IPUK00003B/34

* 9 7 8 1 8 4 7 6 9 5 9 5 6 *